From the Londo

WINTER GARDEN THEATRE, LONDON.... breaking several house records for attendance.

FASCINATING AND CHARMING.... "How fascinating are these tiny fragile girls in glittering gold brocade and gold head-dresses, their dark hair twined with white flowers. Particularly interesting was *Tumulilingan* danced by Ni Gusti Raka and Sampih, depicting the vain courtship of a bumblebee. How charming was ... the lovemaking....The classical *Legong* including a charming bird dance by Raka.... Among character dancers, outstanding was the *Ketjak* ... a male chorus squatting in concentric circles about an admirable mime, Serog, gradually acquire the characteristics of monkeys.The combination of abrupt movement and gutteral barks is quite extraordinary."

—Cyril Beaumont, *Sunday Times, London*

FIRE AND PRECISION.... "delicacy of arm and hand movement ... infinitely plastic use of the body ... the tight swaddling of the girls ... gives them a tenuous elegance, enhanced by their tender age. Ni Gusti Raka ... dances with the fire and precision of a ballerina ... she is the very embodiment of all fairy-tale princesses and as a fierce little bird she is irresistible, putting all western Firebirds to shame ... (and there is some beautifully dressed up fooling)....The entertainment offered is far from being only dancing. The 'gamelan orchestra' is fascinating not only to hear but to watch ... and there is a splendid 'monkey chorus' from the men....The costumes are rich and strange as only oriental dresses can be. Incredibly, they were woven and made in two villages on the island."

—Alexander Bland, *The Observer, London*

UNIQUE DISPLAY.... "a unique display of a highly developed art which should not be missed ... a continuous sinuosity of movement.... Three young girls ... dance the *Legong* ... with superb grace ... the *Ketjak* ... has the most atmosphere, but the highlight of the evening is the *Barong*, a grotesque comedy about a mythical lion who protects the Balinese from evil influences.The show is very ably produced by John Coast."

—P. F. J, *London Telegraph*

A BEAUTIFUL SHOW.... "gorgeous to look at, stunning to listen to, full of vivacity and completely off the beaten track. Ni Gusti Raka, the leading dancer, is an utterly lovely wisp of a girl. Her dancing in the gay and delightful 'bumblebee' number called 'Tumulilingan' is bewitching, and in the more demanding 'Legong' it is truly superb, technically and dramatically."

—John Martin, *New York Times*

THEY LIVE THE DANCE.... "A rich cross-section of the wonderfully varied Balinese dance repertoire. In the intricate choreographies so closely co-ordinated with music of magic sound and complex rhythm, a sensational theatrical art is displayed, like nothing else to be found throughout the East."

—Colin McPhee, *New York Times Magazine*

BEAUTY PLUS.... "William Saroyan once wrote a play called 'The Beautiful People.' The same title fully describes the event which took place last evening at the Fulton Theater where the Dancers of Bali with their Gamelan Orchestra from the little Indonesian villiage of Pliatan, made their American debut. For there was beauty everywhere. Beauty of movement and beauty of sound, beauty of color and beauty of spirit. From the temple doorways, etched against the deep blue sky, came tiny dancers in golds and crimsons and purples, in costumes of breathtaking loveliness and in the wonderfully monstrous garbs of demons."

—Walter Terry, *New York Herald Tribune*

DANCERS OF BALI ARE FASCINATING, FUNNY AND FRISKY
"This Balinese company, visiting here by courtesy of the Republic of Indonesia, is exotic, fabulously costumed, exciting and just plain lightheartedly funny. Its orchestra, called a Gamelan, is a fascinating syncopated ensemble."

—John Chapman, *New York Daily News*

MAGIC CARPET.... "The Fulton Theater, while it shelters the 'Dancers of Bali', is the place to go. The excitement of unfamiliar rhythms and daring volumes, the supreme delicacy of dance patterns and the luxury of broad comedy all combine to make a magic carpet of the exhibition."

—William Hawkins, *New York World-Telegram and Sun*

BALI DANCERS ARE MAGNIFICENT.... "A visit to the Fulton is imperative for those who wish to enlarge their artistic horizons. We found the performance nothing less than magnificent, and the youngsters in the audience were enchanted by it, particularly with the clowning and pageantry."

—Robert Coleman, *New York Daily Mirror*

EAST COMES WEST.... "It portrays a glittering world of make-believe where people never grow up to serious problems of emotions.... Another new experience is the Gamelan orchestra. It can whip up as much frenzy as our jiviest jazz and in the next moment lull you to meditation."

—Frances Herridge, *New York Post*

EXTRAORDINARY.... "From the village of Pliatan, Bali, Indonesia, some 14,000 miles away, came its foremost dancers and musicians to make real the almost legendary accounts of their unique way of life. They provided a choice experience.... There is strange exhilaration as well as fascination in the multi-rhythmic music."

—Miles Kastendieck, *New York Journal-American*

Dancing Out of Bali

John Coast

With a Foreword by
Sir David Attenborough

PERIPLUS

Paperback edition published by Periplus Editions
with the permission of Laura Rosenberg

First published as *Dancers of Bali* by G. P. Putnam's Sons, New York, 1953
Reissued as *Dancing Out of Bali* by Faber and Faber Limited, London, 1954
First Periplus edition, 2004

ISBN 0-7946-0261-4

Publisher's Note
Modern spelling was introduced to Indonesia in 1969 when, for example,
"Dj" became simply "J". Ardjuna is now spelt Arjuna.

"Pliatan" is derived from the original name of Peliatan village, usually
shortened to Pliatan, and so used by John Coast in his book. Peliatan is
adjacent to Ubud which became more famous in later years.

"Luce" was the familiar name of Supianti Sujono, the Javanese wife of
John Coast.

Printed in Singapore

DISTRIBUTORS

PT Java Books Indonesia, Jl. Kelapa Gading Kirana, Blok A-14/17,
Jakarta 14240. Tel: (021) 451 5351; Fax: (021) 453 4987
Email: cs@javabooks.co.id

Asia Pacific
Berkeley Books Pte Ltd, 130 Joo Seng Road #06-01/03, Singapore 368357
Tel: (65) 6280 1330; Fax: (65) 6280 6290; Email: inquiries@periplus.com.sg

Japan
Tuttle Publishing, Yaekari Building, 3F, 5-4-12 Osaki, Shinagawa-ku,
Tokyo 141-0032. Tel: (813) 5437 0171; Fax: (813) 5437 0755
Email: tuttle-sales@gol.com

North America, Latin America and Europe
Tuttle Publishing, 364 Innovation Drive, North Clarendon, VT 05759-9436
Tel: (802) 773 8930; Fax: (802) 773 6993; Email: info@tuttlepublishing.com
www.tuttlepublishing.com

JOHN ALAN COAST
1916–1989

Menanti di pintu sorga

Dancing Out of Bali chronicles John's
most cherished life's work—bringing the people
and culture of Bali to the attention of audiences
throughout the world. It has now been reissued,
fifty years after its initial release, in the hope that
this passionate appreciation will reach an
ever-widening circle of people.

Grateful thanks go to arts consultant and
writer James Murdoch for helping to make this
edition possible, and to Sir David Attenborough,
Jonathan Copeland, Tom Hennes, Ni Wayan Murni
and Ni Gusti Raka for their special support.

Royalties from the sale of this edition
will go towards the continuance of
the performing arts in Bali.

LAURA ROSENBERG
New York City, January 2004
www.johncoast.org

About the Author

John Coast was born in Eastbourne, Kent on October 30, 1916. As Britain entered World War II, he joined the Coldstream Guards and then later the Norfolk Regiment as an officer. He was posted to Singapore, which within days fell to the Japanese invaders, and taken prisoner of war. Coast was sent to Siam (now Thailand) to slave for more than three years on the infamous Thai–Burma Railway. His story of that ordeal, *Railroad of Death* (1946), became an instant best seller and was later to form the basis of *Return to the River Kwai*, an acclaimed documentary he made in 1969 for the BBC. With a multicultural group of dancers, musicians and actors, including many Malays and Indonesians, Coast produced many concert performances during his internment. After the war, Coast joined the press department of the British Foreign Office in Bangkok, but shortly after became press attaché to President Sukarno during the Indonesian struggle for independence. He described his roles in early Indonesian politics in his book *Recruit to Revolution* (1952). In 1950, when Coast moved to Bali to write this book, he became immersed in Balinese culture and dreamed of organizing the first postwar Western tour of Bali's finest musicians and dancers. His perseverance brought such a troupe to Europe and America in 1952/53, with spectacular success. His book *Dancers of Bali* (1953)—published in Britain as *Dancing out of Bali* (1954)—relates the story of this legendary tour. The historic recording made in London of the group's exotic music caused widespread interest and influenced England's great composer Benjamin Britten's three-act ballet *Prince of the Pagodas*. In the mid-1950s, Coast returned to London and became a leading impresario, managing the careers of such artists as Mario Lanza, Luciano Pavarotti, José Carerras, Jon Vickers and Montserrat Caballé. He presented Bob Dylan's first appearance in London and first brought Ravi Shankar to the West. He also contributed articles to *The New Statesman*, *The Economist*, *Ballet* and *Dance News*, and made several films with Sir David Attenborough on Balinese culture for the BBC.

Contents

Acknowledgments

The author wishes to thank Mr Colin McPhee for his technical advice in connection with the analysis of Balinese music made in Chapter 7.

A Short Bibliography

The Island of Bali by Miguel Covarrubias
(ISBN 962 593 060 4)

Dance and Drama in Bali by Walter Spies and Beryl de Zoete
(ISBN 962 593 880 X)

A House in Bali by Colin McPhee
(ISBN 962 593 629 7)

A Tale from Bali by Vicki Baum
(ISBN 962 593 502 9)

Books by the Same Author

Railroad of Death
Recruit to Revolution
Some Aspects of Siamese Politics

Author's Dedication

One day towards the end of February 1954, after the dancers had been back in Bali a year, Sampih was called to dance with the Pliatan group in the palace of the Raja of Gianjar in front of President Sukarno.

He failed to appear. Three days later his murdered body was found in the Ubud River.

Sampih was a very great dancer; and while Luce and I were living in Bali he was like our brother.

The book, which so fittingly could have been dedicated to him and the Anak Agung Mandera, I now dedicate in great sorrow to his memory.

Foreword

There was a time when Bali, to Western eyes, represented all that was remote and exotic. It was the Far East at its most romantic. In the 1930s, a few wealthy travellers, attracted by rumours of the island's extraordinary beauty and the wonders of its music and dancing, started to visit it in their luxury yachts. Occasionally, one or two European painters and musicians went with them and several became so fascinated by the island's rich yet alien culture that they settled there. But they were the exceptions. To the rest of the world, Bali was little more than a name for a distant unreachable island paradise.

John Coast, the author of this book, arrived in Southeast Asia as a member of the British Army during the Second World War. Within days of his landing at Singapore, the island fell to the Japanese and he was taken as prisoner to work on the murderous Burma Railway. There he laboured and suffered alongside others who came from what was then the Dutch East Indies. Such appalling experiences might well have turned many against all things Oriental. For John, they did quite the reverse, and when peace came at last and he was demobilized he returned as part of the British diplomatic delegation in Thailand. From there, he went to Java as a private individual to do what he could to help Indonesia in its fight for independence.

It was then that he visited Bali. He was so overwhelmed by the splendour of the islanders' music and dancing, so unlike the stately traditions of Java and beyond in its fire and brilliance, that he dreamed of arranging a worldwide tour for a group of dancers together with their essential complement, a full gamelan orchestra.

In this book, he tells how he achieved this unlikely and pioneering feat. The story involves intrigue, politics, rivalries and even—tragically— murder. But his pages are also filled with the brilliant clashing sounds of the Balinese gamelan, the flicker of candlelight on the graceful bodies of child dancers, the perfume of incense and frangipani, and the vivid presence of one of the most generous, friendly and talented people on earth.

When his book was first published in 1953, few of its readers could have been to the island. Bali still had no airport of any kind, let alone one that could accept aircraft big enough to bring in visitors hundreds at a time. The beach at Sanur, today lined by towering luxury hotels, was then so quiet and lonely that a stranger could spend the night there, watching turtles come ashore to lay their eggs, looking at the stars, and sleeping on the sand. I know. I did.

So I too became captivated by all things Balinese. On my return, I read this book and eventually met its author. Together we persuaded BBC Television to let us make a series of films that would give some account of Balinese art, and in particular its music and dancing. So I had the huge good fortune of working in Bali in partnership with someone whom the Balinese knew well and held in great affection.

It is indeed splendid that John's book should be in print once more to tell today's visitors of how things once were on the island. But its readers will have no difficulty in imagining that, for there is a miracle about Bali. Its traditions are so vigorous, so deeply rooted in the Balinese character, that they remained astonishingly free from foreign influences for centuries. As a result—if you know where to look—you can still discover and recognize what it was that intoxicated John Coast fifty years ago.

SIR DAVID ATTENBOROUGH
London, October 2003

Illustrations

30. The three Legongs from the wings of the Winter Garden Theatre. (*Baron*)
31. Sampih performing Kebiar Duduk at the Winter Garden Theatre. (*Baron*)
32. The warrior Ardjuna about to do battle with the wild boar sent by the god Shiva to test his prowess. (*Baron*)
33. The Finale: the Barong triumphs over all its adversaries. (*Baron*)
34. Publicity for the "Dancers of Bali" tour of the United States.
35. The "Dancers of Bali" reach Broadway.
36. John Coast directing a rehearsal at the Fulton Theater.
37. The Djanger ensemble in the US debut. (*Arnold Eagle*)
38. Rangda and the Barong with other characters. (*Arnold Eagle*)
39. Sampih performing the Baris. (*Louis Faurer*)
40. Sampih performing Kebiar Duduk with Anak Agung Gde Mandera. (*Arnold Eagle*)
41. Ni Gusti Raka as the bee in the Bumblebee Dance. (*Louis Faurer*)
42. The Djanger dance being performed at the Thunderbird Hotel in Las Vegas. (*Hervey, Southern Pacific R.R.*)
43. Serog, the clown, in the Ketjak monkey circle. (*Colour Processing Laboratories Ltd.*)
44. Oka and Raka sipping orange pop in their dressing room in the Fulton Theater. (*Southern Pacific R.R.*)
45. The Balinese dancers eating ice cream in Manhattan. (*Gordon Parks*)
46. The Legongs with Walt Disney in Los Angeles.
47. The Legongs with Bob Hope and Bing Crosby at Paramount Studios, Hollywood.
48. The three Legongs meeting prima ballerina Alicia Markova.
49. The three Legongs and Luce looking over an American magazine. (*Los Angeles Mail*)
50. A farewell picture in Miami. (*Frank Boran, Miami*)
51. Ni Gusti Raka in 1966 with her youngest child. (*John Coast*)
52. Ni Gusti Raka in a publicity shot for the 1971 Australian tour.
53. John Coast in his London office, 1981. (*Laura Rosenberg*)
54. Reunion in Pliatan, August 1983: Belge, John Coast, Anak Agung Gde Mandera, Raka and Anom. (*Laura Rosenberg*)
55. Pegil, Belge and John Coast, Iseh, Bali, 1983. (*Laura Rosenberg*)
56. Ni Gusti Raka teaching in Bali, 2004. (*Jonathan Copeland*)

Drawings by Supianti Coast

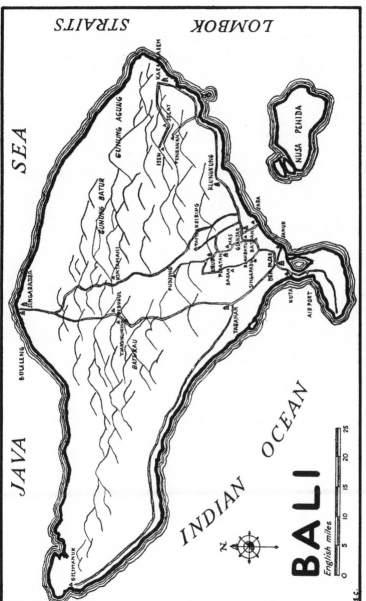

Sketch-map of Bali showing the towns and villages mentioned in the text

Bird's-eye view of our house and compound in
Kaliungu Klod, Denpasar

1

We Decide to Stay

*

We sat in two bamboo chairs, looking toward the beach, where we could hear the breakers gently pounding the white sweep of Kuta Bay. Between our grass-thatched hut and the sea lay only a shallow strip of coconut palms, beneath which the grey, sandy soil baked in the afternoon sun. The breezes blowing in steadily off the Indian Ocean made us want to sleep twelve hours a day. We had only been living in Bali for two weeks, but already we wanted to stay there indefinitely.

Kuta was a fishing village. Along the beach there stood a series of long, ragged huts, placed under trees just above the high-water mark. In these huts were the narrow boats with prows carved like fanciful masks to scare the monsters of the ocean, with their outriggers leaning drunkenly on the sand. But in these huts no Balinese lived; for according to the beliefs of the people, the low-lying sea is the habitat of demons, while always from the sea Bali's invading enemies have come. The sea, therefore, is not to be trusted, but to be placated. It is in the Great Mountain, whose vast peak dominates the whole of the island, that the gods of Bali prefer to live. The real village of Kuta, therefore, lay behind us, slightly inland.

This afternoon had been unusually warm, and we were just thinking of going to the bathhouse to cool off, for the tide was far out and the well water, if scooped over ourselves in empty halves of coconut shells, was cold and refreshing, when our temporarily adopted son, Pegil, came running up to our porch from the direction of the sea. He was a small boy of ten, permitted by his family, who were very poor hill villagers, to live with us and help in our household in return for being sent to school and a promise that we would never take him away from Bali. He was a handsome child, sturdily built, with a wonderful smile, and he lived proudly in a new pair of dark blue cotton shorts. He stood now smiling, nervous, pulling out the joints of his fingers, watching us. First he looked at me; then at Luce. Perhaps Luce looked less forbidding or the more awake, for it was to her that he spoke.

"Excuse, please," he said. "The tide is very far out today. Are you and the Tuan, perhaps, going fishing on the reef?"

Luce looked at me resignedly from her chair and Pegil turned his smile on to me, too.

"Let's all go," she said. "You know you enjoy it yourself quite as much as Pegil does."

"All right, Pegil," I said. "We'll go in a few minutes. As soon as we've put some shoes on."

"Excuse me, Tuan, I will first tell my friends—that is, if the Tuan is going to drive the jeep?"

"Yes, we'll take the jeep."

Inside the hut we pulled on canvas shoes so that we could more safely clamber over the rocks and through the channels. Luce wore shorts and a brief blouse; I wore shorts and sunglasses. Then we were ready. As we walked over to the old wartime jeep, Pegil came forward, seven or eight of his friends from the village with him. Grinning, cheerful little brown urchins, they wore mostly rotting and patched shorts, and in their hands they carried small baskets, heavy hammers, with barbed, yard-long spikes of iron. At my "Okay!" they all scrambled aboard, talking excitedly, for this was a big moment for them; Pegil, however, now kept his face very calm, even slightly aloof, implying that for him it was all a most usual and boring occurrence.

There was a grass track leading to the foreshore, but as the jeep descended the slope on to the beach itself, I had to shift to low gear; then we lurched forward through the soft sand like a tank, the children whooping with pleasure, and chattering like magpies when we finally sped along the firm white sand close to the sea's edge, heading for the reef of white coral that ran out several hundred yards from Kuta Point.

I left the jeep on firm sand and we jumped down. Now it was the turn of a boy smaller than Pegil to lead us. This was Baris, eight-year-

16

old expert on the reef, nimble and wise on tides and races. We had met Baris first during a stroll along the shore at low tide, when he had shown us how to scoop out exquisite black shells living just under the wet sand where the water retreated.

Baris led the way. Luce and I moved cumbersomely after the quickly scattering and light-footed boys. As we walked through pools and over the low rocks, forward to the main reef's edge, where now tame-looking waves lapped at and caressed it, we had to guard all the time against spiky and poisonous sea urchins, amber, black and pale pink, which lay in holes and under ledges everywhere, so that when we stepped or lifted a rock to peer under it, we had always to beware that a groping foot or levering hand did not light upon us.

At first we found only a few clams and some giant, rubbery starfish, bright blue in colour, but presently we caught up with the children busily chipping and prodding for cat's-eyes. These stones, we had learned, were plugs, or stoppers, attached to the bases of certain small molluscs, which, when frightened, retired into their shells, thus seal-ing themselves in, leaving the glaring green and black eye on a white background to frighten off any enemy. The small boys, however, gathered up the shells complete, for they would eat the fish and try to sell the stones to any tourists who came down to bathe. Luce was having one mounted by a Kuta silversmith in a filigree silver ring.

Sometimes, in holes in the rocks, the boys would plunge in their barbed spikes and one would pull out a small octopus, a greatly prized delicacy, or from under the ledges fat eels would wriggle through the shallows to be speared and captured also. In deeper pools shoals of tiny fish of a kingfisher blue would flash and turn, while at the reef's farthest point, where the rocks were crumbling soft, huge and glisten-ing cowries, some brown-black, some fawn-coloured and speckled, were prised away before the turning tide forced us to withdraw to the beach. There we would compare catches with the fishermen, who would try to sell us their too salt crayfish, or huge sea fleas, which they had trapped on the sand ledges between high and low tides. And then we would jeep back to the village.

On the evening of this same day, old Wo Ketut (which means Uncle Fourth-Born) our servant, came to us bursting with excite-ment.

"Tuan," he said, "there is good news. Lotring has come at last. Tonight the Music Club will be rehearsing in Kuta. The Tuan will certainly want to be present. Lotring is my old friend. Let me take the Tuan and the Tuan's wife there after they have eaten."

"This is good news indeed, Wo. Do you know what they will be rehearsing tonight—or is it just a meeting?"

"I do not yet know, Tuan, but later I will find out."

He bustled back to the kitchen, content in his own new-found importance.

For us this really was most valuable information. Lotring had long been one of Bali's most famous musicians, and his home was in Kuta; but so much was he in demand as a teacher that he was being continually called all over the island, and never yet had we found him in his own house. So far the only dancing we had seen had been at the Bali Hotel in Denpasar, where the little girls encased in their cloths of gold, the clowns and masked monsters who fooled and ranted, had begun to work their spell on us. But the dancing had not as yet pleased us as much as the music, that most gentle, hypnotic music of the Belaluan orchestra, hammered out by a percussion of gongs and gilded metallophones—xylophone-shaped, but with keys of metal—played by some five and twenty men. The music fascinated me because I could not see which players so precisely and perfectly controlled it— and I was baffled by the way a piece ended always unexpectedly, as if in mid-phrase, still in mid-air.

After we had eaten that night we went on foot together to the village. The rehearsal was taking place in a small *balé*, or open-air hall, on the earth floor of which the instruments were arranged on three sides of a square. Surrounding the space were crude bamboo slatted shelves on which sat a few casual spectators, the one oil lamp smoked foully, and, as we watched, a fierce argument seemed to be taking place in the thick near-darkness. The men squatted cross-legged behind their metallophones, most of them inscrutable, scratching themselves occasionally, clad only in their workaday sarongs. In the centre of the square two drummers sat leaning across their drums, which they held lengthwise across their knees. One of the drummers, who seemed to be leading the argument, was a well-featured man of some fifty years. Repeatedly he would shout what sounded like: "*Sing!*

18

Sing! Sing nyak!" (No! No! I don't want that!) At last, after some throaty grumbles, the dissidents sulkily eyeing the floor, the rehearsal jerked into life again.

Close by my side old Wo Ketut's voice informed me: "That is Lotring who has been speaking, Tuan. The men of the village say that they are rehearsing for a small festival in three days' time."

We watched Lotring using his drum, his eyes remote, flat palms and beringed fingers alternately caressing, flicking, coaxing and thumping the two end skins. Then suddenly, with no warning, yet all together, they would stop again. Leaning over his drum, Lotring would reach forward toward one of the metallophones, take the light wooden hammer from the player's hand, and, from the reverse side of the keys, beat out the next, unlearned phrase of the melody. Then straight at it they would fly again. If the metallophones hesitated, from Lotring's throat an unearthly, whining sound would issue, his voice thus giving them the lost melody, while his hands continued to punctuate the phrases with the drum.

Amidst laughter and imprecation the rehearsal went on for two hours more. Every half hour or so they would rest. A distinctly musky, fetid atmosphere, purely masculine, clogged the air of the *balé*. During a rest, men would stroll out to relieve themselves, squatting by the edge of the lane. Some of them lit acrid cigarettes flavoured with carnations, but Lotring would always be politely offered a shallow wooden tray whose partitions contained leaves of the sireh vine, some betel nut, lime paste and a coarse black tobacco. Automatically the teacher would fold himself a chew of betel, wrapping the nut and paste in the sireh leaf, putting it well back into his mouth, after which he would rub around his gums with a wad of tobacco, finally leaving the quid between his lips, grotesquely protruding. Presently, as the saliva began to circulate, he would begin chewing; a minute later he would be looking round for a few open inches of floor where he might spit out his first red betel jet.

When it was all over and we were walking home, Wo Ketut, savouring our pleasure, said casually, "Tomorrow perhaps I will ask Lotring to come and meet the Tuan at the house."

And in the morning, when we came out on to the porch to sip our morning coffee, we found Lotring there waiting for us, sitting in one of our chairs, wearing a new khaki shirt and batik headcloth. We greeted him, offered him coffee, but he refused it; out of politeness he allowed us to bring him the milk of a young coconut, but he hardly touched it.

We asked him about the performance in three days' time. Oh, it was nothing—some Baris dancers were coming over from Sanur, maybe, and there would be a little music. But it was of no account.

"How is it," I asked him, "that in your own village there are no dancers, and that this is the first time we've heard music in Kuta?"

"Well, there used to be a club. A Legong club. But the men broke always into factions and squabbled about money. That happens often. But in Kuta the people are very difficult. Beh! very difficult," he repeated. "I have tried several times to hold them together—in vain always. There is nothing to be done about it."

He smiled at us, very unperturbed, his hands lightly thrumming the sides of his chair, as if impatient to be at his drum again.

"Uncle Lotring, we came to Bali to look for dancers and the finest of orchestras. Could you not persuade the men to work with you once more?"

He laughed at us quietly, pointing to his betel-stained, gaping mouth.

"You see, Tuan, I have no teeth. It is hard for me to eat, and I cannot chew betel on my gums with pleasure. But even if you promised me new teeth, I would not be able to make this club work together. It is too difficult, Tuan: too difficult."

"You know, we could look for false teeth for you at the hospital in Denpasar, Uncle."

"Still not possible, Tuan," he grinned. Then a moment later, hands politely clasped, "*Titiang pamit,*" he said, "I go now." And in Balinese fashion, very simply, he was gone.

It was a Japanese mortar shell exploding in my platoon truck during the battle of Singapore that had led me thus to be looking for dancers in Bali. On that far-off day all my glasses had perished in the gutted vehicle, so that later, when I was taken prisoner by the Japanese, I lived for more than three years in a dim, half-seen world. When, in 1944, our main slave task of building a railway from Siam into Burma through hundreds of miles of monsoon jungle and mountains had been completed, we were reassembled for a brief period in vast base camps. There, with our native ingenuity, we built theatres from bamboo and palm thatch and matting, and put on plays and musicals, and I, in order to be able to see these shows, volunteered to prompt. Soon afterwards, in order further to occupy my mind, I had started to learn a foreign language—Malay. By a most singular and far-reaching coincidence, on the day of my first Malay lesson, my teacher introduced me to a young Javanese dancer, a fellow prisoner, whose brown chest was tattooed with the head of a blue tiger and with powerful magic writing.[1]

A month or two later, speaking a limping Malay and having graduated from prompter to stage manager, I was endeavouring to form a company that would put on some Javanese dancing. So absorbed did I become in this utterly new experience, that though a prisoner, I felt perfectly happy.

My first Javanese production, I am ashamed to say, was accompanied by a pair of pseudo-Javanese cymbals played from the matting wings and to the strains of "La Cucaracha" jerked out by the camp band, whose unique instruments were made from such things as telephone wire, soapboxes and gut from locally slain cats. The dancer's costume was made from stolen Japanese mosquito netting, ornamented with lead foil torn from discarded Red Cross cigarette cartons stolen from us by the Japanese Army, and the noble Hindu headdress was fashioned from a cardboard crate that had contained dried fish. To me, at the time, this was magnificent dancing; the other Javanese in camp, fortunately, were too amused and polite to express their real opinions.

This enthusiasm led me, when returned home after the war, to look for the nearest Javanese dancers, whom I did actually find in the end in nearby Holland. They were a student group, and after seeing them dance once in Leyden Museum, my friends and I brought them over to England for a couple of months. This was in the year 1946.

There were only nineteen of them, from princelings to waiters, all amateur, all very impecunious. There were two good dancers among them, both from Solo, in Java. In the theatres we had to use scratchy

[1] See *Railroad of Death*, 1946.

copies of twenty-year-old records to accompany the classical Javanese dance, but for the lighter folk dances of Sumatra, Celebes and Ambon, we used a small, Hawaiian type of band. The finale of the programme was a Djanger dance from Bali, in which, oddly enough, Luce had danced as a student member when studying in Holland before the war.

Our short tour was enthusiastically received in England, and Sol Hurok, the impresario, sent his agent to make us an offer to come to the United States next spring; a Madame Bouchonnet, too, from Paris, suggested that we tour France, Spain and Portugal. But the group broke up, since its members planned to return to Indonesia before the end of the year. And although exhausted after those hectic seven weeks, my ambition had been more than ever fired to bring over a really superb and authentic group, with full orchestra, for the joy and delectation of the western world.

It was my interest in this dancing that led me next into Indonesian politics, so that for some years I was working in Java with the un-recognized Indonesian Government, having unusual adventures as I strove humbly to help in the struggle for Indonesian independence. My eyes, however, remained always fixed on the group of dancers of which I had dreamed, and when, in 1950, after Indonesia had attained nationhood and I was moored impatiently behind a desk in the new Foreign Ministry in the new capital of Djakarta, I spent most of my time working out plans for cultural missions to tour the world. For months I laboured at estimates and routings and earning capacities, and the final result of my research was presented to President Sukarno at ten o'clock one morning in April.

It was a hot and humid day, I remember, as I arrived at the small palace of white marble which is the official residence of the Indonesian President. I sat opposite him in the reception room lined with modern paintings by young Indonesian revolutionary artists, the President cool and elegant in his simple white uniform and black Moslem hat, I perspiring but hopeful in an old sharkskin suit.

Himself a patron of the arts and by blood half Balinese, the President was sympathetic. He recalled, in fact, that in 1948, in the beleaguered capital of Jogja, with Dutch troops trying to force the young Republic to its knees, I had had the temerity to suggest some such venture as this. When I left the palace, in my old battered jeep which often needed a pushing hand from one of the guards, I felt confident.

Imagine, then, my chagrin, when only a few weeks after leaving my memorandum with the President, the chief Palace Secretary, a man with the soul of a true bureaucrat, announced out of the blue that my estimates were ten times too optimistic, that I would need a million dollars of hard currency, that there were many more important things for a young country to think about than mere artistic adventures.

The rejection of my plan, or, more euphemistically, its being "indefinitely postponed," was one of the reasons that sent me on leave to Bali. There, perhaps, was the work on which my heart was set, and together with Luce I hoped to prove my thesis by building up a Balinese dance-group first of all, for I had every confidence that Bali's foreign champions from before the war had not been over-romantic or too grossly misleading in their descriptions of the island's music and dancing.

And already, after only two weeks, and after seeing only three or four performances for tourists and this one rehearsal of Lotring's, we were becoming emotionally entangled. Thus, when Lotring laugh-ingly shrugged off the possibility of creating a club again in Kuta—our first hope—it was a setback to us. It only had the result, however, of making us pull up our roots in Kuta forthwith, for within a few days we had heard from an old friend, Daan Hubrecht, that there was a house for sale in the village of Kaliungu, on the outskirts of Denpasar, a house in Balinese style, set in a delightful compound, hitherto the property of the Government's agricultural adviser, Hans Harten, who was due to go on home leave.

At once we set out for Kaliungu; and when we had seen the house and its walled garden, we found it so charming and so exactly what we wanted, that we decided very quickly to make a bid for purchase. But this meant first sending letters to Djakarta to arrange for a loan on the security of my jeep from Chinese banker friends, while to carry us over the first months Luce and I agreed to pool our capital. This consisted of a Rolleiflex camera, a ring and a few household goods that might well be saleable. Altogether, we hoped that we might be able to live there modestly for half a year or a year.

Our decision thus taken and acted upon, we confounded Hans

Harten by driving over to see him one evening a couple of weeks later and scattering bills of large denomination all over his supper table. Then one day in the September of 1950 we registered the purchase of our house at the office of the Raja of Denpasar, made a new contract for the lease of the land which no foreigner in Bali may own outright, and moved in.

Kaliungu was to become our home and base for the next two years, and when we took over there was not just one house, but two. Both had high, grass-thatched roofs, supported on finely grained pillars of coconut-palm wood. The floor foundations were made from coral, smoothed over with a dark grey cement, and raised a couple of feet above the level of the surrounding garden. Most of the front house was quite open and acted as a cool living room; but one large corner, our bedroom, was walled off squarely with bamboo wickerwork walls, which, on the inside, were lined with a white matting made from finely woven grasses. At the back of this bedroom was a simple dip-and-pour Balinese bathroom, built under the house's extended eaves, and next to it was a lavatory on which we had to squat. Its heart-shaped aperture was hardly the size of a teacup, and there was quite a drop below. We christened it the "high-level bombing sight" and set about having it altered as soon as the equivalent of a plumber could be located.

In both houses almost all the furniture was made from bamboo.

From the front house a passageway ran back past a kitchen, where our food was cooked over charcoal braziers, leading to the smaller, second house, which consisted of two small rooms at the back of a good verandah. Here Hans' servants had slept. The two houses lay in a compound and garden some thirty yards across and sixty yards long.

In the front house, suspended from the eaves by hooked branches, there hung luxuriant ferns and orchids roughly potted in broken open coconut husks and these bordered our entire living space. The passageway was walled with blue-and-white-flowered creepers. In the garden were sireh vines and another vine with creamy, red-tipped flowers called "The Young Maiden chews Sireh," together with flaming red and yellow cannas, and climbing bougainvilleas. A very old hibiscus shrub had grown almost into a tree, and shaded our well and laundering wall behind the kitchen; while we ourselves quickly planted some branches of white and pink frangipani, and some pale mauve hibiscus transplanted from the hills. In the empty sector behind the second house weeds battled with wild potatoes and chili bushes and papaya trees. In the middle of this small wilderness stood a shrine, the former abode of somebody's household gods which no one yet dared to pull down, for perhaps—and who could tell?—the gods still occasionally liked to pay a visit to their old home.

One of Hans' servants, Agung, stayed on with us as gardener and laundryman. He was a lithe boy of about seventeen, but blind in one eye, and his blindness, alas, gave him a fey temperament such as is rarely to be found in a peasant people.

The village took a great and never-ceasing interest in us during the first days. They had heard already, it seemed, that the man was English and although just arrived spoke always in the Indonesian language; and the woman, his wife, was of high caste and from Java, it was said—but she wore shorts, spoke English as if it were her tongue, and was far from submissive. Such people promised to be as good as a shadow play to watch! And watch us they did, curious and full of uninhibited comment, until our new walls hid us. For knowing that the rainy season was fast approaching, we had asked help from our neighbour, Gusti Kompiang, the village head, in looking for carpenters, wall builders and thatchers.

Our mud walls were built up five feet high and then thatched with plenty of the cheap rice straw, so that the coming floods should not dissolve away our walls again this year. Then some ancient carpenters repaired the wooden gates, two on the village road in front of the house, which we then kept shut in an attempt to discourage the pi-dogs, and opposite the kitchen we fixed a new latch on the servants' gate. In a horse cart, blocks of sandstone were brought from the village of Sempidi, and these we placed like stepping-stones the length of our front garden. Altogether there was a friendly and pleasant feeling of work being accomplished in our compound.

While I supervised the building, Luce was tied to the kitchen, for as yet we had found no cook. Old Wo Ketut we had preferred to keep as a friend, not as a cook, and when we left Kuta he had gone back to his own village in east Bali, whence he had already twice descended upon us, chuckling when he heard that we were still cookless, and bringing bottles of the smoky palm toddy and sweet rice wine, with some jars of wild honey, to sell us. Luce, however, knew what she wanted: she was in search of Madé Rantun, the cook trained by the composer and gourmet, Colin McPhee, an American who had lived long in Bali in the years before the war. McPhee had described in a book[1] the excellencies of this Madé Rantun, for, in addition to being a musician, and studying Balinese music, he had also dug deep into the mysteries of Balinese cooking, and Rantun had been his prize discovery.

It was the search for a cook that led us first to Rantun's village, called Pliatan. Here we stopped at the house of the village headman, and met a fat, jovial, perspiring man of middle years, clad in an old batik sarong, and busily engaged in commenting on the roof of a new house in his compound. I complimented him jealously on the depth of his thatch; and he promised us politely to help us look for Rantun. At the time we had no idea that this man knew a note of music; yet he was destined later to be our partner and to travel around the world with us as a leader of the dancers we were searching for. And though he said nothing of it at the time, the squat man whom he was supervising on the house's roof, was the recently divorced husband of the very Madé Rantun whom we sought. The Balinese love to have secrets.

But one morning soon afterwards a quiet-looking woman wearing a neat blue *kebaya* jacket walked into our garden, sat down unobtrusively on a bench in the kitchen, waited for Luce to come in, and announced, "I am Madé Rantun. Is it true that the Nyonya seeks a cook?"

We both liked her manner so much that we wanted to engage her on the spot. But what salary did she want, Luce asked? Oh, the salary was not so important—what she most needed was that her two small children should stay with her and receive their food from us. That could easily be arranged, said Luce. It would be pleasant to have more children around the house. But when could she start? First she must go back to her village, but probably she would be back before ten days had passed—anyhow, she would return with her children as soon as she possibly could.

[1] *House in Bali* (Gollancz)

With Rantun and her children, with Agung and Pegil, our household would be complete.

As our house-building went slowly forward, it became necessary to devise some way of supplementing our living. The local labourers seemed all to be old men, and they worked with a leisurely rhythm that soon frightened my pocket. We discussed, therefore, the idea of building a guest-house.

It so happened that we had seen on the foreshore at Kuta the frameworks of several old houses and huts, and after a trip to take measurements we reckoned that it was possible to move up complete to Kaliungu the seasoned and hard frameworks of two huts, one of which we would turn into a new servants' house, and one of which we would convert into a guest-house bathroom. One day, therefore, we herded our sceptical labourers onto a truck, drove down to Kuta, bought the wooden frames for a song, and arrived back in our village with them intact, though shaken, after the eight-kilometre journey. The wood had been magnificently toughened by more than ten years of weathering the gales from the sea.

This time we could no longer afford the slow Denpasar labourers. But on our travels in search of music and dancing, we had recently been more and more often going to watch the Legong dance in a village called Saba, and I now found some young Saba men who said they would enjoy coming in to work in Denpasar on house building; and since they were very content to be in the southern capital of Bali for a change, the work went ahead rapidly. By the time Rantun reappeared and began to work her magic in our kitchen, the servants' house had been reassembled and a new roof of deep lalang-grass thatch had already been bound and trimmed. Within a matter of days all the servants and children had moved in, and the new labourers were ready to start on the guest-house.

In these ways we acclimatized ourselves to living in a Balinese village. Rantun proved herself a supreme cook of Balinese and Javanese food, and we ate always with our fingers at home so that none of the delectable spicy flavours would be banished by the chill of steel or silver plating. Early in the morning Rantun would leave for the market, buying things at half the prices we had been giving, and soon after eight o'clock she would return, hands laden, a basket on her head, while little Ketut, her four-year-old son, trailed absently behind her, sucking some Balinese sweetmeat, and on his head, perhaps, a live, trussed chicken. Luce, therefore, was now free to think of decorating the two houses.

It was Rantun who looked after our offerings, which made the house a safe place to live in. Every fifteen days, and on all big feast days, she would dress up in her best clothes, her small daughter Sugandi with her, and place offerings of blossoms, fruit, rice and money, arranged on a tiny square cut from young coconut leaves, at all the gateways facing north, south, east and west, and inside the house itself and at various key points in the compound. For this ritual both Rantun and Sugandi would place flowers in their hair, tie an extra cloth around their waists as they would to enter a temple, and as Rantun set down each offering she would flick a little holy water over it and mutter inaudibly some ancient *mantra*.

Agung, on the other hand, introduced us to *leyaks*. Nearly all Balinese believe in *leyaks*, demons that appear as balls of fire or as monsters with flame-dripping tongues, and who suck the blood of unborn babes.

One afternoon Agung was out at the back of the house, ironing. While working he felt a hand push him in the back. He thought it was Pegil, and he swung round quickly to catch the boy: but there was nobody there.

That evening Agung, Rantun and Pegil came together to see us, and to talk about the demons. The Balinese accept these monsters as part of their cosmos, and though perturbed, were no more so than I would have been had I heard an unexpected stair creak in an empty house.

"Tuan," said Rantun, quite happily, "Agung wants to speak to you. He was teased by a *leyak* this afternoon while ironing."

"What is this, Agung?"

Agung twisted restlessly, shyly, and said in a voice almost impossible to hear.

"It is so. I was ironing. I felt a hand touch my back, as if someone were pushing me. I thought it was Pegil. But when I turned around, no one was there. It must have been a *leyak*."

The last words came very softly, but quite surely.

"You don't think it was a muscle twitching in your back, Agung? You feel sure it was a *leyak*?"

"It was a *leyak*." Then in a louder tone: "*Masa!* Is it possible that the Tuan does not know? There are *leyaks* in this village! Many have seen them. A few days ago I saw one in the shape of a flaming monkey, seated on the south garden wall."

So that was that. I thought it best to ask Rantun's advice, for she was older and more experienced in both Balinese and foreign ways.

"What should we do, Madé? Is this serious?"

Rantun laughed good-naturedly at the ignorant Tuan.

"We will make some more offerings. Perhaps the *leyaks* feel that we do not pay enough attention to them. Also, I could ask the *pemangku*."

The *pemangku* is the village priest—not the high caste Brahmana, whose priestly title is *pedanda*, but the everyday and more-close-to-the-people priest.

"But it is nothing heavy, Madé?"

"It is a light matter, Tuan. If the *leyaks* were serious they would do more than push Agung in the back. No, they are perhaps a little offended; we may have been careless not to propitiate them enough. I will prepare some offerings tomorrow."

The matter dropped.

Pegil, who had started going to the local school during the past weeks, gave us our next educational surprise. He came back one day, very tidy and clean, wearing a white shirt and dark-coloured shorts, his satchel in his hands, and said, "Greetings, Tuan. May I speak?"

"But of course, Wayan."

"Tuan, I don't like my name—Pegil. It is not the name for a boy of my age. It's a child's name. So when I went to this school I took another name. I gave my name as Wayan Kusti. Could you perhaps call me Wayan Kusti in future?"

Naturally, we agreed. This was, apparently, a very common Balinese custom. But Pegil had chosen very subtly, we thought. For he was a boy of low caste, and the name Kusti sounds very much the same as the high caste title, Gusti. We appreciated and admired our child's cleverness.

Outside our gateways the village lane was full of ruts and flinty potholes, and little wooden stalls, called *warongs*, lined the road together with scores of the wicker domes of the fighting-cocks' cages. From early in the morning the stall women sold rice and spiced dishes to their customers, who would stroll up, lean against the stall or squat on the ground nearby, unfold the banana leaf wrapping, idly swallow the food, wipe a casual hand on the sarong, throw the leaf down on the road, and without a backward glance walk away. Round these stalls pi-dogs and scavenging pigs, hung-bellied and grey-black, fought for the scraps.

Just before midday the men would begin coming back from the rice-fields, where they had been working since soon after five, their legs now stained with mud, their sireh pouches and knives at their sarongs' waistbands, and near the village *balé* to the south they would buy *tuak*, the smoky toddy brought around at that time of day in long bamboo containers, fastened by the vendor to the front of his bicycle.

Soon the men would tuck up their sarong ends between their legs, crouch down in front of the cage of some favourite fighting cock, un-latch the cage, gently lift the bird out, and then, holding it with one hand under breast and belly, would squat down again, relaxed and content. Then the massage would begin, dreamily given, the man getting as much satisfaction out of the process as the bird.

He would hold the bird in his right hand, and his other hand would caress its back, starting at the head and neck, massaging it with sweeping movements down over its tail. The bird would preen and pretend to struggle, and the massaging would go on for ten steady minutes. Then the man would hold the cock's head in his left hand, fondle and examine the comb and the eyes, blow sharply down its beak, and, after a few moments, still supporting it with his right hand, he would start bouncing it up and down on the ground to exercise its leg muscles, and each time the cock's legs touched the earth it would spring up again as if on a reflex. Next came the tail. The tail had to be bent this way and that way, twitched, fluffed out, blown into. Lastly, if a friend or neighbour were willing, two cocks might be permitted to spar with each other for a few seconds, without using spurs, for practice. Every day this took place; and there was much more to it concerning the hours a cock must be sunned, what it must be fed and when, quite apart from judging the auspicious days on which it might fight. Young boys learned about fighting cocks almost as soon as they could walk: for everything to do with these birds was only man's business.

In a *balé* to the North there was a Djoged orchestra. Each night they would rehearse. The gaily painted instruments had all their keys made from bamboo, and each evening we would hear the madly syncopated clopping of these staccato Djoged melodies. It was strange to hear how melodious a sound bamboo could give out. This club had only just started; how long it would last nobody knew. The Djoged, we were told, was a highly amusing flirtation dance, where any man of the village had a chance to match his skill with the girl Djoged.

The night noises of Kaliungu were various. First, then, the dogs, mournfully, evilly howling, according to the villagers able to see *leyaks* which the human eye could not detect. Then came the usual tropical cicadas, that myriad yet unseen accompaniment to all Balinese nights. Then, the clopping of the Djoged orchestra, stray voices from the nearby *warongs*, and, when the wind was in the right direction, we could just hear the gamelan orchestra of the Belaluan club as they rehearsed near the main road leading into Denpasar.

One evening a car stopped in the lane outside and a boy handed us an invitation to dine at the *puri*, or palace, of the Raja of Gianjar in four days' time, when a performance of a famous Djanger would be put on for us. The invitation came from the very able elder son of the Raja of Gianjar himself, the Anak Agung Gdé Agung, whom Luce and I had known in Djakarta, and who had claimed that the best dancers came from his part of Bali. The Anak Agung was now on a short holiday in Bali before taking up an appointment abroad.

Four nights later, then, we were seated with him and his family watching this celebrated Djanger which he himself had helped create. To our surprise, the leader of the small orchestra was the same fat and jovial headman, or *perbekel*, who had helped us in our search for Rantun.

Though we sat out of doors in a large village *balé*, hemmed in on all sides by thousands of Balinese, we found the dance dull. The twelve pretty girls and twelve young men seated in a square on the floor before us, chanting raucously and making vague gestures with their arms and the upper halves of their bodies, we found monotonous and dreary to watch for more than five minutes. Djanger dances which we had heard from the north of Bali were far more virile and exciting. But this Pliatan group had deliberately softened their Djanger to make it finer, and they had thus devitalized it; also, it had become pretentious, for the dancers first appeared boxed in on a tiny "stage" behind a singularly dirty orange-coloured curtain. This, we feared, was offered as proof of their modernity. We were deeply embarrassed vis-à-vis our host, but to the smiling *perbekel* I gave what I hoped sounded like sincere thanks.

And it became increasingly embarrassing to us because we continued to meet the Anak Agung, who kept talking of his Djanger with the greatest enthusiasm. When he heard that we were hoping to open a guest-house, he very kindly carried us off to a neighbouring village where he showed us a large house which, he told us, we could rent for very little, and would make a wonderful guest-house. It had now been empty a long time, and we would need only to have it rethatched. But it was too far away and too much of a responsibility, so we declined, though we had been sorely tempted on seeing exquisitely carved stands for a gamelan orchestra in the long room upstairs.

Then a series of strange things began to disturb us. One day we asked the Anak Agung to lunch in an attempt to repay some of his generous hospitality, but as he sat down to eat, I chanced to see that in the dispatch case which he kept always close to his side, there lay a revolver. He caught my surprised eye as I noticed this, and he said, "Yes, I'm sorry Mr. Coast; but you see, if anybody tries to shoot me, I have every intention of shooting him first."

This incident left us uneasy. Who, we wondered, would be wanting to shoot the Anak Agung?

Then a few days after the Anak Agung had lunched with us I received a truly astounding post-card through the ordinary mail. At first I thought it was meant for me, but then I saw that it was addressed to some Balinese, whose name I failed to recognize. I called young Kusti, who told me at once that this was the name of the next intended husband of our very valued Rantun: and here in my hands I held a sort of schoolboy-language card threatening his life.

"Traitor to your race," it read. "You, at the time when you were chauffeur to the Anak Agung Gdé Agung, were cruel and oppressive in your conduct against your own people, who were then struggling for their independence. Beware now for your life! Signed: With Pistol and Sword Unsheathed."

And then at night we started to hear gun shots, and we noticed that by nine o'clock at night Denpasar had become as deserted as a city of the dead. When we went out on our nightly excursions, hoping to run into music and dance festivals, we now found that villagers would flee in haste at the mere sound of a jeep's engine, and our headlights would pick them out running as if hordes of *leyaks* were at their heels.

We noticed this particularly near a small town called Blahbatuh, on the road to Saba. And then suddenly we heard that a disaster had hit Pliatan. A girl in the Djanger had been kidnapped by the Military Commander of Bali, who was shortly returning to Java. It might not have been so serious had he not been an Ambonese, and therefore a Christian, and if he hadn't chosen for his bride the prettiest girl of all who was, in fact, the Djanger's fifteen-year-old leader. The Rajas of Gianjar and Denpasar had witnessed the wedding, we were told, so that there was no chance of an appeal.

Very soon after this a new Military Commander arrived, this time a young Sumatran, Islam Salim, and fortunately for us, he was an old acquaintance. From him I learned what I was already beginning to fear: that I had fled from the politics of Djakarta to find that Bali was just about to experience a phase of her national revolution that Java had experienced several years ago. Anything might now happen. People were all at once being killed in a spate of murders of revenge. I began to sleep with a loaded automatic by the side of my pillow. In October the whole island was placed under military law.

2

Our Work Begins

*

Though Bali was the last place on earth where one would have expected to be caught in a "revolution", it was nevertheless some such upheaval which now erupted and which very rapidly entered into the life of every Balinese. But we determined, if it should be possible, to leave their revolution to the Balinese, and, not without trepidation, endeavoured to carry on just as before.

Anyhow, for the time being I was completely wrapped up in my design for the guests' bathroom. It was to be a little gem of modern plumbing, ornamentally encased in the smaller hut taken from Kuta; already it was thatched and connected by another small passageway to the side of the guest house. From a Chinese I had bought serrated green tiles to drain the floor, and green and shining white ones for the bath itself. This bath was not only to be six feet long, but I intended that our guests should have the luxury of hot water. Normally, our baths were filled by Agung with buckets from the well, but for our guests I wanted to heat smooth stones and drop them sizzling into the water to warm it. There was even a real toilet standing in the garden, waiting to be installed.

As it turned out, the Saba workmen should have been sent home as soon as the outside walls and roof were fixed; but their leader, one Gusti Madé, was a garrulous fellow who had married his village's prettiest Legong dancer in days long ago, and he was, it may thus be imagined, a plausible talker. He was perfectly happy to stay in Denpasar and eat in Kaliungu.

"You do understand about tiles, Gusti?" I asked him.

"What is there to understand, Tuan?" he replied—and with such a confident smile that I trusted him utterly.

But this was, in fact, the Gusti's last, too subtle, attempt to draw information from me without losing face. Neither he nor any of the men had handled a tile in their lives.

"How do you fix them, Gusti?" I went on, for I knew nothing of such work. "Do you stick cement on the back of the tile and then lay it against the wall, or do you plaster the wall first and just set the tiles into the plaster?"

The Gusti swallowed—at last he had received a hint as to procedure—and at great speed he answered, "One prepares the wall first, generally. It will all be ready in two days, I reckon."

And for two days they worked like beavers, plastering the walls and themselves with the greatest industry; but I could not help observing that the Gusti's estimate had been a little optimistic. However, on the evening of the second day I went out to inspect. The bath they had not yet begun, and above the edges of the walls they had finished, the cement line was rough and ragged. Very softly, tentatively, I felt one of the top tiles to make sure it held strongly. With no protest at all it fell out into my hand.

There was a very awkward silence. Even Gusti Madé was temporarily checked.

"What's wrong, Gusti?" I asked wearily, as I calculated in my head the cost of redoing the work and feeding those rotund Saba bellies for several more days.

"Wrong, Tuan?" The Gusti sounded hurt. "Why we did it in the very way Tuan ordered!"

I did not recollect *ordering* anything.

"Well, suppose you begin all over again. Maybe you have friends in Denpasar who can give you a little advice."

By the next evening there was one wall already finished by some new method, and on an inspiration the Gusti had laid the floor tiles— so as not to waste time. Resignedly I observed that the serrated edges ran crossways, thus guaranteeing that no water would flow away. The Gusti greeted me with a wide grin as I nodded, hypnotized, at the floor and he smiled easily as I very gingerly prodded the wall put up that day, and when one or two tiles just sighed and tumbled with a squelch into my hand, I silently turned and left them.

That night he came to explain. Luce and I were grimly drinking *arak*, mixed with but little of the sweet rice wine, and we were trying not to think about bathrooms. Cheerfully the Gusti entered and sat on the floor before us, pulling contentedly at the carnation-scented cigarette he had lighted.

"I beg leave to speak, Tuan. Tuan, you must not touch the tiles until after two days. I have been asking a friend. He tells me—excuse me, Tuan—that it is very wrong to touch the tiles for at least two days and nights."

"It seems always to be my fault, eh, Gusti?"

He remained silently smoking, tactfully agreeing that this was so. But I went on quietly: "This is your last chance, Gusti. If in two more days and nights the whole bathroom is not ready, I drive you back to Saba."

Very hurt, the Gusti left me. And at last, using my common sense, the next morning I went to confer in the town with a Chinese contractor.

Unfortunately, the contractor's foreman, a Balinese, came around the following evening to see what the work would entail—for I had guessed that by then the Gusti would have bluffed for the last time. This foreman—his name, he told me, was Nyoman Regog, and he played a metallophone in the Orchestra of the God of Love in a village called Abianangka—walked back with us to witness the state of the bathroom.

I must admit it was uncanny what those three men had achieved. The walls resembled nothing so much as a crossword puzzle, the blanks being the empty spaces from which tiles had already fallen. The long side of the bath had been tiled in what Gusti Madé swore was a straight line, but in what Euclid had long denominated a curve, and ironically, the floor tiles, laid wrongly, were the only ones that had stuck fast.

Luce and I, with Nyoman Regog, stood gazing at my pet experiment, avoiding the workmen's eyes, with Rantun trying to look solemn in the background but periodically unable to contain herself any longer, so that she would have to rush off to her room and explode into what she imagined was silent laughter. It was a depressing sight.

"I ask pardon, Gusti," I said in my politest tones. "Tomorrow I shall drive you home to Saba. It has been all my fault for giving you work that was not suitable."

"May I speak, Tuan? We would have gone home tomorrow anyway, for in a few days there is a temple festival."

Thus face was saved and the bathroom was completed by Nyoman Regog.

Next morning we all drove off to Saba together. The men had bought new *kains* and Hawaiian shirts and the back of the jeep was piled high with their baskets. The Gusti seemed quite cheerful; doubtless he was reflecting on the stories he would soon be telling of his Denpasar adventures. We dropped them on the outskirts of the village, with many polite mutual regrets, and drove in to look for the head of the Legong club, Gusti Gdé Raka. We saw him busy in his house temple, wearing the white *kain* of a priest, so we went to the water garden facing his rice-fields, and sat there to wait for him.

As we rested, looking over the water-lily covered pond to the place opposite where the women came down with earthen jars on their heads to fetch water, we saw one of the Legong girls, a small pot on her head, too. We waved, hoping she and her friends would join us. And presently the three of them came, half running, half holding one another back, soon persuaded by Luce to sit with us, alternately solemn and giggling helplessly, but smoking one of Luce's cigarettes between them.

These were three high-caste children, aged about eight, nine and eleven. They spoke no word of Indonesian, were shy of us as birds, and their charm lay in their earthiness and in their virility of dancing. These three mites lived in a poor village that owned too few rice-fields, especially since the death of the old Gusti, who had pawned or sold so many fields to pay his cockfighting debts. These children, therefore, had to work in the rice-fields daily, and would come home trailing firewood for their mothers. They were burned a dark brown colour by the sun; they had few clothes, and what they did have they saved against the next temple festival or the New Year celebrations, appearing daily in wispy sarongs of great age. They were wild, free, happy, and the village was proud of them.

After a while Raka came into the garden, wearing in his hair,

37

exactly on the top of his head, a white jasmine blossom, a sign that he had made his devotions for the day. He was a stout, youngish fellow, long hair brushed back from his forehead, eyes rather too close together, full of energy and ambition.

"What news?" we asked.

"Oh, nothing. Just as usual."

"Has the Legong played this week?"

"No. It has been quiet."

But Raka was not his robust self for once. His eyes were uneasy, furtive. He looked thinner, too. As he clearly did not wish to talk today, we rose soon to go, and without protest he went with Luce to the gateway, I behind, walking with a young cousin of the family.

"What is the matter with Gusti Gdé Raka?" I asked him, quietly.

"Nothing, Tuan," he replied. But his eyes were wary.

"He looks like a man who has not slept for a week."

"Perhaps that is it, Tuan. A little fever, maybe. That is probably it."

But when we arrived at the jeep, rude though direct questions are, I asked Raka again what was the matter. His disquiet had infected me. And these were the bad days.

"What is it, Raka?"

"Nothing, Tuan. It is nothing."

"Are you sick? Have you not been sleeping?"

He gave a nervous laugh, saying almost under his breath, "It is not so easy to sleep in the *sawahs*."

"Sleep in the rice-fields? What do you mean?"

"Oh, I do not know. I dare not guess. It is better that I say nothing. Certainly it must be a misunderstanding, and my brother Rai thinks he can settle the matter."

"If you tell me this much, I think I should know it all. Is there no way we can help?"

Then: "I have been sought," he said, very simply.

Instinctively my voice went lower now.

"By whom?"

"I don't know. It was some nights ago. Some strange men came to the village from the west. A man gave the alarm on the *kulkul* drum. The village collected at the *kulkul* tower with sticks and knives, but the men had fled. We thought they were thieves, perhaps."

38

"And then?"

"Ah-h, that is the thing, Tuan John. The next night a band of men came from the direction of my rice-fields. We could see electric torches coming from afar, moving toward my *puri*. We all ran away, eastward, to the sea. Later some villagers saw the band going away. It is said they were all dressed in black, and they talked fiercely and several of them carried guns. For the last three nights my family have all slept in the rice-fields to hide. We take it in turn to watch. Where these men came from we dare not guess. But I have told the *punggawa* and the police. They promise to send a bicycle patrol here every night as soon as they can spare the men. But there are many such incidents these days. Since then we have not slept; we are afraid."

"But you are not rich, Raka, and Saba has no politics. I cannot believe that they are after you."

And I told him about the coming of the new Military Commander, our friend Islam Salim, to try to hearten him. But Raka's brother, Gusti Rai, who was listening from a little distance now came up to us, spitting out a piece of grass he had been chewing.

"Tuan, we cannot afford to take stupid risks. This is a time of, well —this may be because Saba has always, for many, many years, been friendly to foreigners. Perhaps this has been misunderstood. Perhaps some people have even thought you were a Dutchman coming to see us. But in Blahbatuh the young nationalists are my friends. I have been to ask their help. It will be better soon. But first we must be patient; and for the moment we choose to sleep in the *sawahs*."

Slowly we turned the jeep around, and Raka made a gallant attempt to talk normally to us.

"Come and eat here next Friday. There is a small festival in the temple in the rice-fields to the west. I have asked the Ida Bagus from Blangsinga village to dance the Kebiar. Also, there may be some trances."

"Thank you, Raka. We'll try to come. But I think we'd better meet you at the temple and not bother you for a meal on such a day. Perhaps someone from your *puri* could guide us over the rice-fields. And now—we ask leave to go."

"Peace on your going."

Feeling very sorry for Saba we headed the jeep next in the direction of Pliatan. We wondered what we could do to help our friend Raka. And since we had heard that President Sukarno was coming to Bali soon on one of his semi-annual visits, I thought it might be a good idea to try to persuade him to see the Saba Legong. If the President favoured the village Legong, automatically the position of Raka would be secure.

Arrived in Pliatan we drove straight to the fat headman's house, for I had decided by instinct and from what I had read in Colin McPhee's book that he was still my best hope. Entering his *puri* by the small side gate—for in Bali ceremonial gateways are for decoration, not for everyday use—we found our friend at home with a towel wrapped around his vast middle, a pair of spectacles on the tip of his nose, sitting at a table and laboriously copying out some document for a peasant who sat hopefully on the floor below him.

"Greetings, Anak Agung," we called, for he was of high caste.

"Greetings, Tuan John. Greetings, Nyonya." He hurried to his feet, turning chairs on the porch in our direction, hastily pulling on a soiled shirt. "Where have you come from?"

"From Saba."

A cloud crossed the face of our headman.

"I was forgetting," he replied, somewhat overpolitely. "The Tuan is a great admirer of the Saba Legong."

"We both are. What do you think of it, Anak Agung?"

"I have not seen it."

This time the coldness of his reply was unconcealed.

Wondering whether this was another old rivalry, I turned to other topics. We discussed the now imminent rains and the excellence of Rantun's cooking. We walked around his compound, which consisted of eight separate houses, some new, some dilapidated, a kitchen, a washhouse, a large *balé* where women were pounding rice by hand with long bamboo pestles heavily weighted at the ends, and a walled-off house temple. There were many children, two rows of fighting cocks in their cages, several girls sitting down weaving at hand looms, and two great trees of pomelos, known as Bali limes, which are like sweet and pink-fleshed grapefruit.

At last we were seated again, drinking coffee, and I dared continue.

"What about the future of your Djanger, Anak Agung?"

"Adoh!" A large sigh. "What can I say? The girl who was kidnapped was my elder brother's child. If we cannot protect our own family, the village certainly will not permit their daughters to join the Djanger club. When the present girls are married in their turn, no fresh ones will come forward to take their places. So, the Djanger is finished."

At which he smiled cheerfully, which is the polite way to hide sorrow or regret, since it is considered childish and stupid to be miserable over something that you can do little or nothing to change.

There was another pause. Luce admired some fine orange-coloured hibiscus outside the house temple gateway.

"If you like that hibiscus, Nyonya, I would be glad to give you a cutting. But you must take it on a Thursday. Thursday is the auspicious day of the week for taking cuttings."

"You are very kind, Anak Agung," said Luce. "Another time I may remind you of it."

Then, hoping that I was not moving too rudely, I made an attempt to come to the point.

"Excuse my ignorance, Anak Agung, but I keep thinking of what I have read about Pliatan's famous gamelan in the years before the war. Although you do not need it for the Djanger—and we must say frankly that we do not think the Djanger a real dance—would it not be possible to start rehearsing your gamelan again?"

The Anak Agung rested his hands on his paunch, thinking; then answered, "I would have to persuade the club. But for what reason should I press them to begin rehearsing again? It is known that Pliatan only has a Djanger now."

"Couldn't you train some other dancers, as well? Has Pliatan only talent for a Djanger? And what has happened to Sampih—whom Colin McPhee entered as a member of your club? We heard he was a wonderful Baris, and still we haven't seen a Kebiar worth anything at all."

The Anak Agung became animated.

"Does the Tuan know my friend Tuan Colin McPhee?"

"Alas, no, Anak Agung. But thanks to him I know you and Sampih and others by name."

He smiled at me, very charmingly, with a most subtle expression on his round face.

"I think the Tuan has much to say to me. What is the Tuan planning—why am I being asked all these questions?"

"It is quite simple," I said carefully. "I want you to rehearse your famous gamelan, train new dancers and work together with me. As you progress, we will look for tourists to bring up to watch the club at work, and you will fix a fee for them to pay. Then the club will gain heart from receiving extra money, other than from the Djanger's performances. And if we get on happily with one another and are satisfied with our work—well, my great ambition is to take a really first-class group of dancers abroad."

Anxiously I watched the Anak Agung's reaction to this proposal, for on this could hinge everything. But he beamed, wagged his head several times without saying anything, flavouring the idea, and then he said, "*Beh!* I would like to go abroad again. The Tuan knows that in the Dutch time we were taken by Tjokorda Sukawati to the Paris Exposition with the orchestra you are talking about? But we were hidden away, we Balinese, like serfs, and we saw little of Paris or foreigners. But today, Indonesia is a free country and it would be all quite different." He chuckled. "It is a fine idea. I think I can persuade the club to such a scheme."

"Wonderful. You call the club together and let me know their opinion. Then we'll try working together for a month to see how we *tjotjok*—fit together."

"*Tjotjok!* That is certain! I will call the club tonight. And tomorrow I will come by the morning bus to Denpasar and tell you what is decided."

We got up to leave, the Anak Agung accompanying us to the jeep, sighing to himself, recalling already, perhaps, his few glimpses of Paris in 1931.

"Till tomorrow, then. We beg leave to go."

"Peace on your going."

In the jeep I said to Luce, "Now we have Saba and Pliatan—two irons in the fire. But I like this old headman. I think we're all going to *tjotjok* like anything."

Soon after breakfast the next morning the Anak Agung arrived, stepping with a puzzled air over our stepping-stones in the still dry compound. In the old Balinese manner he carried one end of his long *kain* in his hand as he walked. Behind him there came a tall, dour-faced man. We called for cups of coffee and sat down to satisfy Eastern etiquette by talking for a while of nothing that was related to our purpose.

"*Beh!*" said the Anak Agung. "The Tuan has some noble moon orchids."

His eyes flew around the house, looked pityingly at my thatch, taking in every detail. After a few minutes Rantun entered with the coffee and at once our guests came to life.

"*Beh!* Young sister Rantun!" they both exclaimed.

Rantun smiled and nodded and addressed the Anak Agung so enthusiastically that the coffee was almost lost, and the tall, hitherto solemn-faced individual who had come with the Anak Agung now became animated too, slapping his knee, asking questions like a machine gun of Madé Rantun. Finally, shaking his head, the Anuk Agung said, "Now only Sampih is lacking. Then Tuan Colin's family would be complete. I was his friend; Rantun was his cook; and Madé Lebah, here," he indicated the tall man, "was his chief instructor of Balinese music and his chauffeur."

I could be patient no longer—for what could be a better omen than this?

"But, Anak Agung," I asked rapidly, "did the club meet and did you decide anything last night?"

I could almost feel the disappointed surprise of the Anak Agung. Could not this young foreigner restrain his impatience for half an hour? Why should we rob ourselves of the pleasant anticipation of the news soon enough to be imparted? Oh, well. These white men were all the same. He sighed, put on his most imposing manner, and said, "The club decided to start rehearsing again. Lebah here is my right hand man in the club. But first we must wait for an auspicious day— the omens need not be perfect, but good—so I hope we shall begin within two weeks."

The Anuk Agung here was referring to the need of consulting an astrologer, who would advise the club when would be a lucky day to start work. In Bali, as in much of Asia, astrology plays a big role in both personal and national decisions.

"But, Tuan, the club makes one request. That you and the Nyonya don't come up until several days after we've started. The club would be ashamed."

"Easily agreed!" And then: "What will you choose first for a new dance, Anak Agung?"

"We thought we would make a Legong. A real classical Legong. Then you can have pleasure making comparisons."

This was to pull our Saba-prejudiced legs.

"And for the *guru*—who will you ask to come? The little girls, too, have they been found yet?"

"Slowly, slowly, Tuan. Little girls are not hard to find in our village. As for the teacher, perhaps the Tuan knows of Lotring? Long ago he and his wife made a Legong in Pliatan."

"Yes—we met Lotring when we lived at Kuta. We know his house. He won't be there, but we'll drive you down now, if you like, to look for him."

"That would be good."

So we climbed into the jeep, and when we had arrived in Kuta and walked down the hot sandy path between grey-white walls of coral to Lotring's compound, the teacher was not at home. Four delicate metallophones for the Shadow Play music lay dismantled on the floor of his house, awaiting tuning. The children told us he had gone back to Sempidi, where a new dance he was making was nearly ready.

"If we take the sea road through the rice-fields it's only fourteen kilometres to Sempidi. Let's go now, Anak Agung. Lotring never can be found at home."

So we bumped along through miles of flat, water-filled *sawahs* beneath a hot blue sky, at last emerging on the main road to Tabanan, turned right to Sempidi, and very soon found Lotring seated before a coffee stall. He was so astonished to see the four of us together that he forgot all manners. "*Beh!* Greetings, greetings! What brought you all here today? Heh! Elder sister—" this to the woman at the *warong*, "four more glasses of *tuak* for my friends."

We sat down on the bench running in front of the stall and slowly the Anak Agung began to explain . . . to tell about the Djanger . . .

44

that the gamelan club wanted to train new dancers . . . that the English Tuan wanted to try to help . . . so we were wondering whether perhaps Elder Brother Lotring would honour the club by coming to teach again in Pliatan. . . .

"Hah! So that's it. When?"

"The gamelan will be rehearsing soon; and we have three little girls in mind whom we think suitable. But you must see them first, of course."

"I could not begin soon." Automatically Lotring's hand strayed to his *sireh* pouch. "For weeks I have delayed going to Bangli. I have been called by the Lord Raja. I must see what it is that he desires. Perhaps he wants a Baris dance—perhaps a little music. But I must expect to be gone a month."

His *sireh* now ready he slipped it into his mouth, watching the Anak Agung out of the corner of his eye. I had the impression that this was all a game—that Lotring had no intention of going to Pliatan.

"*Arroh!* that is ill news," answered our headman. Yet I could hear no surprise and fancied that I could almost detect a note of relief in his voice. "I will tell the club tonight. Then perhaps I must come to seek you again."

"It is indeed a shame," said old Lotring; and yet I could have sworn his eye was merry. Effusively we took leave of one another, Lotring joking to the last, asking us, "And my teeth? Perhaps the Tuan found some growing in Denpasar?"

At first there was a silence in the jeep. Then the two Balinese started talking rapidly together, laughing and quite unperturbed, it seemed. But perhaps this was their way of telling me that it was not possible to make a Legong.

"So what now? No teacher, no Legong?"

"Who said so, Tuan? The best Legong teacher perhaps in all Bali lives in Pliatan itself. Her name is Gusti Madé Sengok and she will teach our Legong."

"I am stupid, then. I do not understand. Why did we come all this way to look for Lotring?"

It was a very Balinese reply. Oh, it was good manners . . . Lotring had taught them long ago, before modernizing himself and when he still listened to his wife's advice . . . they had known that Lotring was very busy and had gambled on his not being able to come . . . so now everybody was happy . . . respect had been shown to Lotring, the Pliatan teacher would be used . . .

We dropped our cheerful friends in the Denpasar market place, for they had shopping to do before the bus left at one o'clock, departing packed to the roof with its passengers, and on its roof baskets of fruit and fish and pottery and even bicycles.

"Just let us know when we may come and hear your music, Anak Agung."

"Certainly; it will be soon. We go now."

On the day of the Saba Temple Festival a puncture delayed us and it was eleven o'clock before we arrived. However, the moon was just coming up and we feared no incidents of violence during a festival, because no nationalistic youth, however disposed to violence, would dare risk the wrath of the gods by desecrating their celebrations.

The *puri* was deserted, but in the water garden we found Raka's servant asleep on a bench and guessed that he had been left there to guide us. I woke him.

"*Adoh!* But you are late, Tuan. The Legong is over. I heard the music just now. But if we hurry perhaps you will see the Ida Bagus dance his Kebiar."

So saying he led us, barefoot, through a small stream and into the rice-fields. With my torch I picked out a path about ten inches wide which lay along the top of the earth banks between the fields; it was sometimes slippery with mud, sometimes prickly with coarse grasses. Some of the rice had just been planted and was barely discernible by night against the shimmering water, but when we passed the tall, ripe *padi* we could see that whole fields were alive with fireflies, mysteriously and silently flying through the rice stalks, making patterns of great intricacy with their glowing tail lights as they heard us coming. We walked in single file and the hum of the great crowd in the temple came loudly to our ears.

This temple lay on a grass oasis in the middle of the sea of rice-fields. Thousands of gaily dressed people, with sweet-smelling flowers in their hair, made walking almost impossible. On all sides the *warong* women were selling drink and food, while men and boys

46

played games with cards and counters in numberless temporary shacks. The air was filled with smoke, the scent of flowers and coconut oil. Our guide pushed and dragged us through the good-humoured mass, sometimes shouting back at us, "Can you not hear, Tuan? That is the Kebiar music that has started. We will miss everything. *Adoh!* this crowd . . ."

But when we reached the top step of the main gateway into the outer courtyard and saw the jammed humanity below, we decided to stay there. We could see the rectangle of earth gaily decorated with streamers and woven palm leaves where the gamelan was playing under the white glare of three kerosene lamps. We could make out Raka at his drum. And in front of the orchestra we could plainly see the Kebiar dancer. For fifteen minutes we watched him dance—the fluttering of long-nailed fingers, the flirtatious eyebrows, the pivoting and hopping about the floor, all in a seated position. But though the dancer had grace of a sort and rhythm, he was entirely without the magic quality which we sought—the quality that the dance's creator had had in the nineteen-thirties, the great Mario.

As the dance finished, the crowd slowly flowed in our direction, while we waited flat against the gateway till they had gone. Then we went forward to apologize to Raka.

We were greeted with laughter.

"*Beh!* The Tuan is perhaps becoming a Balinese. How late is it, Tuan?"

So we sat joking at a *warong*, sipping a little *arak* mixed with the pink, thick rice wine, called *brum*, till Raka asked, "Are you tired or do you still want to see the trances—if they come off?"

"But we would love to see the trances."

"Good. Then we will go into the inner courtyard."

It was now dark in the inner courtyard. Over in a corner we could just see an old priest, waited on by some women who sat before him on the ground, with a pot of charcoal burning there in the darkness, and a few small offering trays nearby. The sound of rising and falling voices was wafted over to us.

Suddenly a bunch of neatly dressed girls, hand in hand, brushed past us, one of them turning toward us and smiling, for we saw the flash of white teeth. Raka laughed when we asked him who the girl was.

47

"It was Soli, the Legong dancer," he said. "She is nearly a woman now. She goes with older girls these days, seldom any more with the other Legong girls. It is a nuisance, but soon we shall be looking for another Legong dancer."

"But Raka—how old is Soli? Eleven? Twelve?"

"Maybe. She doesn't know how old she is. But she has a young sister who has already menstruated. Soli will be carried off soon. Tuan has noticed perhaps that when she dances her eyes sometimes glance at a man? That is very bad indeed in a Legong. It is good if she marries."

We waited, kicking our heels.

"You haven't really told us what is likely to happen . . ." I was beginning, when Raka turned to us quickly.

"It is starting now," he said briefly. "Just watch."

In front of the incense arising from the charcoal brazier we could see the old white-robed priest getting to his feet, while attendants stood tensely, protectingly around him. All the while he kept muttering, and then a sentence of the old Kawi tongue, incomprehensible, would be flung out across the courtyard. Then came more mumbling, sometimes a deep-throated chuckle, ending in a laugh or snort. A weird, eerie act of ventriloquy in the night, it seemed to us, for the priest was seemingly carrying on conversations with himself in several voices.

"What is he saying?" I whispered.

"He is in trance. He goes into this state so that he can become an empty medium through which the gods can speak to the village and tell us whether they are satisfied or not with our offerings. So far all is well."

But a moment later a fierce altercation seemed to break out. Stormy voices were raised—all issuing from the one throat. It was uncanny. Snarls, grunts, whines, imperious orders, poured through the old priest, who was swaying tempestuously around the yard, in the end facing the high altar where the sacred and powerful masks of the Barong and Rangda lay displayed on top of the boxes in which they were normally stored. The Barong, a purely animistic symbol of Good, was in Saba represented in the form of a great black boar, inside which two men would dance and act the Barong play at the time of the New Year festivities. Rangda on the other hand, was the Demon Queen of the *leyaks*, in another manifestation being Durga, the Hindu Goddess of Death. And it was towards the mask of the terrible Rangda, flaming of tongue and sabre-toothed, that the priest was now clawing his way, a torrent of bestial growls bursting through his old lips.

The few Balinese present seemed to be watching closely, but showed no sign of fear. Raka breathed excitedly. "Na-a-a! So that is it. Rangda has said that not enough offerings were made for her. She is complaining and cursing through the priest. More offerings will have to be made, and more propitiations."

The priest, meanwhile, shivering all over as with a fever, was clamouring for the Rangda mask to be put over his head.

"Now the spirit of Rangda is in him," said Raka.

Strutting, shaking, the old man stamped around the courtyard, making his way back awkwardly to his place before the brazier. There the mumblings continued, until after a while, when he was calmer, the mask was gently lifted off him. But he himself remained deep in trance, mouthing incomprehensibly. Some voices started chanting, to break the trance, and holy water was made ready to sprinkle on him when the trance should leave him. At last the priest opened his eyes, staring, and then frenziedly plunged his hands into the brazier, upsetting it, tearing out two or three burning husks of coconut fibre, which, still red and aflame, he dusted through his long hair, even crammed in his mouth, sparks scattering all around him.

"The trance is now leaving him, Tuan," said Raka solemnly. "There remains only the sprinkling of the holy water. Then he will go home."

Stiffly we got to our feet. Fantastic scenes such as these, full of beauty and sincerity, probably take place many thousands of times in one year in Bali.

Raka walked with us to the road.

"Thank you for a wonderfully interesting experience, Raka. And peace on your sleep."

"It was nothing. Peace on your going."

When the President arrived in Bali I was fortunate in being able to speak with him for a moment at the airport, where I was eyed suspiciously by my old opponent, the Palace Secretary. And though his planned holiday was to become a week of solid political speech-making, he agreed that he would like to see the Legong of Saba. Luce and I, therefore, almost lived in Saba, timing the dance so that the President should not be bored, and patching up the costumes and headdresses as best we could.

But before the evening for the Legong came, I heard that the President was to make one of his speeches in the Wisnu Cinema to young nationalists from all over Bali. And for once I broke my rule. I was so interested to hear what the Head of State's attitude would be to the dangerously growing lawlessness throughout the island, that, together with Jef Last, a renowned Dutch writer who was teaching in a school in North Bali, and was my valued friend, I found myself seated with the representatives of the press in about the fourth row. Behind us the hall overflowed with long-haired young men, oddly garbed, whose tenseness communicated itself to us, and who were the force which, if uncontrolled, would bring Bali into terrorized anarchy.

Straight from an Army Day parade came Sukarno, dressed in very simple, man-of-the-people khaki shirt with open collar and rolled up sleeves. He was greeted with a frightening welcome of cheers in which patriotism and hysteria were blended. But at first Sukarno took his seat in the hall's front row, and a Balinese youth leapt to the stage, where, with raised fist and staring eyes, he led those young national-ists on a sweet orgy of verbal revenge against the ills of Indonesia's past colonial sufferings. My skin was a-prickle with gooseflesh. Myself an emotional person, I have learned to be profoundly distrustful of emotional thinking. And that this could happen in Bali, depressed and worried me.

Then Ruslan Abdulgani rose to take his place. He, since the revolutionary days in Java, had been the Secretary-General at the Ministry of Information, and he poured cold douches of reason and logic over the hot heads before him, mixing his reason with a subtle sympathy for their cause, till he judged they were ready to receive the speech of the President himself.

Having folded his sleeves a trifle higher and urged some gaping market women standing at the rear of the hall to come forward and fill the empty front seats, Sukarno led his listeners out on a brisk attack on the classic enemy, Imperialism. The young nationalists roared their applause. Having thus shown them that he, too, could eat fire, and when he sensed that he had them tied emotionally to him, he broke off, paused, and in a quite different, hushed voice, descended from the realms of generalization to the present moment.

Did they think that Father Sukarno did not understand their aspirations, he asked them? Did they not guess how completely he was in sympathy with them? Then, very gently he underlined the points where he agreed with them. He, too, wanted Bali to progress with the rest of Indonesia; he deplored, also, the old Dutch policy of keeping Bali in a museum state; the old feudal system which had been banished in Java must meet the same fate in Bali, he said; and was he not the Father of his People and thus the greatest believer of them all in a united country . . .? But . . .

When Pandit Nehru had come to Bali with him six months ago ("and don't forget, my friends, that Nehru's India is politically perhaps our closest ally as well as the ancient source of much of Bali's Hindu culture"), well, Pandit Nehru had said: (and here the President's voice faltered, and tears coursed down his cheeks unashamed, bringing a deathly silence upon the hall): "In Bali I feel that I am seeing a people and country as it was in the morning of the world . . . *in the morning of the world.*" Therefore, whether they liked it or not, Bali and the people of Bali, did have a special position in the eyes of the outside world, and thus a unique responsibility to the State of Indonesia.

And having brought his young hearers to this firm, even primeval earth, he abandoned all oratorical tricks in order to urge, no, in order to *command* the nationalists to act henceforth in a disciplined way. In the most lucid language he instructed them to throw away their methods of violence and terror, and to use such techniques as they had just heard outlined by Ruslan Abdulgani.

It was a masterpiece of a speech. And to me it was now encouragingly clear that the Indonesian Government in Djakarta regarded the disorders in this inconveniently well-known island as a danger to the name of the whole archipelago. It was for this reason

51

that the President was prepared to spend a whole week touring the island with Islam Salim and the head of Denpasar's civil administration, Sutedja, in an attempt to restore peace.

A few nights later, on a lawn in front of the Government house, the President saw the Saba Legong. We sat exactly behind him, and to us, hoping for his approval, the dance this night seemed infinitely long. We watched anxiously to see if he yawned. But when the Legong and his favourite dancer, Tjawan, had both danced, he turned around and asked, "This Saba—is it a very poor village?"

"It is poor, sir."

"Tell their leader to bring the small girls to see me tomorrow about noon. And tell them to work out the cost of a new set of costumes. I *like* this Legong. It is truly of the people."

Next day Gusti Gdé Raka appeared at our house just as we were finishing lunch. His face was positively smug with contentment. The Legong children and several members of the club followed behind him. He sat down, breathless, unable to speak. Then: "*Beh!* That Bapa Sukarno!"

"Well—did he promise you new costumes?"

"New costumes? That was nothing! He told us that he would call us to dance in the palace at Djakarta soon. We are exploding with happiness. A greater honour we could not have. And then, as we prepared to take our leave, he told us that we could spend up to a thousand *rupiahs* on making new costumes so that we should not be ashamed in Djakarta."

Raka was so overcome that he could say no more, not even utter a word of thanks; but the double-hand grip he insisted on giving both of us as he left with his party to catch a bus, nearly broke our fingers.

The sequel to this story came some months later. We were eating one day in Saba with our friend, Theo Meier, the Swiss painter, when out of the night there sprang a man waving a broad knife, and who, instead of cutting our throats, started haranguing Raka fiercely. Raka, very calmly, sent this fellow about his business, saying to us, "His daughter has been kidnapped for marriage. He swears he knew nothing about it and wants me to help him go in pursuit of the man.

But it is nonsense. It was all arranged." He paused, then went on: "There are two kidnappings tonight, for it is a lucky day. The other girl that I hear is to be kidnapped is our Legong—Soli."

And so it was. Nor had Raka trained any substitute for her, nor was any good understudy for the respectably married Soli ever found. Her place was at length taken by a little mouse of a thing with no personality at all.

But when Raka said to us, very soon after her marriage, "It is rumoured that Soli's *kain* was clean this month," so that we knew she would soon be bearing a child and unable to dance the Legong ever again, we told Raka bluntly that he was risking the future of his club if he found no suitable replacement.

"You try to find one, Tuan John," Raka would reply jokingly. "I've looked at every little girl in the village. There are no others."

The sad truth, however, was, that ever since the President had looked with favour on his Legong, Raka's manner had become more and more overconfident. He was compensating for his former fear by becoming very self-satisfied. There was no arguing with him. The little mouse came to stay. And so timid a little mouse was she that when the summons to the palace came, many months later, he dared not use her and the Legong was danced by a young mother, Soli: which was all very wrong.

It was fortunate then, that a car stopped in our lane one morning soon after the President's departure, and its chauffeur, Madé Lebah, entered our compound bringing news from the Pliatan gamelan club.

"Greetings, Tuan and Nyonya. Well, we have been rehearsing three nights. It is very bad at the moment—very bad. But if you are brave enough to listen once, the Anak Agung hopes you will dine in his *puri* tomorrow evening soon after nightfall. Then you can hear the gamelan and see our Legong candidates."

"This is the best of news, Madé. We shall meet tomorrow."

I turned to Luce with a smile: "It seems that the Pliatan iron is warming up just as Saba begins to cool off."

"By tomorrow night we shall know," answered Luce.

3

The Club in Pliatan

*

A tall, spare man with grey hair and a deep voice was waiting at the gateway of the *puri* in Pliatan to meet us and bring us in. He was spotlessly tidy in a starched khaki shirt, with a green sarong and sandals.

"I am the Dewa Gdé Putu and the headman is my brother," he said, introducing himself, "I am to welcome you to our home. We hope that tonight's will be the first of many meals you will both eat here with us," and motioning with his right hand he beckoned us to follow him in.

"There is great excitement tonight," he continued. "The club will all be here; perhaps you will care to say a few words to them. Also, the old Legong teacher may come later, and then you can see the three little Legong girls whom we think suitable, for we want also to ask your opinion. And Sampih has come over from Sayan and is here tonight, too."

So saying he was leading us through the courtyard, which was made into an outer and inner courtyard by being divided by a broad house, set exactly in its centre, and the rear wall of which was sculptured with a magnificently carved Garuda bird, the Hindu phoenix, steed of the God Wisnu. Passing a verandah in this first courtyard our eyes detected the gleam of gold paint on the metallophones of a full gamelan orchestra. The compound was alive with people in the dusk, with scores of naked children, arms around each others necks, and waists, happy already in anticipation.

We were to eat in the farthest, newest house, a thatched replica of a very simple modern bungalow of three rooms The sitting room and dining room combined was lit by a kerosene lamp which revealed four bamboo chairs round a low table on a cement floor, while in the background we could see another table where plates were already piled high with white rice.

The headman came in, rubbing his hands, beaming: "Welcome, welcome! I am just this minute finished in the kitchen."

"You have been cooking yourself, Anak Agung?"

"Of course. Balinese men are the best cooks, and if it is for a feast or for guests, I always do the cooking myself. Now, we have here some special *arak*, mixed with *brum* and wild honey. It is a very strong *arak*. Do you and the Nyonya dare to join us?"

So we sat there drinking together while night fell swiftly across the courtyard outside. Then, apologetically: "Anak Agung," I said. "Before we begin working together, forgive my ignorance and please tell me exactly what your full name is; also your brother's. We are terribly confused by all these titles in Bali."

But it was his brother who quickly replied, "Of a truth there are many titles, Tuan. You see, in our Hindu religion there are four castes. First, the caste from which the high priests are chosen—the Brahmana. The priests have the title *Pedanda*; but an ordinary Brahmana man we address as Ida Bagus, and a Brahmana woman as Dayu."

"Then not all Brahmana are priests?"

"Certainly not. But high priests can only be chosen from the Brahmana caste. Then next comes the Raja caste, the caste of the warriors, the Ksatriya. Their titles are Tjokorda, Anak Agung and Dewa, and to that caste our family belongs. Next there are the Wesya, whose title generally is Gusti. There are thousands of these titles all over Bali, and the three castes together make up our aristocracy.

Lastly, we come to the ordinary people—the Suddras. They have many castes and crafts among themselves, but possess no titles. A first-born child of a Suddra family is simply called Wayan, a second born, Madé, a third, Nyoman and a fourth, Ketut."

"And if there is a fifth born?"

"Then they start all over again with Wayan."

"And will you explain your names—your own and your brother's?"

"I am Dewa Gdé Putu. Dewa is my title; Gdé means great, but is just a sort of honorary prefix, and Putu means a first-born Ksatriya.

My brother the *perbekel* (which means "headman") is Anak Agung Gdé Ngurah Mandera. Anak Agung is his title, and Gdé is the same prefix as mine; Ngurah means he is the head of the family, and Mandera is his personal name. We live in Puri Kaleran, which means Puri of the North, and a *puri* is any house where men of the Ksatriya caste live."

"Well, thank you, Dewa. That was quite a lecture. You spoke like a professor."

"It is possible," he laughed, "for I have been teaching for thirty-four years and am now headmaster in the village of Mas."

"In that case, please, here and now, both of you become our instructors and guides in everything Balinese—not only in music and dancing, but in the Balinese way of thinking and living."

"Gladly, gladly, Tuan," said the Anak Agung. "Then let us continue your education with some real Balinese food."

So the four of us sat down and the food was brought in by the tall Madé Lebah from the adjoining kitchen; and this food was different in some subtle way from our Rantun's.

"It is sharper, stronger," said the Anak Agung. "This is men's cooking; Rantun's is woman's cooking. Now, here is Pliatan's speciality—*bebek tutu*—spiced, smoked duck."

We ate, as usual, with our right hands, and this made the brothers happy and at ease, and finger-bowls of water were quickly brought us. The food continued to come in, and we were pressed to put more and more on to the slowly disappearing mounds of our rice. There were two sorts of *saté*, meat grilled on little sticks, of pork flesh, both, but quite differently cooked and spiced; the famous smoked duck was pungent, but its flesh flaked away delicately; there were young ferns from the hills, tenderer than asparagus; there were crisp, dry, fried chicken joints, chopped up small; then bean sprouts and bean curd in soya sauce; there was the crackling outer skin of a very aromatic pork; lastly, chillis, little onions and rock salt. On and on we ate, trying, but failing to keep up with our hosts, until, hardly able to stand, we moved from the table to drink coffee in the front of the house again.

Then the Anak Agung shouted an order, adding to us, "I want you to see the Legong children. I wonder what you will think of them. And I've just sent a man to look round the *warongs* for Sampih. He should be here soon."

In a few minutes the little girls came, entering very shyly, smiling, pulling down the ends of their jackets in their nervousness, and the three little tots sat in one chair, politely not looking at us. Their features were far more aristocratic than the three in Saba.

"Well?" asked the Anak Agung.

"But what do we know about Legongs!" replied Luce and I together. But I added, to pull his leg for a change, "You see, we are only really familiar with the Legong in Saba. But I can see three very delightful little girls here—where are they from?"

"Heh! You children come and give your hands to the Tuan and Nyonya," called the Anak Agung.

They sidled forward, smiling awkwardly, utterly captivating. Each gave us a limp hand in turn, smiling sideways at us, then ran back to the chair.

"This is Oka," said the *perbekel*. "She is my own daughter and her mother was a Djanger from Kedewatan village. She is in the top class of the Lower School. And this is Anom—the child of my brother here. These are our two Legongs, we think. Oka is of strong character and will take the male roles in the story; Anom, as you see, is gentle and soft, with huge eyes—she will be the Princess Langkesari. And now this is Raka, who is Oka's friend and lives just over the road. She will be the important Tjondong—the Attendant on the two Legongs."

"They look exquisite. Have they begun rehearsing?"

"No; but if you like them, we will start tomorrow or the next day. Whenever they are not at school. It will be easiest with Raka—she always runs away from school."

"You will find us living in your compound, I'm afraid."

"Good. Then you will learn fast." He clapped both his hands to his vast stomach. "And now—if the Tuan and Nyonya are ready, the club is waiting for us."

We walked over together, servants bringing the kerosene lamp and chairs for the Dewa and ourselves, and by the lamp's glaring light we saw the rehearsal place clearly—a long, stone and brick verandah, fifteen yards long, whitewashed throughout and opening on to the first courtyard. On its inside wall hung a photograph of the gamelan club in 1938, just after it had won the 1938 all-Bali gamelan competition; and also a strange, blue picture of a white man, holding a gun

57

in his hand, seated in a rowing-boat by the lake shore, with a tiger just about to leap into the boat from the overhanging bank.

The instruments were all arranged at one end, covering about a third of the floor space. Our chairs were placed facing them. At the very back of the gamelan we could see the great bronze gongs on a wooden stand, then some tall, heavy metallophones, played by men seated on stools, and in front of them the main metallophone section, eight of them, of which the largest, in the front row, was under the hammer of Madé Lebah. On the floor nearest us sat the men who played the pair of small cymbals, with the two drummers. The leading drummer was the Anak Agung himself, who gripped the larger, fèmale drum across his knee, and his partner was a fine-featured man, introduced to us now as Gusti Kompiang.

For a brief minute they talked among themselves, while the children crowded in from outside, squatting all along the step. A man pumped the lamp up for the last time. The Anak Agung straightened his back a little, shouting across to us, "We are going to start with Tabuh Telu—Melody Three."

"I think this may be a little loud," I whispered to Luce, for the verandah was low and narrow, and no less than twenty-four players sat with hammers poised before us.

Madé Lebah gripped his hammer firmly; then he and the Anak Agung exchanged a lightning glance, and drum and metallophone started on a terrific chord that I shall never forget, and straightaway we were drowned in the music—drowned, overwhelmed, carried away, submerged. For such music as this we had never heard in our lives, never heard hinted at by the dozens of gamelans which we had already listened to.

This gamelan had a percussive attack, an electric virtuosity, a sort of appalling precision, which, as it echoed and rebounded off that long wall, almost pulsated us out of our seats, bringing tears of astonished emotion to our eyes.

Where was the melody? I had no idea! But an incessant cascade of sound rushed through us and around us and deep down inside us. The two drums thwacked and throbbed, the deep gongs boomed, the cymbals chattered and clacked; but it was the metallophones and a battery of twelve gongs of descending size on a long, low stand, played by four men, which swept us away. The metallophones hammered out patterns of such intricacy, such crisscross elusiveness, and with such a dazzling, brilliant zeal, as was most assuredly outside my comprehension; and from that long battery of gongs came a baffling, staccato syncopation which nothing out of Africa could hope to rival. This music broke its way into us, possessed us.

"Tabuh Telu" came to an end. It took several seconds for the quivering sound to die away. Twenty-four peasants looked impassively at me—most of them very humble, poor people, who had been working that day in their rice-fields. As the Anak Agung got to his feet, profusely sweating, and came to sit with us, the orchestra members broke into grins, reaching for their cigarettes.

"It is still very bad," said the Anak Agung, mopping his forehead. "I must ask pardon for allowing the Tuan to hear such imperfection." But his eyes gleamed with pure pride as he awaited my beginner's verdict.

But for an embarrassing half minute I was speechless, moved so deeply that I dared not open my lips. My whole Balinese horizon had been violently broadened in these few minutes. Not only did the gamelans of Denpasar now sound tame and insipid, but that such great music as this could have been devised had never entered my senses. When at last I felt I could speak, we all went and sat on the floor with the club members. I told them, I think, that this was the most wonderful music I had heard in my life, anywhere, ever: that the western world must have an opportunity to hear it: that I hoped we would date our working together from that same night.

And then the rehearsal went on again. They practised the music of Sampih's Kebiar, which made "Tabuh Telu" sound gentle and simple. But after that first initial shock I was only aware that night of one thing, and of this both Luce and I were absolutely sure: this was the orchestra for us, and if ever we went abroad, it would be with the Pliatan club.

When we left the *puri* to go home, feeling still dazed, exhausted, as if those lightning fast little hammers had been rippling up and down our spines for hours, we were conscious of the Anak Agung's voice again: "Tuan, here is Sampih."

We saw a still boyish-looking young man, rather short, neatly, compactly built, snub nose and cheerful eyes, curly, unruly hair. Though twenty-five years old, he seemed much younger—this Sampih, whose child's face had appeared in almost every book written about Bali before the war.

"Greetings, Sampih. We have been long looking for you. Do you think you could dance a little Kebiar for us next time we come to Pliatan?"

"*Beh!* It is long since I tried to dance the Kebiar. These days I work in the rice-fields, and if I dance it is always Baris. Working in the fields is no way to keep supple for dancing the Kebiar, Tuan."

"Well, all we've seen of the Kebiar is the Ida Bagus from Blang-singa and the ones who fumble their way round the Bali Hotel stage," I replied. "You have not much competition."

"I can try, Tuan. But you must not blame me if you find me a stiff peasant."

"I know you've been dancing the Kebiar for eighteen years, Sampih. Tuan Colin introduced you to us with his book many years ago."

I turned happily to the Anak Agung.

"This has been a fateful evening, Anak Agung. Within two days we will be back to see Sampih dance and the Legongs take their lessons."

"You must regard my *puri* as your second home, Tuan John."

"And our hut in Kaliungu is yours whenever you care to visit us, Anak Agung," I replied.

And so it began.

Just as the rainy season set in, our first visitors from the outside world began to find their way to our compound, although the Bali Hotel office would always profess to have no knowledge of our address, since even a rumoured guest-house of two rooms was a puncture in their age-old hotel monopoly. These strangers, arriving in our garden through the garage door, would come across Luce with her mouth full of tacks, lining the guest-house walls with soft white matting, and me at my typewriter, clad in a Siamese sarong.

Now at the hotel were two entertaining Danes, the Nielsens, who planned to stay long in Bali, taking moving pictures.

It was these two who dropped in one evening to sip at Luce's *arak* and *brum* cocktails, and gave us the news that the luxury yacht, the *Stella Polaris*, was shortly due in Bali with a cargo of millionaires, and it was this that prompted us to plan for a first tourist trip to Pliatan. For we already considered that there was enough of interest there to justify taking people up to watch an evening's work.

We had gone back to see our first Legong lesson only two nights after the gamelan started rehearsing in public, and the technique of instruction was fascinating. Further, we had seen Sampih dance his Kebiar.

After seeing Sampih's Kebiar we began to understand some of the excitement of its first beholders in the nineteen-thirties. Sampih, however, was a pupil of Gusti Raka of Tabanan rather than of the noble and unique Mario, for, as Gusti Raka had done of old, Sampih danced a Kebiar that was brilliant technically, full of tricks and of a dash that could only have come from many years of dancing.

His facial expression was amazing. In perfect time to the music his eyes would open and shut from pin points to saucers in size; his eyebrows he could lift on the drum's beats, fast as a butterfly's wings; so supple was he still that he could bend over sideways until his entire trunk and head was level with the ground, and with legs tucked up under his *kain* like steel springs, he could swoop and pirouette around the floor in a seated position, flirting with the Anak Agung at the drum, almost fighting with the cymbals player. And when first we saw it, this dance lasted sixteen exhausting minutes, with Sampih, at its end, hardly able to rise to his feet and walk off the floor.

The old Legong teacher, we had discovered, was a dark, craggy-faced woman, her mouth red-black from the everlasting chewing of betel, with piles of thick, wavy grey hair falling about her face. She wore only an old *kain*. We were told to call her Gusti Biang—which means Mother Gusti. Gusti Biang's elder sister had married one Dewa Ketut Blatjing of Pliatan, a man who, forty years ago, had raised Legong dancing to its most perfect classical form, working with another great teacher of Sukawati, Anak Agung Rai Prit. She, too, in her day, had been a famous dancer, and her teaching now was in the great tradition.

Picture, then, the Anak Agung seated on the floor of the rehearsal

61

verandah with the other drummer, on a hot afternoon, both of them stripped to the waist with towels tied around their middles to check the flowing sweat, while behind them, perhaps, sits just one man picking out the main melody on a metallophone Then in front of them Gusti Biang holding one of the children, facing the drums, while the other children sit quietly watching, fanning themselves after their own exertions.

At the very beginning the little girl's body would be tucked into the enveloping form of Gusti Biang behind her. The child's head would fit under the teacher's chin, and that chin and the guiding palms of the teacher's hands would indicate the head movements. Arms pointed out warningly before the child's eyes would anticipate the side glances of the eyes. The whole body would be precisely fitted into the teacher's, the child's back stemming from the teacher's belly. The teacher's arms would outline the child's arms, her hands holding and manipulating the child's hands and fingers; behind the child's legs would be the teacher's legs, which would shuffle, push and firmly kick the child's legs and feet into the right positions and sequences.

Though the drums gave the tempo and the metallophone the tune, from the teacher would flow a procession of noises quite impossible to reproduce accurately, but these sounds would underline and represent every instrument in the gamelan. Gusti Biang was famous for her musicality. Fifteen seconds of such instruction might sound a little like this, with the music starting and the teacher pushing and guiding the little girl's body, speaking to her all the time.

"Now, go! That's it—like that. Sink your body lower—lower—but gently. Your hands! Hands! To the south that upper hand! South! South! That is better. Now—ready for those eye glances . . . *tju-dèt* . . . *tju-dèt* . . . *tju-dèt* . . . Yes, yes, there is hope. Now *listen* to the drum beating . . . ready . . . yes! *tju-det* . . . *tju-det* . . . *gu-pak-u-pak-u-pak: tu-tjèng!* So, you can follow it. Keep moving! Keep moving! step, step, step: *Pong!* march, march, march; *Pong!* stamp, stamp, stamp: *Pong!* . . . there, the kempli is clear enough to guide you isn't it? Now to the end of this section. Watch that foot—turn it out, out, OUT! More, to the east a little. Here is the last phrase coming: *Gu-pak-u-pak: tjeng! Gu-pak-u-pak, tu-tjurrrr!*"

And the little girls, with their fragile bodies, would work till the sweat coursed down from their necks, their faces miraculously expressionless and patient in spite of angry commands from the perfectionist drummers, never answering back, never complaining, meek and slender like reeds, six hours of instruction every single day.

But even after such training their work was not over. The Legong had to possess them body and soul. If not at school or at work, we would come across them in some quiet corner of the *puri* being loosened up by Gusti Biang, their bodies being massaged every day, so that their every joint should be softly supple. And as they were massaged they would be lectured about the dance.

"Now, Raka, you are the Tjondong, the attendant on the two Legongs. That is very suitable, for you are a Wesya and they are Ksatriya, although your friends. It is very cleverly chosen by the Anak Agung. But you have no need to think your dancing is less important. Any good attendant can steal the dance. It is the most vital role. And at the end of the dance it is you who become the Bird of Ill Omen. Then you must try to feel that you really are a great black raven attacking the Raja of Lasem, many hundreds of years ago, in far-off Java. When you put on your wings of painted buffalo hide, you must fly! And you must look *fierce*. Your eyes, little Raka, must glare like a hawk's. You must feel, *feel*, forgetting altogether that you are Ni Gusti Raka . . . for then you are no longer Raka but a great black bird attacking a Raja!"

And then she would talk to Oka and Anom, telling them how in Bali, where everything went in pairs, male and female (from drums and metallophones to gods and humans), so, in the Legong, one dancer must be more masculine, and one more feminine, thus making a complete and harmonious dance. Then into little Oka she would instil a mood of arrogant pride suitable to her role of an evil Raja who kidnaps the daughter of the neighbouring Raja of Daha; and into the gentle Anom she would implant the feelings of despair, pathos and all-pervading sweetness, so important in the kidnapped Princess Langkesari.

Whenever it was humanly possible Luce and I were in Pliatan during these next four months of creation. By day, eating the great pink-fleshed pomelo limes and watching the Legong being built up section by section; at night, lying on mats drowning again and again in the immense music, but now surfacing occasionally to sit up and try to take a more intelligent interest in how the music was put together and controlled. And during this entranced period we found that Sampih seemed to have been living with us for about a month already, so we borrowed two metallophones to add to the drum we had been given in Saba, and brought them to Kaliungu for Sampih to instruct us with them.

The coming of the *Stella Polaris* was useful to us for two reasons. One passenger bought a painting I had long possessed, the work of one of Java's more publicized modern artists, and the price paid for it, though moderate, enabled us to live in Bali another two months; and another passenger collected a group to see a first try-out performance in Pliatan.

We put on for them some of the Djanger choruses, Sampih's Kebiar, and part of a Legong lesson, for which the little girls had their hair finely combed and decorated with *tjampak* blossoms, their tiny bodies being wound in the long pink strips of cloth normally used by Djanger girls.

And at the end of the performance, which was given in a *balé* outside, and which was attended also by about a hundred thousand flying ants which circled and hummed round the kerosene lamp, the club collected a sum of about two hundred *rupiahs*—or twenty dollars. To us, however, the reaction of our audience was more interesting. They universally praised the gamelan and marvelled at the skill of Sampih; and the Legong lesson fascinated them by its giving them the feeling that they were seeing something secret, something very unusual. They loved the little girls. But the proud Djanger came in for the same comments that would be applied to any dance routine based on a line of pretty girls. This was, on the whole, most encouraging to our embryonic work.

But these were not people from the theatrical world, and it was our good fortune that quite soon afterwards, on one of the days when our dove orchids, small, white and heavily scented, were all in flower, there walked up to and hammered at our front gate a tall American, ruddy, direct-eyed, white eyebrows jutting, and with him an elegant little figure in pale olive-green Chinese pyjamas and sunglasses.

Kusti ran from the kitchen to the gate, bringing these guests in to our house.

They introduced themselves as Martin and Connie Flavin, and as we sat talking it gradually transpired that though now a novelist, formerly he had been a playwright, and had had quite a few of his plays on Broadway. When I outlined to him our work, he showed the liveliest interest, and by a natural sequence of events we spent much of the next few days together. With considerable anxiety we took the Flavins to watch a rehearsal in Pliatan, and he, while admitting, mark you, that he was no musician at all, said bluntly that he was convinced we were working with material that had limitless theatrical potentialities. He became our first expert enthusiast, giving us confidence by writing down for us his address in Pebble Beach, California, which at that time sounded as remote as if he had said Seventieth Crater West, Moon. But his imagination seemed tickled by our project and also by our struggle to exist in Bali with a nationalist revolution boiling around us. He invited us to his room in the Bali Hotel, where, in his shirt sleeves, he cross-examined us further in between slicing fresh pineapple for some powerful rum drinks of his own recipe.

"How do you live?" he asked.

"Well, we're selling things at the moment." We told him about the painting sold to the *Stella Polaris* traveller, rings, Rolleiflexes. "But we are also hoping to open a guest-house and take in a few carefully selected guests."

"Have you built it yet? I'd like to see it.

"We'll show it you—including the new bathroom."

"I imagine it must be something like Hawaiian style. But will you be able to live off it when you've finished selling your household goods?"

"Probably not. But we're getting to know a lot of Balinese painters and carvers, and we may sell their work, too. Then various people in Denpasar have asked us to teach English—wives of the Indonesian Army officers want Luce to teach them, and there are Balinese, Chinese and Javanese here in Denpasar who have asked me to take classes."

"Well, you might get by, I suppose. It's quite an adventure."

Then: "Tell me—what's all this about not being able to photograph bare Balinese breasts?"

"Its national sentiment—a new sort of pride."

"But what is back of it? Do they really fine you and take away your camera if they see you?"

"Not only that. They also fine the woman two hundred *rupiahs* if she allows herself to be photographed. That's a lot."

"God bless my soul!"

"You'd understand the modern Balinese viewpoint better, though, if you'd seen tourists posing Balinese girls as if they were dolls and photographing them as curiosities. You can't let modern education reach Indonesia and expect these people to remain unaware that this is considered primitive. Personally, I sympathize with some of their new ideas—and anyhow, most breasts after they've suckled a couple of children are not exactly aesthetically pleasing."

"There's probably something in that."

"Of course the funny thing is that to the Balinese the breast has little sexual appeal—you become used to it. I think I shall develop a fetish about ankles, myself. But to the Balinese it is unthinkable to bare a thigh—and that's why the Esther Williams pictures in Denpasar always sell out. They stop their women's breasts being photographed, and have a wonderful time whistling in the movies when they see bathing beauties. Don't you think that's rather amusing?"

He turned to his wife, not answering.

"And what do you think about it, my dear?"he asked.

When the Flavins dined with us on their last evening in Bali I was laid up with a chill, which I feared was a return of malaria. To the last they encouraged us, and as Luce dropped them back at the hotel they shouted in farewell, "Don't forget: keep in touch."

From their seats in the Great Mountain the gods now sent another infliction to trouble Bali during this rainy season. As the New Year came and the auguries seemed better, because, thanks to Islam Salim, murders and rumours of murders were becoming steadily fewer, a pestilence descended upon the villages.

Our first realization of it came one morning when we were driving up the road to Sayan, Sampih's village. Sampih was learning to drive the jeep, and we often used this route to Pliatan because it was quieter, the road passing only small villages and wide expanses of *sawahs*, gradually ascending to the foothills. As we entered the villages I noticed by the sides of the road rough gateways made from bamboo poles crudely interwoven with fronds of coconut palm, and outside one village, in the middle of such a gateway, I glimpsed a black, painted coconut husk, grinning at us like a skull.

"Look Sampih! What is that?"

"I don't know," he answered.

"Oh, come on, Pih—it must mean something."

"Well, perhaps it means that there is sickness in the village. That might be a warning to strangers."

And this is how we learned for the first time that a plague of small-pox was sweeping through Bali, a tragic legacy from the Japanese war-time occupation followed by years of political strife afterwards. To the Balinese peasant, however, smallpox was a gift from the gods, to be accepted with resignation. They made many offerings, set up the warning gateways and waited for the scourge to pass.

But one day a messenger came to us from Kusti's village, telling me that one of the favourite models of Theo Meier, who was still on leave in Switzerland, was sick of the dreaded *tjatjar*. I was asked to bring medicine So, taking Kusti for company and also so that he could visit his family, I put penicillin and sulpha powder in the jeep and drove up the sixty-five kilometres to Iseh village, half-guessing that this would be a Balinese wild-goose chase.

Iseh is a poor mountain village lying at the foot of the Great Mountain, perched on the rim of a deep, fertile and most beautiful valley. The people, however, live in dingy hovels, roofed with re-versed bamboo tiles, in small, muddy compounds. Life is far more primitive than in either Denpasar or Pliatan. The sick girl's uncle met me in one such wretched yard, in his hands holding a piece of white-pink, albino buffalo horn which he was laboriously carving into an exquisite figure of a crowned *pedanda* high priest. My visit was in vain, he feared—the child had the smallpox—it was from the gods—nothing could be done—he was sorry the Tuan had been bothered.

In the next yard I was met by the girl's grandfather, who irritated me by his polite and lengthy welcome, but who gave me hope, nevertheless. It was nothing, he said, just a few spots—perhaps nothing heavy at all. Thank God, I thought to myself, for this was a lovely young girl, and I patted my sulpha powder in my pocket, foreseeing a patch of septic scabies.

They took me inside a hut almost pitch dark—a wise precaution, this, for modern science and Balinese doctors know that smallpox scars are shallower and the pain less maddening if the sick person is kept in the dark. And in this filthy shack I made out some old women and the girl's mother. They looked blankly at me. "Greetings, Tuan," they said, and chased some chickens away that were on the bed and kicked out a fair-sized pig which had been sleeping on the black mud floor. As my eyes became accustomed to the gloom I could see the bamboo bed, or shelf, where the child lay. I groped my way towards her.

"Greetings, Gusti," I began. "I have brought . . ." and found myself retching and running from the hut. The women followed me to the door, watching me, not criticizing but perfectly calm.

"A moment, Gusti Mother," I said. "In a minute I will enter again. I have never seen this sickness before."

And presently, partly from shame, partly from pride, but mostly from pity, I forced myself back into the now evil-seeming atmosphere of the hut.

On the hard bamboo bed lay what had once been a beautiful little girl. I saw a grossly swollen red body, entirely covered with disgusting pustules from its head to the soles of its feet. Eyes and mouth were almost invisible beneath the swelling. Her nose, madly irritant, the poor child had rubbed so that the skin was broken and its shape already destroyed. This awful bloated shell was so unrecognizable that I could not have told whether the body was that of a young girl or an old woman. It was a terrifying and pathetic sight.

Making a sorry job of it, I tried to speak to her. "Gusti Ayu, I am glad to see you are not so very ill. I have brought some good, strong medicine for you. And very soon Tuan Theo will be back from Switzerland to look after you. I will send you milk and foods up from Denpasar. And I will go now to find a medical orderly and ask him to come here every day to give you injections to make you strong.

Try to feel that the orderly, Tuan Theo and I are all working for you; and try to help us by fighting to get better quickly, little Gusti."

And by God knows what miracle, live she did. I persuaded the orderly to come and give her penicillin injections daily against the secondary infections; Luce sent up tinned milk and other foods from Denpasar, and Theo came back in time to give her a long course of body-restoring injections. Her hair fell out, but began to grow again slowly, thinly; and with a ruined nose and pitifully scarred, the brave child was hobbling around her village again within a few months.

But on that first day, frightened, feeling saturated with the foul germs from that stinking hut, I drove back to Denpasar like one possessed, straight to the hospital and the resident doctor, where Kusti and I were vaccinated at once; and on the next morning our entire household was vaccinated, too.

The smallpox went on spreading. In some of the villages the *baleans*, village doctors, advised against vaccination, so that the Government eventually had to pass a law ordering every man, woman and child to receive the vaccine. But we would hear of three hundred people who had died in Boeg-Boeg, four hundred in a village near Gianjar, a hundred and fifty around nearby Sanur, until the casualties soared into the thousands.

One evening we met two young tourist doctors who had just qualified and had never seen smallpox. They jumped at the chance to see some, for we told them we were off to Saba, where a relation of one of the Legongs had just succumbed. On the way, just outside Saba, we were held up on the grassy track by a long and strange procession of villagers. All of them held wooden staves with pieces of green foliage tied to them, and as they walked they chanted and shouted savagely, banging their sticks on strips of metal or gongs, journeying to the sea, where they would make a special ceremonial cleansing for the effigies of their gods, whom they were bearing along on little raised shrines supported on their shoulders. This must be some sort of *metjaru*, we explained to the doctors, to drive out the evil spirits who had brought the smallpox, and which had now become an intolerable punishment.

But it was not until the vaccination was completed and the dry weather had come again that the smallpox left Bali.

The Legong lessons were interrupted in February by the approach of Galungan, the great Festival of the Balinese New Year.

"A pity," the Anak Agung said. "We still need more than a month before the Legong will be ready to perform in public. Also, the costumes are not yet made. The club would have liked to have had the Legong danced for the first time during Galungan."

But since this was impossible, the work of the club stopped, and only the little girls continued to work just as hard as before with Gusti Biang.

"What is the meaning of Galungan, Anak Agung?" we asked one day. We were sitting gossiping idly while old Gusti Biang was massaging the children, noting the increased bustle about the *puri*.

"At Galungan we celebrate the New Year—that is, the Balinese year of two hundred and ten days. For ten days the ancestral gods come down to receive our offerings at their shrines and to enjoy the feasting with us."

"Then it is not Hindu, it's more of an ancient (I wanted to say animistic, but did not know how to) festival?"

"It is Hindu-Bali, Tuan," he replied solemnly.

"So offerings are made to the gods, and—what else?"

"Oh, many things. It is the gayest time of the year, and we all dress up in our best and newest clothes in order to *melali*—to go out and enjoy ourselves. At dawn, or even in the middle of the night before Galungan, we all get up and kill our fatted pigs to make *lawar*, and . . ."

"*Lawar*? What is *lawar*?"

"You have not yet eaten lawar? *Beh!* You have pleasure in store! *Lawar* is made from many meats, but for Galungan we make it from pork. We shred the meat and skin of the pig, mix it with raw blood, chopping it all up very fine, we spice it and mix in many excellent herbs—and then we have *lawar*."

"It sounds . . . interesting. May we try some *lawar* with you, Anak Agung?"

"Tuan John, Tuan John—*adoh!* you are always running ahead of me. Do *you* wish to invite yourself to *my* feast? It was on my lips to invite you and the Nyonya to eat with me and the whole club on the day of Penampahan Galungan."

"I'm sorry, Anak Agung. My western haste again! But we'd love to eat with you and the club."

"Good. And besides the feasting, this is the season for bringing out our Barong. You'll see two in Pliatan. One from the *puri* of the Punggawa, and one being made now, a sort of toy Barong, by the village children."

And so indeed we did celebrate our first conscious Galungan since we'd been in Bali. First, we made presents of new clothes to Rantun, Agung, Kusti and Rantun's children; and then, with a magnificently dressed Sampih, wearing new *kain*, new shirt and a gaudy headcloth, we drove to Pliatan and ate *lawar* and yellow saffron rice with the club. Enormous plates of yellow rice, with four variants of *lawar* and *saté*. It tasted dry, hot, and partly what the Balinese call *asem*—a little sour. The little girls were not allowed to eat with us and the men of the club, but ate somewhere in one of the wives' houses. This was on the Galungan Eve.

On Galungan Day we found Denpasar packed with brightly dressed people, many villagers having come in from afar, pacing the roads to demonstrate their finery, while all the buses and taxis and private cars were jammed with people out to enjoy themselves. The road to Pliatan was overhung with tall *penyor*, giant bamboo poles thirty feet high and more, bedecked and ornamented with flowers and woven coconut leaves, their tips weighed over like immense fishing rods straining against a catch, but instead of a fish, from the end of the *penyor* would be bobbing fantastical figures in traditional style, again cut out by the women from young palm leaves.

Galungan was a family celebration. The ancestral gods were made welcome with lavish and exquisite offerings of fruit and flowers and meats and rice cakes, piled high on flat red trays, and in the evening the air was filled with the blue smoke from the incense placed with each offering before the gateways, while dogs fought and snarled to pick out the edible scraps.

And all during this week, and through till the Day of Kuningan was past, the fabulous monsters, the Barongs, gambolled and played, preceded or pursued by their perspiring orchestras with slung instruments. The two dancers inside one of the Barongs from a hill village north of Pliatan was said to have played its way through Ubud village, actually chasing some children up a mango tree, so that this mythical, shaggy monster with its red and gold leatherwork harness and myriad

71

glittering small mirrors, was to be seen looking down into the Ubud *puri* from the mango-tree's branches.

For two or three weeks all serious work in Bali ceased. Then suddenly Denpasar looked normal again, and we knew that Galungan and Kuningan had passed.

4

Our Legong: and the Great Mario

*

When the little girls had been learning to dance for about one month, the Pliatan orchestra started to rehearse the Legong music with them, and we had been able to see each section of the dance, phrase by phrase, built into a full classical Legong lasting just under one hour. Later, we were told, they would learn other parts: the Love Dance, or the story of the witch, Tjalonarang. And this gentle Legong music, played by a smaller, lightened gamelan, was to me more attractive and elusive than that of the magnificently flamboyant Kebiar.

In Kaliungu we had placed our two borrowed metallophones in the front house, and all the time I would be asking Sampih to play the Legong melodies for us.

"Pih," I would say. "How does that tune go where the attendant picks up the fans ready to hand them over to the Legongs?"

Sampih would then play some very slow melody which I had never consciously heard before.

"No, it can't be that, Pih. The fast one when Raka has the fans actually in her hands and is dancing with them. It's very rippling and very fast."

"That's the part I was playing. The *gending pokok*. The melody."

"But how is that possible? I didn't recognize a note."

"He played it quite correctly," Luce would say, nodding her head and looking irritatingly sure of herself.

To prove it to me, next time we went to Pliatan and the Legong was rehearsing, Sampih and Luce sat on either side of me, and when my ears were ringing with the rapid surface notes of the smaller metallophones, Sampih said patiently and humouringly to me, "Now, listen only to the Anak Agung's metallophone. Watch his hammer—" for in the Legong music the Anak Agung played the leading metallophone, which sang under his hand, and Lebah with his long, bony fingers took the light drum.

And the Anak Agung's hammer, to my surprise and disgust, did move in the precise slow rhythm that Sampih and Luce were humming in my newly awakened ear. So, during the next weeks I made an effort to sit or lie in the middle of the gamelan every night, and there I just began to pick out a few of the parts that went to form these complex pieces; but the fastest-playing metallophones, sit beside them nightly though I did, remained as untrackable as ever.

The night was now approaching for our Legong to perform in public for the first time. The Anak Agung's family had woven the dark green and purple cloth, which was decorated in traditional patterns with gold paint; the jackets were cut out, and then *kains* and jackets were hung out to dry in the courtyard. Fine oxhide was bought, scraped white, and prepared to make the elaborate headdresses; the dressed skin was carved by hand with tiny chisels, and into it were encrusted jewels of glass and the whole was painted with gold leaf. The shallow crowns were studded with scores of little wire springs, each fastened by hand, and on each of which would be tied one quivering frangipani flower on nights of dancing.

On the first night we were taking up with us in the jeep an old teacher named Ida Bagus Boda, who had actually taught Lotring. He was to be the *tandak*, sitting in the orchestra, where in a high nasal voice he would sing his commentary on the Legong story. From Gianjar the Raja was coming, Anak Agung Gdé Agung's young brother, and from neighbouring Ubud we had invited the Tjokorda Agung, a lesser Raja whom we knew quite well.

Very early that afternoon we drove up to the *puri*. Luce brought lipstick, eye pencil and rouge with her, for Balinese make-up is only crude due to lack of materials; and I wanted to supervise the lighting. The performance was to be given in front of the *puri's* main gateway, and many offerings were made against rain.

"I shall ask the priest from Tampaksiring to bring his kris," the Anak Agung had told us.

"Is that a holy kris?" we had asked.

"It is very powerful against rain," he answered, "Many times it has been used between Pliatan and Ubud, and each time the rain has fallen in other villages—but not where the kris lay."

We arrived up in Pliatan just as the little girls were coming back from the Temple of Gunung Sari, where they had made their offerings and received purification before dancing, and now they were squealing gaily and trying on their stiff jackets, watching anxiously to see whether the *perada*, the gold paint, would flake off. After drinking a little coffee with a harassed Anak Agung, we went over to watch them get into their costumes.

First they fastened their *kains*, purple and gold, and then their insect bodies were wound in long strips of white cloth, so that they appeared like slender cocoons. Then the miniature jackets, with safety pins for buttons. Then the ornamental belt and side pieces, their long bibs, sequin flashing and red, and their gold-painted arm bands.

Very soon it was dark, and seated in the rehearsal verandah with one kerosene lamp sputtering on the floor, the second drummer, Gusti Kompiang, began to work on the make-up, while Luce, sitting near him, added the final touches. First he smeared on a yellow base, made from *atal*, a clay imported from China, which had been mixed with a rice powder; with a razorlike knife he shaved the eyebrows and the whole forehead, too, for imaginary fluff; then, with a match, he lengthened the eyebrows, accenting them with China ink, and there remained only the round, white beauty spots, which he applied with a leaf stalk dipped into a lime paste—placing one above the bridge of the nose, and one at the side of each temple. From Gusti Kompiang the children shuffled over to Luce, who smoothed over the powder, softened up its too-saffron yellow, and added a small touch of lipstick.

On the main gateway, Madé Lebah and I were busy. The children of the *puri* were setting out more than forty hollowed pieces of coconut shell filled with oil, placing them on each ledge of the ornate gateway to add to the beauty of our decor; and the three kerosene lamps which had been borrowed for the evening we placed on special wooden

75

stands, affixing shields of thin metal to divert their usual hot glare from the eyes of the audience.

The club, meanwhile, had put on their new headcloths of silver and green, with white shirts—for it was thought old-fashioned, these days, to perform with bare torsos or shoulders—and outside their ordinary *kain* they all had tied an outer cloth of wine colour, heavily flowered. They sat gossiping on the mats that made our stage in front of the gate of entry.

By now the Legong were being put into their hard and heavy headdresses. First, Gusti Kompiang tied up and twisted their hair into the tightest knots; then he balanced the headdresses on their heads, holding them level, and pulling the stiff leather down, firmly and gradually, onto the wincing heads of the girls After that ordeal was over, they were ready, and each in turn ran into the Anak Agung's room, where, in an ancient wardrobe glass, they saw themselves in full costume for the first time.

"*Beh!*" they said accusingly, to one another. "I will be ashamed. Clearly this headdress is not on straight." Or, "Look at Anom's headdress," Oka laughed. "It's all bent up at the back." And there they sat, joking and bickering friendlily, growing silent as their headdresses grew heavier and heavier, felt tighter and tighter.

"It's already very late, Anak Agung," I exclaimed, looking at my watch. "Do you think the Raja is not coming?"

"Oh, he has been here a long time. He is sitting in the *punggawa's puri* just down the road. Perhaps he will soon be here."

And we were lucky, I suppose, because this smiling, plump young man, whose subjects all sat on the ground with hands clasped as he passed, kept us waiting only one hour. But at last we saw him walking up the road with a flashlight and his family, and we brought him to the chairs of honour, sitting down with him to hear his comments on our Legong.

The two drummers took their seats, backs to the audience and facing the gateway from which the dancers would descend. To the right was the metallophone section; to our left was the long battery of gongs. The village audience surged forward, eager. Around the floor were rows of naked children, and on one side stood the women, turbans of towels twisted into their hair, some bare breasted, some

76

with gay and pretty jackets, while opposite them were bunched the men, laughing, talking, raising their eyebrows invitingly at the girls, scarlet hibiscus flowers behind their ears. Hundreds of people had walked to Pliatan from afar, for this was the first time any real dancing had been seen in the village for years. At the back of the crowd we could hear yelpings as the *warong* women kicked at scavengers who snatched too greedily, and sometimes a wretched mongrel would sniff its way across our stage, where nobody paid any attention to it. The atmosphere was heavy, musky, sweetly scented, mixed with blasts of herbivorous wind.

For the overture we played "Tabuh Telu," and then the Anak Agung handed over his drum to the care of Madé Lebah, and got up and waddled over himself to play the leading metallophone. With a flourish his hammer picked out the slow, hesitant introduction on the lead instrument, and on a first, soft chord, the gamelan flowed in to join him.

At the top of the steps, the figure of a tiny girl appears, looking shyly down at her first audience, her gold and purple costume, darkly glittering, outlined breathtakingly against a blue-black gash of night in the narrow doorway behind her. As her musical cue comes near, the little girl vanishes, transformed into the Attendant of the two Legongs, and in time to the music she begins to move, easily, calmly, introducing the dance, while the voice of our old *tandak* in the gamelan hails her appearance.

Slowly still, with careful measured rhythm, she descends the high steps, reaches the matting-covered floor, and the dance of the Attendant begins. Like a dragonfly skimming over a pond she hovers before us, first to the north, then to the south, moving in sweeps with her knees half bent, dipping and rising as light as a leaf in the wind. Now stationary, she forces her arms down beside her and her shoulders shiver to the rapid drumbeats, and, as the melody is punctuated, so she phrases her dance with side-glancing flicks of her eye or with sinuous undulations of her neck and head. Her arm movements are clean, brisk, square This is pure dancing.

A break in the music and we see her bending on one knee, coolly sighting the fans which she must pick up and hand over to the Legongs, and which she now spies on the ground before the drummers. Then starts her swerving dance toward them, and when she is almost upon them, with a lightning stoop she picks them up and turns to face the gateway where the two Legongs now appear. Solemnly, too, the slender, delicate Legongs pause on the top step, then sway in unison down to the floor, where they trace exquisite patterns at high speed, as their Attendant dances before them. The three small bodies weave expertly in and out of one another, knees bending as they turn and fling around, working up to a crescendo, it seems, when suddenly, on an instant, they stop—all three of them—and the Attendant hands the fans to her Legongs.

Now a new, stronger melody enters, and the two Legongs look with starting eyes at their Attendant before dancing off again in their intricate patterns, the Legongs holding their fans now before them, now stretched out to arms' length at their sides, weaving and interweaving, till the three meet in the very centre of the floor, and each like a slender hoop, bends slowly backwards, till their headdresses touch the matting; as their reed-like bodies straighten, they roll first sideways to the left, and sideways to the right, then miraculously they are upright again, and faster and faster they dance, floating over the ground, until the three of them reach the bottom of the steps, and there they turn in line and suddenly face the audience; the Attendant takes a half step forward, and with a captivating little shrug of leave-taking, becomes Raka again, walks up the steps, out of sight, to await her next entry

The *tandak* now raises his voice, for here begins the story proper. One Legong is now the Raja of Lasem, that is Oka, and Anom is his courtier. As they regard each other from opposite corners, Lasem is proud of feature and bold of gesture. His courtier apes his every move, like an echo. Then the Raja stands in the middle of the stage, testing his strength, examining his armour, demanding praise, and faithfully his courtier prances and stamps around him, admiring, flattering, assisting. Again the music changes, and the proud Lasem is beating his breast as he bids farewell to his faithful wife, the same Anom, who now crouches, softly kneeling, in her new role before him.

Once more the melody shifts and an ominous, pulsating rhythm is sped on its way by the now restless metallophones. The two Legongs, king and courtier, king and wife—or whoever they now represent, are

78

torn apart as the moment approaches when the Raja must go out to battle against the Raja of Daha, whose daughter, Langkesari, Lasem has carried off. Lasem is left alone, making heroic poses, trying to give himself courage, for he has dreamt that today he will meet his death.

And then through the black gateway there storms down and swoops in the golden-winged Bird of Ill Omen, again Raka. Immediately and frantically she assaults the Raja, dashing her wings into his face, and they swirl and clash, swirl and clash as they sweep madly around the stage. At times the bird leaps up the gateway's steps, where, as if from a tree, she looks down fiercely upon the Raja, who flourishes his sword and threatens her from below. In fury she sharpens her beak on a branch and falls once more into the attack. They battle and part continuously, the white frangipani blossoms flying off their headdresses in every direction, neither able to win, until at last, exhausted, the bird is driven by brute strength up the steps and away. The story has ended.

Now Anom returns from the stool where she has been sitting quietly on the edge of the gamelan, and to a more formal, simple tune, the two Legongs advance upon us, paying their respects; their fans make weaving patterns, held at arms' full length, until at last they sink to one knee just between the drummers; their arms drop languidly to their sides, their eyes are lowered, and modestly glancing at nobody, they get to their feet and walk slowly up the steps again into the *puri*. The dance is over.

A few days later the Anak Agung brought the three children down to our house to spend the day with us. We took them to the Wisnu Store, owned by our friend, Chan Ling Siong, and we gave them presents of bright coloured cloth which they chose themselves to make new *kebayas* with. Then we drove down to Sanur, where they paddled and ran in the sea, while Luce and I, with the Anak Agung, sat in a bougainvillaea arbour in the garden of the Belgian painter, Lemayeur, chatting with his statuesquely beautiful wife, Polok, and who, when a child, had been an enchanting dancer herself.

In the evening they ate Rantun's food and then we took them to see their first cinema. And though Luce and I sat between them and tried

79

to explain the story with Sampih's help, to them it was all very confusing, and they hooted with laughter, holding their hands politely before their mouths, every time a man and woman kissed in public. *"Beh!* They don't know shame!" they cried. Only the Anak Agung seemed fully satisfied.

"That was very fortunate," he said as we walked out. "The children understood nothing."

"It wasn't a good film for them, I know. But I'm sorry they understood so little."

"I am glad. They've seen one bad film and they won't want to see any more. It will be less trouble for me."

Driving back that evening to Pliatan, feeling even closer to these friends of ours after a whole day spent in each other's company, we asked the Anak Agung to drop the formal Tuan and Nyonya and to call us by our Christian names.

"With pleasure," he agreed, "when I can become used to it. But you must then call me Agung Adji, Father Agung. For to tell you the truth it is quite wrong, according to Balinese manners, to call me Anak Agung all the time. Agung Adji is not only more friendly, but more Balinese."

And on the same evening I became Bli, elder brother, to Sampih, and Luce was his M'bok, his elder sister.

I now told the Anak Agung with absolute sincerity that his Legong had so convinced me of Pliatan's possibilities that I was going to redouble my efforts to look for contacts abroad. I could have added, though to him it would have meant nothing, that the Pliatan Legong had something of the same perfect quality of "Les Sylphides", a ballet of which I could never tire.

Accordingly, I typed out a six-page proposal for the tour of a company of Balinese dancers, and in it outlined a programme consisting of the six types of dancing we then contemplated. The group, I suggested, would be of about forty people, and my main selling contention was that thanks to the glamour, false or real, attached to the word Bali, such a company would bring its own impetus with it. This proposal I sent off to my actress cousin in London, Joan White, and to Charles Landstone in the Arts Council. In America, through my friend Matthew Fox, I was already in touch with several booking-

1. John Coast envisioned and organized the project of bringing Balinese dancers and musicians to audiences in London, New York and other Western capitals in the postwar period. He first met Indonesians during his captivity following the fall of Singapore to the Japanese in 1942. He learned their language (Malay, the lingua franca widely used throughout the region), admired their culture and later joined in their struggle for independence. This 1950 photograph was taken in Bangkok where Coast had been with the UK Foreign Office. He was later appointed by President Sukarno as his international press attaché.

2. John Coast (second from left) and Luce (Supianti), later his wife, in their house in Kaliangu, Bali. On either side of them is star dancer Sampih (left) and Mr Suriono (right) from the Indonesian Department of Information. After Indonesia had won its independence, Coast retired from political life and withdrew to Bali to write. He soon found himself deeply immersed in the music and dance of the island.

3. Mario (I Ketut Maria), the great Balinese dancer, training Ni Gusti Raka for the tour. Here he is shaping the young dancer's body with his own.

4. Balinese dance and its music is not notated but is learned by endless repetition. Mario took Raka through weeks of rehearsals for the tour.

5. The gamelan orchestra of metal gongs is led by the principal drummer. Here Raka, guided by Mario, learns the rhythmic patterns of the Bumblebee Dance.

6. Coast commissioned Mario to choreograph a new dance, the Tumulilingan Mengisap Sari (The Bumblebee Sips Honey), better known as the Bumblebee Dance, for the Dance Company of Pliatan village. It used two dancers, a litle girl (Ni Gusti Raka), and a virile young male (Sampih), and had a simple story: the small girl would be a bumblebee flitting around a garden, sunning herself. The male bumblebee would enter, be attracted to her, be rejected, and in his frustration and despair, would be driven to flirt with the instruments in the orchestra. Here Raka and Sampih rehearse the Bumblebee Dance in Bali.

7. For its first public appearance, the Tumulilingan was danced by Raka and Sampih in front of about 150 United Nations delegates invited by the club at Pliatan to a feast followed by dancing. It was only after this that the dance entered the club's repertoire. The dance was later pruned from its original 28 minutes to half that time for the group's tour of Europe and the US. In the background is part of the 23-strong gamelan group which went on tour.

8. Mario in his prime during the 1930s, in his own creation, Kebiar Duduk (Seated Kebiar). Most of the dance is performed from the waist up from a sitting position. This photo demonstrates the astonishing suppleness of Mario's body.

9. Sampih in a photograph taken as he emerges from childhood. In the mid-1930s, when he was nine, Sampih was adopted by Colin McPhee, the American composer and author of *A House in Bali* (1947). He learnt to dance under the best teachers, including Mario, and was hailed as a child prodigy. He was famous for his Kebiar Duduk by the time he was ten.

10. Sampih rehearses Kebiar Duduk in Bali with Anak Agung Gde Mandera, the lead drummer and Artistic Director of the Pliatan Gamelan orchestra. Two years after the "Dancers of Bali" tour ended, the 28-year-old dancer was murdered in Bali, purportedly a victim of jealousy generated by the fame and the small wealth he had brought back from the tour.

11. The Legong, Bali's great classic, is danced only by three very young girls, who mime and dance the tale of King Lasem who seduced and abducted the daughter of an enemy with whom he was at war. It alternates pure dance with dramatic episodes. Here the girls rehearse with the Anak Agung Gde Mandera (left) in the grounds of his house temple.

12. The attendant of the two Legongs, the Chondong, dances before a typical Balinese festival audience. The three girls portray various characters and events in the story of King Lasem.

13. Ni Gusti Raka as the raven, the golden bird of ill omen, who encounters the wicked King Lasem as he prepares to do battle with his enemy.

14. The dramatic episodes of the Legong reveal the ardent king; his suit to the captured Princess Langkesari, who rebuffs him; his departure for battle, and his encounter with the fierce little raven, omen of death. Following this is his death-struggle with the brother of the captive princess, both warriors impersonated by the small dancers whose fans are symbols of swords.

15. Ni Gusti Raka poses in front of the Garuda Bird, carved on a wall from local paras sandstone. The mythical Garuda became the national emblem of Indonesia, and was the name chosen for its national airline.

Opposite: 16. Anom, in the role of Princess Langkesari, weeps in fear as King Lasem, danced by Oka, approaches her from afar.

17. A public performance of the Djanger, a modern folk-dance. A mass flirtation between a group of girls and young men, the Djanger progresses from the provocative singing of nonsense rhymes by the young girls to the boys' excited reaction—a response matched in the orchestra by lively tempos and syncopation.

18. Djanger dancers wearing the typical headdress.

19. Anak Agung Gde Mandera directs a Djanger rehearsal in Pliatan.

20. Rehearsal from the dance-drama, "The Fasting Ardjuna", in Anak Agung Gde Mandera's palace courtyard. The tusked figure is Rangda, Queen of the Witches.

21. "The Fasting Ardjuna" story rehearsed by the roadside outside the palace courtyard in Pliatan, 1951.

22. An open-air rehearsal of the gamelan in Pliatan village.

23. A section of the handsome sarong-clad gamelan players from Pliatan village. The cross-sections of the orchestra skilfully blend the complex layers of decorated melodies.

24. *Chengcheng* (grounded cymbals) players from the Pliatan gamelan supply rhythmic accents.

25. Anom, Raka and Oka stitch costumes of multi-coloured silks and brocades, stamped with gold-leaf decoration, for the tour abroad.

26. Tjokorda Oka, with Luce, fitting a costume for dancer Ni Oka, who was also deft with a needle. Tjokorda Oka designed and made the magnificent masks for the Barong and Rangda and other mythical creatures taken on the tour.

27. President Sukarno with the three Legongs in the palace in Djakarta prior to the tour. The President adopted the three little dancers as his wards and saw to their education. The President of Indonesia regarded the arts of Bali as one of the most important elements of Indonesian life, and one to be supported.

28. Twelve-year-old Ni Gusti Raka, the diminutive star of the show, and one of
the nine girls in the group, aged from ten to fifteen. Richard Skinner, Columbia
Artists' company manager for the American cross-country tour, described the
girls as "delicate in size and proportion, dressed always off the stage in their
charming Balinese prints, with their sleek glossy black hair pulled straight back
from the forehead and decorated with a single flower, their blouses pinned
together with large American safety pins, and their sarongs tightly bound, all
worn with simplicity and charm."

agents, one of whom had to date only shown interest in a group so small that we would have had insufficient human material to build up a full programme. I was determined that we would do it perfectly, in a big way, or not at all. We were being helped, too, by the Nielsens, the Danish photographers, who had seen the first performance of the Legong and become our enthusiastic supporters. One whole morning they had filmed our Legong, the Kebiar, and some masked dancers we had brought up from the village of Batuan, and they had promised to send us some publicity "stills" with a hundred feet or so of coloured movie film.

Whenever I explained the need for such work to the Anak Agung, or told him of my correspondence, he would reply, "Good! But that I leave all to you. I follow."

We were in fact already beginning to see that our vast friend, if far away from his drum, was never sure of himself. As the Legong first night had amusingly illustrated, in times of urgency he ran round in puzzled circles, leaving everything to his deep-voiced brother and ourselves. We had observed, too, that in common with most of his village, he was a Balinese on the old pattern—feudalism was deep in his bones and instincts. Though theoretically a feudal serf is as distasteful to me as is a petty Raja, in Bali this worried me little, for I had long abandoned the idea that any one way of life was either better or even desirable for all peoples. In my work ahead, though, I could sense difficulties looming.

Many foreigners have admired the integration of Balinese daily life with its religion; but since the basis of both lies on a caste system, it appeared obvious to me that the Anak Agung's loyalty would lie always in the direction of his Raja in Gianjar. We had to hope, therefore, that this young Anak Agung Gdé Oka would be sympathetic to our work—while politically keeping his distance. For the Rajadoms of Gianjar and Denpasar stood at opposite poles: for the Old ideas and the New. And when, in March, 1951, Islam Salim decreed the end of his military law, the whole island was again under the rule of the twenty-eight-year-old Anak Agung Bagus Sutedja, father of nine children and of the new nationalist ideas dominating the island, the head of the Civil Government Council in Denpasar.

One morning a letter came from Djakarta telling us that our first guests were due to arrive by the afternoon plane. Frank and Martha

Galbraith were of the American Embassy. Frank I had known in Djakarta as one of the few younger diplomats who spoke fluent Indonesian. Accordingly, I tried to make a final attack on our pi-dog problem, the pariahs, and Sampih assembled the entire household to discuss what could be done.

"Pih, these are our very first guests coming to stay with us They simply must get a good impression. Now—what can be done about these dogs?"

They were all silent, for on how many occasions had they seen me driven crazy by the continuous yelping and howling of these detestable curs, who crept out into the lane each night, and only stopped their banshee chorus the following dawn, in time to sleep during the day and pick up strength for the next night's ululation.

"Tuan," said Rantun thoughtfully, "if the children throw stones, other dogs join in and make the noise louder. That is no good, then. The Tuan has put down poison, but only one of my chickens was killed. Both Sampih and I have tried to buy the dogs—but the people say they are useful watchdogs, who howl, perhaps, when they see *leyaks* that are invisible to the human eye. I think we have done all that is possible."

I turned to Sampih again.

"If we none of us can think of anything, and our guest-house becomes nicknamed a kennel, it will be difficult for us all very shortly, Pih."

"You have not heard the latest story about the black and white dog that lives opposite us?" asked Sampih, referring to one demoniac dog that I would gladly have slain with my own hands.

"No—what happened?"

"Well, knowing that our guests were coming I went to see the dog's owner. I told him that I sorely needed the liver of just such a black and white dog to make medicine. I asked to buy it. The man looked at me, perhaps not believing my tale, and he said I could have the dog—he would give it me, cheerfully, only I must catch it myself."

He paused, grinning at the memory, and all the children laughed with glee, for Bli Sampih was a favourite of theirs.

"Well—I called all the children and we chased that dog till we were all nearly dead. The dog just laughed at us—he is a real devil—

82

we could not even touch him. So, Bli, we don't know what to do. I admit I am beaten."

"Perhaps it will go on raining," said Rantun, with solemn face. "Then the dogs will stay inside and not come out into our lane."

So, with only this problem unsolved, and knowing that under Luce's hands the guest-house was looking very attractive and full of flowers, Sampih and I set out in the jeep for the airport that evening. As we brought the Galbraiths back into Denpasar, they told us how exhausted they were, that they could hardly keep awake, that they wanted to sleep for a week.

On their first evening we sat talking together in our front house, rather shamefully drinking the bourbon our guests had brought with them.

"What do you both most want to see? I mean, we can easily show you lots of dancing, in Pliatan, in Saba, in many other places—even here in the Bali Hotel. But what else do you want to see?"

"Oh, we thought some wood carvers and painters, and maybe some festival or cremation or something. Anything that seems to be happening."

"That should be easy, though, in this wet season it's unlikely you'll see any cremations. But our jeep is terrific at ploughing its way right into tiny villages. We can take you right to the mud-wall door of painters' and carvers' houses and let you see them at work."

"That's just the thing we want. Oh yes—we want to see some of Theo Meier's pictures; *and*—we want to see Mario dance."

"What! See Mario dance!"

"Is it impossible?"

"Well, just a minute. We've long wanted to meet Mario, but we never thought he'd dance for us. He's too old." Again I turned to Sampih. "What do you think, Pih? Would Mario be able to dance again? Do you know his house?"

"I know his house, Bli. It's in Tabanan. But as to whether Papa Mario would dance—that is another matter. Doubtless he is old. He has not danced since the Japanese time, that is certain."

"We'll try it then, Frank. But we'll choose a day when it's not raining for that trip."

That night Frank and Martha christened our new bathroom. And it worked, except that Agung had tidily thrown half a broken bottle down the closet, not having come across a swan neck before, and Nyoman Regog had to be summoned hastily on the morrow to remove it. But it rained steadily, and they slept well.

Next morning it so happened that we had a visit from one of our hill-village carver friends, a cunning old fellow named Pan Bedil. He sat damply on our floor, for he always refused our offered chairs, and we offered him cigarettes and coffee while he slowly emptied the coconut-leaf bags he brought with him, spreading out over our floor the most truly astonishing collection of carvings, such as only he and his friends made in the hill-villages of Pudjong and Sebatu.

I went over to fetch Frank and Martha, explaining that this was odd, but unique work, which we generally considered true "primitives," and which were very reasonably priced. On that particular morning old Pan Bedil displayed for us: a rampaging *leyak*, with long teeth, about to devour an infant in arms; a minute human head, of sphinx-like expression, with an arm and hand growing straight out on the top of its skull; four very primitive monkeys on a tree stump; a woman lying in childbirth, two attendants squatting by her, pressing her sides, all with faceless Henry Moore faces; a delightful, simple figure of a child *sanghyang* dancer, her body bent over backwards in a perfect arc, long hair touching the ground; a seated figure, cross-legged, doubled over and hiding his face in cubistic hands; a very ancient old man, each rib showing, hobbling along with a stick, his *sireh* pouch at his waistband, and every sort of peasant figure of the countryside with which the carvers were familiar—but all caricatured, all made grotesque.

"What incredible things," said Frank, and down we both sat and started haggling.

During the next few days the rain fell steadily and our stepping-stones were no longer laughed at by our neighbours. In between the storms we took the Galbraiths down to Renon village, near Sanur, where Theo Meier's wife was building herself a modern brick box of a house and there we also introduced them to Rudin, a young painter whose delightful India ink and water-colour paintings of dancing figures were made, we had discovered, not from life but from the series of sketches by the Mexican Covarrubias in his famous book.

84

But so that they should see a very different sort of wood carving from Pan Bedil's, we took them to Mas, the village just to the south of Pliatan where Dewa Gdé Putu was headmaster at the school, into the compounds of two Brahmana artists, Ida Bagus Ketut and Ida Bagus Nyana.

The elder of these two, Ketut, was the puppet master of the local Shadow Play, the leader of the nearly extinct *wayang wong* Theatre, a *topeng* (masked) dancer who made his own masks, as well as a wood carver. His masks were good, and seldom could a visitor resist buying one when old Ketut wore one to demonstrate the character it represented. He would don the mask, say, of a deaf man, and with head cocked to one side he would look up at his visitors, his eyes, though seen through slits, somehow pathetic, and he would quaver: "I'm a very poor man, Tuan."

Nyana, his cousin, was not only the antithesis of Pan Bedil, but he was also an artist as opposed to the slick craftsmen who chipped out, year after year, those soulless "Bali Heads" for Denpasar's tourists. He was the son of an aged *pedanda*, and had a finely featured Hindu face; his son, twelve years old, was already working under his father and had bought a bicycle from the sale of his own carvings.

On the morning we visited him, Nyana was slowly chiselling at a tall, elongated figure of a fasting man, made from hard ebony wood that came from Borneo. He rose to his feet to greet us, but we slipped quickly in and sat on the edge of his *balé*, asking him to go on working.

"How long does it take you to make a carving, Ida Bagus?" asked Galbraith.

The Ida Bagus laid down his work, thinking, then answered in his soft voice, "If it is made from this iron-tree wood it takes twice as long as when I work with what we call crocodile-tooth wood, which is white and soft. But it is like this, Tuan. I cut the wood first to roughly the size I will use, and I let it dry out for two or three months. And at one time I may be working on several pieces. So I cannot tell how long each carving takes—but for a big one, in soft wood, I should guess at least one month."

"And for how much will you sell the one that you are carving now?"

"For about four hundred *rupiahs*," he answered, as if that were unimportant.

"Isn't that very expensive?"

"I don't know, Tuan. People seem gladly to pay my prices." He smiled. "There are more than twenty mouths to feed in this compound."

As we left I told Frank that we so admired Nyana's work that we never bargained with him. Once, in the past, he had made two small pieces which Luce and I had greatly coveted, and we had asked him, apologetically, if he could lower his prices a little. And at once his young son, Tilem, before Nyana could open his mouth, had replied, *"Sing bisa!"* Impossible! So that, rebuffed and amused, we had nicknamed the boy Singbisa—but we never attempted to haggle with him again.

We went also to Tjampuang, the place where two rivers meet, above Ubud, and we pointed out the site of Walter Spies' house, built toward the top of a gorge and facing an unreally perfect small temple, its courts laid out under a *wairingin* tree on the very point below which the two streams rushed together. Spies was a German painter and musician who had lived in Bali before the war, and who had greatly influenced both Balinese painting and dancing. He, in fact, with an American dancer, Katharane Mershon, had been responsible for selecting the trance chants and movements of the now famous Ketjak, or Monkey Dance, where a hundred and fifty men seated in brown concentric circles by night, chant and dance with their hands, while, by the light of a branched jungle torch in the circle's centre, parts of the Ramayana story are enacted, telling the tale of Hanuman, Prince of the Monkeys, who brings his hordes of monkeys to help Prince Rama rescue his wife, Sita, who has been kidnapped by the Demon King, Ravana.

Then journeying on past Tjampuang we reached Sayan and walked to the edge of the great cliff where Colin McPhee's house had stood. Here, pointing downward, Sampih said, "You can almost see my house from here—it's just around the corner where the river disappears. *Beh!* Those black dots—you can just see them? I think that is my sister and her husband." And he shouted with all his strength, till the tiny figures looked up, waving vaguely at us.

As far as the eye could go, up and down this immense, steep valley, bisected by its boulder-strewn river, there was nothing to see but water-filled rice terraces, irrigated so perfectly that even the fields on the crests of the hills grew good *padi*, and everywhere water trickled and fell, incessantly. For me, there is no more beautiful sight in the world than such terraced rice-fields, with their grey or palest yellow-green seedlings just pricked out in them, reflecting the sky or rippled by the wind, making a shimmering patchwork that slowly rises or descends, that climbs over and falls down the multitudinous volcanic chasms and valleys of this richly blessed island.

At home in the evenings I would try, for our guests, to look under the serene-looking surface of this Bali we were living in.

"About Balinese feudalism," I would say. "The young nationalists are right—I think all serf or serf-like mentalities are regrettable. And the Balinese art that I admire, I believe, has been developed in spite of, not because of, the Rajas; because in Bali art springs from the ordinary people, everywhere, all the time. I would guess that Bali's handful of Rajas have grabbed off and made umpteenth wives of as many Legong dancers as they helped train or foster."

"But what would happen to Balinese art if the castes disappeared? Would the art disappear, too?"

"That's the great question. Of course, all the Rajas and people of high caste say that that would be the case. But I just don't yet know enough to estimate how fundamentally the Rajas and feudalism are bound up in the Hinduism of Bali. If the ending of feudalism meant a religious disintegration, two symptoms might emerge. There would be a tendency to an anarchic collapse until a new basis of society could be secured, and perhaps some of the *occasions* for dancing and music would vanish."

"How do you mean—what occasions?"

"Well, the Balinese dance at temple festivals, at tooth filings, at marriages, at the New Year, at big ceremonies after cremations. If a reformed religion meant banishing these ceremonies, then, as I say, some of the occasions for dancing would go."

"Do you think a 'reformed' Balinese religion is possible?"

"I don't know. It might be. The Balinese are very resilient and receptive. And I don't believe that the Balinese gods would collapse if all the castes intermarried, or if the people didn't grovel on the earth in front of their Rajas and address them as Tjokorda Dewa—don't

87

you think it's bad for the dignity of any human being to address another mere man as a 'Limb of God?' "

"Maybe that's only our Western way of thinking."

"Yes—but I feel that changes are inevitable. You should read the Denpasar newspaper. And if the 'Limbs of God' do disappear, I believe, or maybe I hope, that Shiva and the Bali-theon, together with such innocent symbols of Good and Evil as Barong and Rangda, still remain—and therefore ceremonies and festivals will remain. But anyhow, Frank, the souls of these people are filled with natural music and with the desire to dance, and that doesn't only come from their religion—much of it must spring from the fantastic beauty of this island."

"I hope you're right."

"So do I!" I laughed. "A week or so ago a well-known Denpasar family had a birthday party in its garden. I happened to drive by in my jeep, and I saw no Balinese decorations to speak of, heard no gamelan. But I saw Balinese men and women sitting around formally in nice 'burger' squares at tables, all in western clothes, and those of the women incredibly childishly cut, while in front of a microphone was a nice little Balinese girl of twenty years old, in pigtails, singing, in English, 'Home, Sweet Home.' I presumed that was thought to be 'modern progress'."

Frank, a good diplomat, made no comment.

On the day when the sun first broke through enough to encourage us to jeep over to look for Mario, a variant of this problem occurred to me on the way.

"Everything's so very contradictory, I find. Just listen to these two things. The *balean* doctor in the village of Boeg-Boeg in east Bali used his influence against vaccination, and the smallpox casualties there were among the worst in the island. That was terrible. But when the young nationalists in Karangasem started burning the Djoged gamelans in the public square in an excess of puritanical zeal (the Djoged, they said, was bad for national dignity), this same old doctor courageously led a mob of angry villagers to Karangasem in protest.

"Then the breast question. They ban the photographing of breasts and urge their women to cover themselves in public, but they don't realize how much more offensively primitive it can be to see women

88

pausing beside the roads, legs astraddle, lifting a grubby sarong with a free hand, and relieving themselves. Their ideas are in a muddle; but they've certainly got me confused, too."

It was twenty kilometres to Tabanan, a twisty road through level rice-fields, and we found it a neat, small town. We turned down a narrow lane near the Raja's *puri*.

"Mario lives in a very small hut," Sampih warned us. "He was given some money by Tuan Koke who had a hotel at Kuta before the war, but he simply was *forced* to spend half of it on fighting cocks."

And it was indeed a dismal place where Bali's greatest dancer lived. He had one small shack, very grubby and musty, and its roof was leaking. His wife, who must have been very pretty when young and who still had charming features, received us nervously, rapidly questioning Sampih. In the end, since it was again raining hard, we sat around a sordid table while a girl went to look for Mario.

"Bapa Mario works in the Government Office," Sampih now told us. "He gets enough money for his rice and the work is very easy. It is mostly to open the office in the morning and to close it in the evenings; if anyone wants to send a message from the office, they look for Mario in a *warong* in the market." It began to seem not so bad a life for a retired dancer.

Eventually a tall figure came cautiously up the slippery path between the neighbouring houses, wheeling a dripping bicycle beside him.

"This is Mario," said Sampih, laughing with pleasure as Mario jumped up the steps into the house.

"*Beh!* Can it be possible? The boy Sampih grown up!"

"*Beh!* Pa Mario—unalterable, the same as ever!"

"And your friends . . .?"

Grinning, Sampih introduced us all. And at once we were delighted with Mario, for we had heard so many stories of his sicknesses that we had imagined a white-haired and reprobate old skeleton. Instead, we saw a handsome man of about fifty, greying hair well brushed back from his temples, eyes that puckered easily into laughter, a good nose, firm chin, a head set nobly on a strong neck, and a personality immediately attractive by its natural charm.

In five minutes we were talking like old friends; in half an hour

Luce and I had returned from the market with some food and we were all sitting around the table drinking and eating contentedly. After the food, like two buffoons, Mario and Sampih sat cross-legged on a bamboo bed where Mario demonstrated for us the sad decline of the modern Kebiar.

"*Beh!* These young fellows—" he complained. "They hold themselves like nothing—ugh! like Sampih sits now—and they think they can dance in five minutes. But dancing is hard work, Tuan; it is *work.*"

Again he posed Sampih in a painfully incorrect position, exclaiming and laughing. Then he turned to us again, pure tragedy in his eyes.

"That's how they sit nowadays," he moaned. "Terrible, terrible!" And burst into more laughter.

"And what sort of a pupil was Sampih, Pa Mario?"

"Difficult, Tuan—very difficult. Always he was difficult." And he had to break off, for the two of them were now shouting at each other as reminiscence overcame them.

"Then the best thing, Bapa," I said calmly, "is for you to come to Pliatan and show us how the Kebiar should be danced."

An astonished face.

"*Beh!* What, me?"

He sat very still. His face became most solemn. He shook his head glumly.

"I am old, Tuan. I never dance. I do not even take pupils any more."

At once Sampih intervened and another hilarious Balinese altercation began. Frank and I argued with him for almost an hour, all of which flattered Mario immensely, and at last, with a martyr's sigh, he capitulated.

"I will try, then. But I am old—and stiff. I cannot move. You will make me *ashamed*, Tuan. In front of Pliatan, too. I will attempt only the '*Pelaion'*—the introduction when I play on the *terompong*."

"*Terompong*, Pih? What's that?"

"Oh, we don't use one generally in Pliatan. It's like a *reyong*, with twelve gongs in a row, but designed only for one player."

"Agreed, then. Perfect. And perhaps you will find some child in Pliatan whom you may think worthy of teaching the Kebiar. Now— can you find our house in Kaliungu? Good. You come by bus to

90

Kaliungu, and we'll drive you up in the jeep to Pliatan. You can sleep on the couch in our front house if you like."

"Good, Tuan. So be it then." We left him looking mournful a little.

But when he danced in Pliatan we learned that the old books about Bali were still right. There is no Kebiar dancer like the man who created it some twenty-five years ago.

Though he danced only for five minutes in an old costume borrowed from Sampih, and though he sat behind the *terompong* and only reached from one end of it to the other with his long arms, his quality remained. Technically, perhaps, Mario was never as brilliant or as full of fireworks as his first pupils. But his quality was not to be stolen: for it was Mario himself.

He had taken the Kebiar music of North Bali, and made this sitting dance that was ideally suited to his own physique. His expression is infinitely subtle and serene; his body is long and straight, so are his arms and fingers, too; and his head is set on his neck and shoulders with the perfection of a Roman statue.

He sat, then, behind this *terompong*, two slender white batons in his hand, and behind him the gamelan started a quiet, floating introduction to a Kebiar. Then he played that *terompong* with superb and nonchalant gestures; on his face, as he twirled the batons which descended in perfectly elegant yet in sometimes almost hesitant timing, was an expression of fastidiousness, of aloofness, of nobility. At a break in the music he would drop the batons and draw back, and with arms and body dance a fraction of his old Kebiar. Mario's eyebrows did not flutter with great speed—he hinted, rather, that he was raising them, very gently and with the most subtle innuendo; and a split second after his eyes had started out of his head they relaxed back into a suggestion of quite urchin humour—but only a suggestion.

Without that supremely mobile face and its quality of unconscious greatness, no other dancer could hope to compare with Mario.

When it was over he sat there fanning himself, panting, laughing and shouting at us all, "I told you so. I *told* you. I am old. I cannot dance any more. I cannot!"

But clearly he could; and he did, many times sleeping in our front house, before continuing on his way home by the dawn bus to Tabanan from Denpasar.

When we eventually said good-bye to these Galbraiths at the airport is was we who felt indebted to them. Not only had we discovered Mario together, but they had proved to us that a guest-house could be a pleasant way of looking for a living in Bali.

5

Shaping a Programme

*

One of the most delightful things about living in Bali is the way the servants become part of your family. For our relations with Rantun and her children were of this nature, just as we felt Sampih to be our younger brother and Kusti our adopted son. To talk with Rantun, and to ask her questions about her Bali, was to reveal that we lived in the same yet utterly apart worlds, seeing and evaluating the same things quite differently, and her account of the now imminent solar Day of Nyepi illustrated this perfectly.

To me Nyepi was a nuisance. Either I had to go to the Raja's office and queue up with all the local Chinese to pay the customary fines; or else, for twenty-four hours I must light no fire, burn no electricity, use no typewriter, eat no food cooked that day, and under no circumstances go out in my jeep. It was an irritation, merely.

But to Rantun it was quite otherwise. She told us her story of Nyepi with that mixture of seriousness and laughing incredulity which colours and makes sane so much of the Balinese religion.

"They say it is like this, Tuan. On the day before Nyepi the gods drive out all the devils from the outer worlds. And alas, we fear they may fall on Bali and plague us. So, at the time of the spring equinox, we make special offerings to attract all the devils that are already here. And of an evening, when they have collected at the crossroads where we have laid out the offerings, we all go out and make a fearful noise, the children banging and shouting, beating old tins and striking the *kulkul* drums, and thus the devils are driven out—either to another land, or to . . . well, that does not matter. And then the next day all our villages keep silent. Nobody shouts or makes a noise; no cars are allowed on the roads to show that Bali is inhabited; no smoke from cooking fires. All is still. And the devils are deceived—for luckily for us, Tuan, these devils seem generally to be rather stupid—and they think that our Bali is empty, deserted, with no people to annoy and with no people from whom to receive offerings. And in this way we get rid of our devils each year."

Nonsense, do I hear you say, gentle reader? Well, one day we told Rantun the story of the Gadarene Swine. But she and her children were embarrassed at the end of it, silent, because they were far too polite to tell us that this sounded a very naïve and childish tale.

Nyepi came at about the end of March, and thereafter, thanks in part to the Galbraiths and in part to the end of the wet season, our guest house often came to have one or two guests staying in it, while yet other people, who came to Denpasar but preferred the more certain comforts of a hotel, would come to our house and ask to be taken around the villages to meet the Balinese in their own houses. And this, together with the English lessons we started to give in the dry weather, five evenings a week, meant that we had plenty to occupy us outside our work in Pliatan. With our guests we had to develop two techniques. If we liked the look of them we invited them to use our front house as theirs, too; but if we only took them in from dire economic necessity, I would lead them to the second house, say firmly to them, "This is *your* house," and walk off down the passage-way again, by mental suggestion contriving to slam an invisible barrier at the end of that connecting passage so that we would not be bothered too often.

As the hot season approached—and in Bali only April and May can be considered at all uncomfortably hot—we received a visit from two Belgians, one Henri Fast and his wife. He was the head of U.N. Information work in the Far East; and his dry Gallic intelligence was a refreshing thing to encounter after the superficial and ill-founded ecstasies which we heard so often.

Henri Fast was very perceptive. He saw our collection of primitive carvings and asked us at once:

"Do the Balinese themselves use such carvings and paintings in their own homes, or are they purely a tourist commodity?" Very few people asked us that question, because it was generally presumed that since the Balinese carved and painted, their houses must be full of such things.

"They all work for the tourist trade," I answered.

"Then where do the artists find their place in their own culture?"

"Oh, they can still do work in traditional style if the village requires it. The painters make friezes in the old Hindu style around temple altars; the wood carvers make magnificently carved doors and screens, they carve the frames for the gamelan instruments, they decorate the pillars and beams of the village meeting halls, and make ornamental wooden figures for the temples As for the sculptors who work in the soft *paras* stone, just look at the temple gateways and walls or at the guardian figures and gargoyles outside the temples. That's their real work."

Later we drove them over to watch the men sculpting a new temple in Ubud, under the eye of the old Tjokorda Ngurah; and afterwards we visited the Halls of Justice in Klungkung, where some fine artists had painted around the inside of the roofs friezes which began their story in Hindu mythology, and ended with a Japanese soldier falling into the sea with his rising sun flag right into the mouth of an attendant shark of the year 1945.

On our way home we saw a cremation just finishing on the outskirts of the village of Batuan.

"May we watch a moment?" asked the Fasts.

So we walked over to the burial ground, where the Temple of the Dead was, and near which we could see a few people still standing and gossiping while the flames licked sluggishly at the blackened frames of the tall wooden towers which had held the bull-shaped sarcophagi. The corpses had long ago become ashes.

"Greetings," I said to one of the bystanders. "Was there a fine cremation today?"

"It was nothing," came the reply. "Of seven persons only."

"Of high caste, perhaps?"

"No. Ordinary folk who had been sick."

So we guessed that this was one of the many quick cremations following on death from smallpox. Often the Balinese wait months and years before disinterring the bodies to cremate them, waiting for an auspicious day and a time when they have money to spare.

"What a pity we just missed it," said Henri Fast.

"I'm rather glad," said Luce.

"Oh, but why? Is it not very interesting?" He turned to Luce in surprise.

"It's very interesting—once. But although I know a corpse to the Balinese is only an empty shell, an 'earthly encumbrance' which, until it's burnt, merely prevents the soul's liberation, I just don't like to see bits of bodies being tossed about by laughing relatives; nor do I much care for the stink of putrefaction."

"But where is your anthropological curiosity? How will you understand the Balinese if you don't sympathize with what takes place in their minds at such important rites?" This time he turned to me, and he was part mocking.

"The trouble is that you must stick to your own 'ology'. Bali is interesting enough to give a life's work to many anthropologists, ethnologists, archaeologists, musicologists and others. So we concentrate on our own chosen field. I could tell you little about cremations; further, I would admit cremations don't especially interest me. But I could tell you quite a lot of the history of the classical Legong in the last sixty years, and we have ideas even for creating a new dance. And don't forget we have our living to earn, too—looking after delightful people like you."

"You flatter me. But tell me one thing—by studying dancing and music, do you also get to know the people and the way they think?"

"You do. But I would say that five years in Bali and a good knowledge of the Balinese language, quite apart from Indonesian, would be necessary to understand much of the Balinese. I'll tell you this much: the recently arrived Javanese and Sumatran officials in Denpasar often admit to not being able to understand them."

"Well, what sort of people do you *think* they are?"

"I know one thing. They are the least romantic of people. Like peasants all over the world they are superstitious, full of natural lore, necessarily opportunist. In their personal relationships they are direct and simple. They are so uninhibited that they must have driven Margaret Mead to distraction. Complexes can only be projected into them, for they own none of themselves. Oh, they can be devastatingly natural! But their structure of society, their religion, their ways of thinking, their rules of conduct—that is where the complications come in."

"Please don't dispel my romantic illusions," said Madame Fast. "I do so enjoy them."

"Good. You keep your illusions, then. And Luce and I will continue to be mad about their music and dancing."

We took the Fasts up to see the dancing in Pliatan, of course, and he at once offered to put me in touch with an impresario in Belgium.

"It would be a tremendous success in Brussels," he said. "As for Paris, it would go crazy about it."

Before going back to Djakarta he told us, "We have to hold a regional conference somewhere in Indonesia during July. I am thinking that Bali might be an ideal place to hold it. Don't be surprised if we meet again before too many months have gone by."

The lights in the compound at Pliatan were dim. On the floor of the rehearsal verandah sat the Anak Agung, his two right hands, Madé Lebah and Gusti Kompiang, Sampih and our two selves. The night was hot and still, and our cups of thick black coffee which the *warong* just outside the *puri* gates bought from a plantation in the mountains near Bedugul, remained untouched. The three children had long ago climbed together onto one thin mattress and were asleep, sprawled out over each other. The members of the club had all carefully laid down their hammers on the metallophone keys and wandered back to their houses in the dark. The only sign of movement in any of the houses, where now only coconut-shell lights burned steadily, came from the house nearest us, where a "mother" of the Anak Agung, his father's last surviving wife, could be heard yawning. This vast woman, we had recently learned, was the real head of the family, for she controlled the monies of the *puri* and thereby every adult and child within its four walls. What she thought of our work we did not know. We could see her as we talked, sitting mountainously on her bed, an old towel wrapped around her head, and scratching her large, still firm, bosom.

The cement of the verandah floor was cool, and we were discussing what next to add to our programme. We had a Legong that lasted over an hour, with Sampih's Kebiar and the overture. There was the

Djanger, which could go on indefinitely; and there were masked dancers whom we used to call in sometimes from outlying villages. Already we had at our disposal a repertoire almost unique for one club, and our friends were conscious and proud of this.

"If we were to go abroad, Agung Adji, do you know how long our Legong, with the Kebiar and Djanger and Tabuh Telu would play for?"

"That is for you to tell us," was the comfortable answer. The Balinese love talking into the night and he was in no hurry.

"You mean the dances are too long?" asked Lebah.

"Of course they are," growled Sampih, who living in Kaliungu and poring over books on ballet and the western theatre was already our invaluable adviser.

"*We* love to see the Legong play for an hour, Madé. But abroad our whole programme will have to be cut and condensed. So far, we have perhaps nearly half a programme. There is still much work to do."

"*Beh!* I thought we were nearly ready."

"Agung Adji—could we not make some agreement with three or four masked dancers from another village and make them honorary members of the club? We should find the right people and ask them to start rehearsing with us, because masked plays go on for hours and hours and I want to have two stories rehearsed and shortened to about twenty or thirty minutes. To make it worth their while, we could agree that if and when we go abroad, they would go with us."

"That would be possible. In the village of Singapadu there are such people."

"And in Batuan, too, perhaps? I admire Kakul very much."

I was referring to a famous teacher and dancer, who by day was a hard-working peasant, each afternoon a fancier of fighting cocks, whose children from the ages of seven to fourteen all were good dancers, and who, himself, was able to teach some six sorts of dancing.

"Pliatan has no relations with Batuan. But doubtless John and Sampih together could influence Kakul. He is your friend and Sampih's old Baris teacher."

"All right, Agung Adji—that means we have Legong, Kebiar, Djanger, and Sampih's Baris dance to put in a masked play. Now Luce and I want something *new*."

"Something new? You mean . . .?"

"We mean just that. Bali is the only island in the whole of the Far East where new dance forms are being created. How old is the Kebiar, or the Djanger? Less than twenty-five years! Well, we want an entirely new dance created for our club to take abroad."

They considered this, open-minded, with none of that scorn or conservatism that such a suggestion would have received in other eastern lands. Then Lebah, who perhaps had nightmare visions of western choreography being forced upon his gamelan and dancers, asked us cautiously, "And who would teach this new dance, Tuan?"

"Mario."

They looked happier as they thought this over. Then the Anak Agung sucked his teeth loudly and said, "It might be possible. Have you perhaps any ideas about what sort of dance this should be—or did you talk it over with Mario?"

"No, we've said nothing to Mario before asking for your approval. But Luce and I had two ideas only. We'd like this to be a dance for a man and a girl, not another solo dance; we would like a real Balinese dance created for, say, Sampih and little Raka, because so far we've seen girls take male roles and men take girls' roles, but never—apart from the Djoged—have we seen a *fine* dance of this sort. And then Luce wants to design a truly feminine costume for the girl dancer— for similar reasons—because girls dancing in male Kebiar costume we think are ugly and dull. Luce wants a really delicate, feminine costume. Perhaps it will have just a little Javanese or Serimpi influence in it."

"*Beh!*" Another silence.

Then the Anak Agung looked at the other Balinese, raised his eyebrows, shrugged, and turned to us grinning: "That is settled then. Has John any more ideas that we could discuss?"

"Only this, O Limb of God, my dear Agung Adji—when do we board the jeep together and invade Tabanan to carry off Mario?"

"Most excellent Tuan," he replied, laughing, "who has never known patience: shall we say tomorrow morning at precisely ten o'clock from Kaliungu?"

And so the siege of Mario began.

On our first trip to Tabanan we found him just leaving the Government office on his bicycle to go on a message. So we were compelled to tell him that we wanted him to create another new dance for us under the patronizing gaze of the white-shirted and smartly trousered officials, who found it a ridiculous thing that a foreigner should drive all the way over from Denpasar to look for their messenger boy.

Mario was astonished at our proposal, yet also delighted. Since he must have leisure to think it all over, and since he had no immediate ideas for a new dance, he played for time. But this we gave him gladly, at first, merely telling him that we hoped he would make a dance with Sampih and Raka in it, and one that would contain the essentials of "boy meets girl." He guffawed, saying, "Good, Tuan, very good."

A week later we drove over again at the time his office closed. Perhaps there had been many cockfights, or perhaps no inspiration had yet come. He was full of excuses, and desperate as we blocked them.

His wife was sick, he said—truly sick. We replied that we had just come from his house, where indeed his wife had seemed a little pale, but we would gladly take her to Denpasar's hospital or to Dr. Suhardi, a Javanese gynaecologist friend of Luce's family, who was now practising there, too. Then he changed his ground, whispering to us confidentially that he must first ask permission of the Raja, who was still the nominal head of the civil administration. We said yes, this was reasonable, we would gladly go with him and tell the Raja why we were asking for him. So Mario, with his back to the wall, said that he must stay in Tabanan a while because very soon it was the anniversary of his house temple—and furthermore, he added on an inspiration, if he left his house, who would feed the fighting cocks?

We gave him another four days to think it over, and when we returned next time we drove straight to his house. His wife met us, laughing. "Mario has gone to a cockfight," she told us.

"Do you know, perhaps, in which village this fight is?"

"I did not ask. There is one almost every day."

Again we were defeated. But the following day we came back in the morning and found Mario in the market, drinking coffee. He greeted us with pretended contrition. "A great pity that my foolish wife did not know where the cockfight was yesterday." Then seriously: "I have not yet asked the permission of the Lord Raja to go to Pliatan, Tuan."

So we invited him to get into the jeep and solemnly and at once we drove up before the Raja's Office, and after we had apologized for the informality of our dress, the young Raja received us together and at once. He was a dark-skinned, round-faced man in his thirties, and most helpful.

"So you are starting Mario off again as a teacher," he commented. "That is very good. He should be teaching Kebiar here in Tabanan, also."

And he graciously gave Mario permission to absent himself for a week or ten days at a time, provided that a reasonable deputy could be found to do his work.

"Easy, easy, Tuan," he told us. "My friends in the office will do that for me."

So we agreed to wait in Kaliungu till Mario came over on the morning bus, and then to take him by jeep to Pliatan. But next day no Mario came. We telephoned the Tabanan office from Denpasar, but he was not there. Next morning again we telephoned, and from another messenger we gathered that Mario's friends were not so willing to take over his additional work.

Then one afternoon I said to Sampih, "Come on, Pih. Let's go to Tabanan for the last time. Wherever Mario is we will find him and bring him back to Pliatan this very day."

Of course, he was not at home. But his wife told us to ask for him at a sort of *warong*, or club, where there was a billiard table, near the central crossroads of the town; and here we met a friend of Mario's who thought, though he was not sure, that Mario had left for a cock-fight in a certain village some twelve kilometres distant, riding his bicycle. We left in hot pursuit, driving over grassy roads through rice fields which sloped down to the seashore, until we knew we were on the right track because we began to pass Balinese figures hurrying along, in their hands the coconut-leaf meshed baskets, out of which the fighting cocks tails could be seen projecting. Of one such man we asked the name of the village where the cockfight was being held; he directed us but he dared not claim a place in our jeep for fear it should alarm his cock. Another mile, and we could hear the roar of the betting crowd above the jeep's engine, and then the track, which was running through the very rice-fields, became so narrow that it would be impossible to turn if we went further, and the last hundreds of yards we walked.

As is the normal custom, the fight was taking place under a temporary awning made from loosely laid palm fronds. Around the square earth floor were hundreds of peasants—no women at all were visible save those selling *arak* or palm toddy at the inevitable *warongs*—and they were in much the mood of a boxing crowd, the only differences being that they chewed betel, drank *arak* and squatted or stood in densely packed layers, talking and shouting loudly. We soon spotted Mario, in the very front row, with a smile of satisfaction on his face, but seeming to take no active part in the animated discussions surrounding him.

The whole of the centre of the floor was filled with squatting men, mouths plugged with their chews of tobacco, hoarsely offering their birds for a fight, holding them up to challenge some onlooker. When two men thought that their birds might be well matched, they would squat facing each other in the ring, where they exchanged birds, felt them, weighed them, fancying their chances, calculating whether the day and the hour and the colour of their opponent's bird was auspicious for their own bird or not. When any two of them had agreed to a contest, they would take out a slim wooden case the shape of a slender axehead, and from it select a spur, three or four inches long and as sharp as a razor, which they then bound firmly to their bird's right leg, where its own natural spur had long been removed. When three or four pairs were thus suited, the next round of fights would begin.

Seated prominently at one side of the ring was an elderly man, wearing a gorgeous new headcloth in honour of his position as the referee. By his side was a bell to sound the rounds, and also a bowl of water, near which was set a half coconut shell into which had been bored a tiny hole. A wounded bird would be "counted out" in the time that it took the coconut shell to sink in the bowl of water.

The first two owners now squatted in opposing corners, their birds held up in one hand above their heads, where their fine points were offered for the betters' inspection, and then bets began to be placed uproariously by every man. Two men would make a bet by one catching the other's eye, indicating the bird they each fancied by an outward thrust of the chin in its direction or by a shout of their bird's colour, then eyebrows were raised in mutual satisfaction and with a firm nod the bet was on. Professional betters also made their rounds, placing or accepting bets at even prices, at two-to-three or at two-to-one. Those who wanted to place their bets tried to find takers by shouting out the colour of the bird they fancied and by raising a hand with their silver coins exposed in them. *"Djau! Djau! Djau! Djau!"* they would shriek, this being the betting abbreviation for *hidjau*, meaning green.

When it was judged that most of the bets had been made, the first two men set their birds on the ground, facing each other in the centre of the ring and only an inch or two apart, where, with serpentine necks and bristling combs they measured and lunged at each other, while their owners inflamed them further by bouncing them up and down within range of their opponents' beaks, then pulling them back again, until the birds crowed and were frantic with rage. The two men retreated again to their corners while the last bets were made in a storm of noise, and at a signal from the referee, released them to fight.

The two cocks run at each other, meeting beak to beak in the centre, measuring each other up and down, circling, eyeing one another redly, snakelike necks dipping and lowering, head and neck feathers angrily ruffled, always beak to beak, looking for an opening. The crowd is deathly silent.

Suddenly one cock leaps up—an immediate, long-drawn "Ah-h-h!" from the crowd—but he has timed it badly; only a few feathers fly. At once his opponent leaps up against him again, and, as they fall apart, the keen spur is drawn in a vicious slash into the breast of his enemy near where the wing joins the body. As if on a reflex both birds leap up a third time together, breast to breast, and this time there is a great falling of feathers as they tumble asunder again. But the green bird is now seen crouched to the floor, a tell-tale trickle of dark blood showing through its bedraggled feathers. It tries in vain to rise to its feet again, but its eyes are already filming over and half shut in death. The owner of the winning bird, meanwhile, walks gingerly after his cock who still tries to attack the dying bird, and very carefully he slips a hand under it and lifts it cleanly aloft. If a bird is too excited, or its owner careless in picking it up, the spur can cut through a man's hand to the bone, while a frightened bird flapping desperately into the spectators has been known to send men to hospital with terrible wounds.

During three bouts the spectators urged on their favourites and groaned over their losses, making the most colossal and exciting din, but each time the fighting was over they pulled out their money and paid or accepted their debts with poker faces. Then out came the *sireh* pouches and the *warongs* were surrounded by men slinging down tots of the fiery *arak*. There was a wild-eyed, rather alcoholic atmosphere, aggressively masculine, and the usual musky smell was heavily impregnated with *tuak* and *arak*, with betel and cigarettes acrid and carnation flavoured.

I met Mario and Sampih on the edge of the throng. Mario was looking very happy.

"*Beh!* A pity the Tuan arrived so late. He would have seen my bird win." He indicated the winner's tail sticking out of the palm-leaf bag in which he was already encased again, and to which there was also now tied the corpse of his late enemy.

"I think cockfighting is like a religion to you, Bapa."

"Indeed, it is *very* important, Tuan. Even when I was always dancing I had to fight the cocks as well. If I had smelled blood at a fight, I would dance better."

To my relief, Mario made no trouble about coming with us. He told a friend to take his bird home and handed over his bicycle to the man as well. I hoped this meant that the new dance was ready in his head.

An hour later we were waiting in Mario's house while he changed into a fine dark green sarong, put on a new headcloth at a jaunty angle, slipped on a bright pink shirt which he wore outside the sarong, and added a clean towel tied round his waist.

"Are you ready, Bapa? Nothing else to bring with you?"

"I am ready," he replied. "What more should I need?" And we left, Mario shouting out to his wife, asking her to remind his friends to take over his work at the office on the morrow.

When more *arak* had been served in Kaliungu and the meal was being made ready by Rantun, we asked Mario to tell us more about the dance. What was the story, we wanted to know—and what music was he using?

He walked over to one of our metallophones, calling over to Sampih, "Learn this tune, Pih. I will need you to play this at first in Pliatan while I am holding the girl." And he played out a most simple, silly little melody, repetitive and catchy. In ten minutes not only Sampih but Kusti also could play it.

"What tune is that, Bapa?"

"It is nothing, that tune; but it is good for us to use at first. I must teach this Raka her basic movements and steps before using the true music. This will be a new style to her."

"And the story—you say it is about two bumblebees?"

"Oh, don't worry, Tuan. It will be a simple story. Raka will be the girl bumblebee, Sampih the male. It will be enough, don't you think?"

"Perhaps, Bapa. But the details of it are not yet clear?"

"They are not yet thought out. But it will come; I must see Raka dance first. If she is suitable, the story will come of itself. You will see, Tuan. Do not trouble yourself."

And that is just what did happen. For three days Mario held Raka or danced before her until his pink shirt was dark with sweat; and when he was tired, Sampih took over. And in those three days several very important things developed. First we had the pure joy of watching Mario teach. Mario has probably the most superbly mobile actor's face in the world. When he taught it was as if he was giving a performance, one eye cocked always on his audience. He held Raka in the same way that Gusti Biang had done. He showed her each movement and phrase a score of times, most patiently, watching her try to mirror him with eyes as alert as a cat's, sometimes squatting on the ground looking up at her, then jumping up to flip some Legong-haunted hand into a bumblebee position, clicking his tongue, sighs of satisfaction nicely mixed with anger and feigned or real disappointment. But it was when he danced in front of her, showing her precisely what he wanted, that I was open-mouthed at Mario's genius. This tall, noble man of fifty odd years became a little girl, every emotion necessary to a timid, delicious, bewildered and finally angry and frightened small child passing over his face, till the compound was filled with villagers, who watched amused, but greatly puzzled, for the quality of Mario's greatness was beyond their ken.

But in Ni Gusti Raka he had found a worthy pupil. She learned with a speed that embarrassed her teacher's inventiveness. Her ability to copy faithfully the right movements was matched by an emotional echoing of Mario's superb face in a way that was unbelievable in a ten-year-old child. In the end Mario left for Tabanan again to fetch Pan Sukra, his drummer, so that the club could begin learning the true music. As he left, he praised Raka, but added deprecatingly, "It is often like this, Tuan. In Bali this is *normal*." But I believe that Mario was running away from Raka till he could think out the dance more wholly. But our friend the Anak Agung, too, would also not yet admit anything unusual in little Raka. When we understood this we became careful, for we realized that his pride was slightly hurt—the two Legongs were of his family and Oka was his very own daughter; and we were selecting for the honour of this new dance a Wesya, a neighbour, someone from outside his family. So we went gently, since we valued both him and the Legongs very highly, and I explained that if we were to go abroad, it would be necessary for the other girls also to learn this role; and that if I had chosen out Raka, I was daring to select her from more international standards, whereas I was quite prepared to admit that as Legongs, Oka and Anom had no rivals at all.

Mario was so excited, it seemed, that two days later he went directly back to Pliatan by bus, taking Pan Sukra with him. He called at Kaliungu for the briefest of moments, eyes gleaming, "Greetings, Tuan. I come for a moment only. Here is my music composer, Pan Sukra. We go now to Pliatan. Will the Tuan be coming up tonight?"

"Of course, Bapa. We'll see you then." And off they hurried, a most remarkable phenomenon in Balinese, Mario's long legs impatient with the small, sturdy figure of Pan Sukra beside him.

When we arrived about nine o'clock that night in the village we found the gamelan well into the first melody of the new dance; and it was Kebiar music, though new, Mario told us, having been composed originally by Pan Sukra for a club in Marga, near Tabanan: but it had never been used. And anyhow, these tunes were arranged for a girl dancer, while the original ones had been for a man.

It took about three weeks for the thirty minutes of music to be perfectly mastered by Pliatan, and at the end of that time Pan Sukra went home to his village. Then the Anak Agung, Madé Lebah and Gusti Kompiang grinned freely. "Now it is our turn," they said.

106

"What do you mean?" we asked.

"*Aggh!* This is crude music. Now it is a matter of *tabuh*—style. You will see. It must be rearranged and polished by the club."

And during the next couple of months Mario would keep coming up to the *puri* for a day or two at a time, but never stopping longer than three days because he could not bear to be away from his fighting cocks for a time longer than that. And Luce and I camped in Pliatan, daily eating our food there, which Rantun wrapped for us in little banana-leaf bundles, so that we had no need to bother the generous hospitality of the Anak Agung.

And we saw the story of the dance unfold, as Mario had told us it would, creating itself bit by bit, with ideas thrown in from us all. We saw Raka as the little bumblebee sunning herself in a flower-filled garden, in moods of surprise, delight and fear; we saw the gaudy male bumblebee enter, and Sampih could pick up Mario's ideas with the speed with which a western ballet dancer follows an *enchaînement* in class; we saw him spy the delectable little bee, zoom towards her, court her, frighten her by his advances till she fled from him. Then Sampih danced alone in baffled fury as the Kebiar music raged around him, and in the last rollicking melody he danced a Kebiar of sheer frustration around the whole gamelan, flirting desperately with its members. This was a development out of Mario's original Kebiar, and he called it now in full: Tumulilingan Mengisap Sari—the Bumblebee Sips Honey.

Luce was meanwhile busy with the costumes. Sampih's was to be that of a normal Kebiar dancer, but in the boldest gold and purple bee-like stripes, Raka's *kain* was to be long and trailing, and of gold and green cloth and very feminine; her body was to be encased in glittering purple, and at her hips were to be two *ontjers*, streamers of apple-green chiffon which flowed as she danced like transparent wings; on her head was to be perched a crown of golden flowers, with gold antennae quivering. All our Pliatan family were engrossed in this dance, for it was a new thing and it was ours.

This was when we first began to know the characters of the three little girls, and we even made serious and round-about enquiries of Raka's family, for we let the Anak Agung know that we found her a most attractive and perfect child, and had there been any chance of

107

adopting her as ours, we would have loved legally to have taken her. But her family were living and proud of her, and she was inseparable from her friends Oka and Anom.

As we sat long hours with the children, we began to hear some of the secrets of the *puri*. They told us, for instance, that Djero Wanita, the young wife of Dewa Gdé Putu, had fear and respect for rats—which many Balinese designate with the superstitious title of Djero Ketut—"Fourth Born of Unknown Caste." Each day Djero Wanita would feed them with her own hands in the neat *balé* of the Dewa. Then, when we asked Oka how it was they all had lice in their hair, so that, in common with all Balinese children, they were for ever de-lousing one another, they answered, *"Beh!* We don't like lice! But just try to persuade everybody else in the *puri* the same thing, and then ask Agung Adji's permission to burn all our bedding!"

Dewa Gdé Putu told us amusing tales about his brother.

"Adoh! But my brother is hopeless with money," he once said. *"Tjoba!* He never gives money away to anybody—as if he were a miser, hating to give it even to his wives. Yet he can't keep it—*always* it vanishes! If he has any cash, all the *puri* knows it will be in the pocket of his shirt hanging up in his room. So the mother of Bawa, maybe, needs money and takes a few *rupiahs*. My brother does not notice. Then comes the mother of Oka—perhaps one of her children needs a new anklet, so she, too, takes some money. It is like a *bank*, that pocket! Then the mother of little Bangli, the son who is the apple of his father's eye, only two years old, goes in her turn to the shirt pocket and it is empty. So she asks my brother for money. Give me my shirt, he replies, gruffly. There is nothing there, shouts the mother of Bangli, and so once again we have a KRISIS in the *puri*.

"Oh, we are a funny family. Always it happens like this; and never does my brother act differently. At first he suspects everybody in the compound. Then, if he suspects one person, *"Itu bangsat!"* he will mutter—"That louse!" But never does it dawn on him that the culprits are his own family and that he himself leaves them no other method of finding money. Yet at other times I think this is a clever trick of my brother—that he deliberately puts there the money he doesn't mind losing."

It was June and the dance was almost ready when we had a letter from Henri Fast telling us that the U.N. Conference was indeed to take place in Denpasar, beginning at the end of July. Furthermore, he, as the host to the conference, wanted to know whether the Pliatan club, at a not too exorbitant price, could put on a Balinese feast and dance performance in the Anak Agung's *puri* for the hundred and twenty delegates. The arrangements of it he would gladly leave to us.

That evening the club and the Anak Agung agreed that this would be a fine occasion on which first to present the new bumblebee dance. So that night there was no rehearsal, but instead Kuwus, a butcher in the club, and Bregeg, a pig dealer, and the Anak Agung and his wives, worked out the cost of the necessary roast sucking pigs, the smoked ducks, the chickens, the goat for the Moslems, the *lawar*, the *saté*, the fruits, the traditional Balinese decorations, the oil for scores and scores of lamps, the hiring of chairs for the guests and glasses and plates and spoons to feed them, and lastly, the fee for the dancers. Next morning I wrote off to Fast, and we soon came to a satisfactory agreement.

Then, by some misfortune, but largely, perhaps, because the Foreign Ministry in Djakarta was in part responsible for the conference, I found myself elected on to a committee in Denpasar as the man to plan four days of entertainment for the conference. Here I became surrounded at once by parochial jealousies.

It was now that we met the teacher, Nyoman Kaler, for the first time. An old, old rival of Lotring's, we had more admiration for the latter, but had kept outside their two factions in Denpasar, which had existed even in Colin McPhee's time. Both of them had been the pupils of our aged neighbour in Kaliungu, Ida Bagus Boda, with whom we preferred to chat.

But Kaler now started coming to our house in the evenings just after dark, entering always by the back gate. A gaunt man in his fifties, protuberant-eyed and of a cold personality, he drank *arak* with us and seemed friendly enough. He came to discuss "basic fundamentals" with us, he said mysteriously, in a deep, staccato voice; but he ended by inviting us to eat at his house where there might also be some dancing. So we went and ate a spitted sucking pig with him and saw the dancers and orchestra of Pemogan, which was his real objective, and in that the dancers had newly commenced their dancing, we could only offer this club's orchestra the opportunity to play in the Bali Hotel on the conference's opening night.

The chief Indonesian organizer of the whole project, one Sumarno, stayed at our guest house with his pretty wife all through the week and no unsurmountable difficulties arose. The conference was as tiresome as all such conferences, and Sampih had just got his driving licence and was invaluable in the help he gave Luce and myself in this work.

The U.N. delegates saw the Monkey Dance in Bonah village, and had lunch with Lemayeur and Polok on the beach, where Polok forgot herself far enough to attempt to dance some fragments of Legong; and on the final evening of the conference the Masked Play went on to uncontrollable lengths in the Bali Hotel hall, till in the end the show was for the Balinese of Denpasar only, while the unfortunate delegates were trying vainly to sleep.

On the evening of the feast in Pliatan the whole *puri* compound was lit by hundreds of tiny oil lights, and in the inner court long tables covered with coconut-leaf mats and heavy with bright flowers were ready to receive the guests. No police came over from Gianjar to help us (another little local political matter of "face"), so that most of the delegates had to get out of their cars in an appalling traffic-block and walk from afar into the *puri*, where they at once could help themselves to mountains of the best Balinese food, served in buffet fashion and presided over by Luce. The club and the rest of us were all waiters for the night, and we were defeated only by the Indian delegate, Sir Mirza Ismail, whose strict diet, alas, permitted him to eat only a banana or two.

That night Mario himself played the *terompong* and sparred for a moment with Sampih in a "Cockfight Kebiar"; and as Mario walked off the dancing floor, the music of his Tumililingan began, and for the very first time the dance of the two bumblebees was performed in public. After the Tumililingan we gave the Legong. And packed together uncomfortably though they were in the narrow confines of the *puri* entrance, most of the foreign delegates were entranced. The senior official of the Foreign Ministry sat good-naturedly on the matting floor behind the drummers; and the tired lady who was private secretary to the Indonesian Prime Minister, dozed throughout.

It was a warmly, wonderfully chaotic evening. And when, hours and hours later, it seemed, the last car had borne away the last members of the seventeen-nationality audience, we could all of us at last sit down and eat, too.

But the evening was little Raka's. This child, who had danced perfectly her bumblebee dance for half an hour, followed by her exacting and longer role in the Legong, was still running around as lively as a cricket at one o'clock in the morning; and though we tried to make her eat with us, it was she and the other children who pranced happily around with plates of food and glasses of *arak*, very proud and full of laughter, waiting on their elders.

6

Of Guests and Guest-Houses

*

It so happened that Luce's birthday fell on the day of Tumpak Wayang, the day when all the music and dance clubs of Bali make offerings to Dewa Pergina, God of the Dance; and in that we were members of the club, we celebrated this day with them.

Under the great lichee trees at the entrance to the *puri* a bamboo altar was raised, and onto it each instrument of the gamelan was lifted and arranged, while the families of all the club members brought trays laden with the usual offerings of flowers and fruits and foods, piled in bright pyramids, and these were offered to the gamelan and placed beside and between the instruments on the altar.

Then we all sat on the floor of the rehearsal verandah together, while a *pemangku* priest blessed the occasion, lighting his incense and tolling his small, long-handled bell of brass to call the god to partake of the offerings. And when his prayers had been said and the formulae and sacred *mantras* had been intoned, he rose and with a leaf flicked over us all the *tirta*, holy water, which the Balinese received eagerly in cupped hands, clamouring for more, raising it to their lips or anointing their own faces.

Earlier in the morning the three Legongs had walked up the shady road to the temple of Gunung Sari, which had an especial affinity for dancers, and there the same priest had drawn magical patterns and designs on their foreheads, their closed eyes and all their limbs, so that the God might thereby make these his servants attractive and beautiful in the eyes of their beholders.

There were, in fact, many customs connected with the gamelan itself, and we had learned, for instance, never to step over an instrument but always to walk around it; and when we had asked the Anak Agung the meaning of this he told us that it was a matter of respect—a gamelan had a soul, not a human soul, but a power of its own that enabled the players to draw fine music from it. And, said he, it thus came about that a club which respected its gamelan would more easily prosper, for in truth it was paying respect to its own standards. A club which treated its gamelan as lifeless blocks of wood and metal, would damage its own artistic spirit. In Pliatan the discipline in connection with the gamelan had always been great, and this in part explained why they had been able to enjoy so fine a name for such a long time.

This seemed essentially healthy to us, and we tried never to break any of the customs which our friends found to be right. On this present day we merely pledged ourselves to do all we could to see that the next Tumpak Wayang be celebrated abroad.

During our work in the last few months, though, we had again been forced to recognize that we were still living in a period of tumult. Hitherto, incidents which disfigured the peace of Bali had been purely internal, affecting only the Balinese. But we few foreign residents were now dismayed to hear that the seventy-year-old Lemayeur had been seriously wounded by a gang of men who attacked his house by night, while soon afterwards, only a thousand yards from his house, two Dutchmen had been brutally murdered.

The Koopmans, as their name implied, were merchants. He was a retired civil servant of stubborn, hard-headed character, but a man straightforward to deal with. With his shrewd wife he lived by the edge of the sea near Sanur, and the two of them together ran the Sindhu Art Gallery, which held by far the best collection of carvings and paintings on the island.

One night Koopman and his wife were playing cards with the manager of the local Dutch bank and a Eurasian friend. With no warning, a group of masked men sprang out of the night into the house, firing a sten-gun as they rushed in. Koopman and the bank manager were instantly killed, but Mrs. Koopman and the Eurasian threw themselves to the floor, where at first they shammed dead. When the criminals began to ransack the house, they were able to escape into the garden and run away. Since Koopman was no fool, he

113

kept no money in his isolated home, and the bank manager happened purely by chance to be there. A generally accepted theory of the murder thus arose which alleged that the premature firing of the gun was probably due to inexperience, nerves or hysteria. There were no profits from the two crimes.

Now these wanton murders caused a great dismay among the white population of Bali. Lemayeur and Koopman could hardly be considered persons of any political consequence, and these incidents looked like cases of pure robbery with violence against foreigners. So, we all began to wonder who could count themselves safe—for who, in those days of racial sentiment and personal revenge so often misleadingly obscured by political camouflage, could guarantee not to offend some village cut-throat who might thereupon gather a gang together to revenge themselves on an alien "imperialist"? I looked around our compound, defended by mud walls and gates of bamboo wattle. I scratched my head as I walked through our houses, more than half of which were quite open verandahs and whose only half-walls were of woven bamboo which reached eight feet above the floor and thus not halfway up to the roof. My pistol I had been forced to surrender to Islam Salim when its licence date had expired, and we now had no weapon of any sort. All I could do was collect some Chinese firecrackers, tie them on a long string around our bathroom, place some matches ready nearby, and had any marauders come I would have tried a loud but harmless bluff on them by setting of a magazine of firecrackers.

So once again I was sleeping, as I had done for weary months at the end of 1950, uneasily and with eyes alert. Rarely did I drop off before two in the morning. We suffered, however, nothing more annoying than occasional sneak thieves, who would creep into our houses at night, barefoot and silent, to steal cups and saucers, or shoes or clothes or even a burning lamp; and on one occasion they fished with a long pole through the open window of the room we had built for Sampih and Kusti, thus robbing two Balinese of their best *kains* and shirts. It was not worth while bothering to report such luckily minor occurrences to overburdened police headquarters.

In this somewhat anxious period, Luce, who was far more intrepid than I, became ill. For some time her fingers had been irritated by

114

outbreaks of blisters, which came in patches, and now, to our distress, her hands swelled and the tips of her fingers right up to her wrists became entirely covered in odourless yet water-filled blisters, which soon quite crippled her. The local doctors diagnosed it as heat rash, as an allergy or as a sort of eczema. They were quite certain that there was no drug known that would cure it, but they all said she must go to a cooler climate if she wanted to recover.

Since the poor girl was quite unable to look after herself, and was desperate and furiously frustrated at her own helplessness, she agreed at length to go into the mountains and stay with our friend, Captain McConnell, a retired Naval officer of the old school who had lived some eighteen years in Bali, and whose house commanded the crest of a hill overlooking the blue lake of Bedugul. This was fifty kilometres to the north of Denpasar, on the dusty road to Singaradja.

McConnell was our orchid adviser and a great horticulturalist. He lived on local pork and tinned foods in a house of wood that was really a conservatory and laid only a very secondary emphasis on any human, habitable purpose, and in his amazing garden I had seen sweet peas in bloom, also lilies of the valley, and once, even, an astonished tropic daffodil! But it was when it came to orchids, which he himself imported from every corner of the globe, that the captain was a master. His enthusiasm he shared with our best English pupil, Chan Ling Siong, who owned the Wisnu Store in Denpasar and was building an orchid house on its roof.

Whenever our orchids looked stagnant, we would take them up to Bedugul for treatment; for the captain had his own theory about orchids in his mountain climate.

"It's the lake," he would say. "The lake and the morning mists. In the mornings the mists rise off the lake and simply *fling* all the moisture and foods which orchids need from the air, straight into my house. You can't go wrong up here." And he would smile down from his six feet two and jerk out his jaunty white beard at you.

So we had always brought our plants up to him for rejuvenation, and after barren months of sulking and producing leaves only in Denpasar, with only a week or so to imbibe the lake's magical atmosphere, out would shoot the flower stalks again. The orchid bond had led us to become much attached to this robust, middle-aged gentleman, who lived for the most part in his garden and dressing gown.

I, therefore, now drove up to Bedugul to see McConnell to ask him whether he would try the magic of his weather on Luce. And characteristically he offered her a room for as long as she needed, and I urged that Rantun accompany her, both for Luce's comfort and in order to cast her influence a little over his kitchen. In a depressedly silent jeep on the following day, armed with net gloves and boracic powder and food and magazines, Sampih and I took the two exiles up into the mountains, hoping that the fifteen degrees difference in temperature—seventy-five instead of ninety—would manage quickly to dry up her painful and maddening wounds.

Soon after Luce had gone to Bedugul and while I was trying to exist on the cooking of Agung, Sampih and Kusti, which was amusing in the cooking but not so funny to eat, the brigantine *Yankee* sailed into the harbour of Benoa, eight miles south of Denpasar. To Irving Johnson, her skipper, we had not only an introduction from Daan Hubrecht, but there was now living in the old guest house of Walter Spies, in Ubud, a retired New Zealand doctor, Ted Lucas, who had sailed around the world on the *Yankee*'s last cruise as the ship's doctor. He was now living in Bali as a result of having fallen in love with it on that first visit.

When I had walked over the shingly paths of the hotel to greet the skipper in person, I found a thin-faced man, very tanned by the sun and with a chest on him like a gorilla, who introduced me to his crew, and in particular to Jim Ford, a man who had lectured on the fine arts at Princeton. Jim was a man in his middle thirties, round faced, with small features, a compact body, brown eyes and hair which he wore in a "crew cut". He was as alert as a sparrow. He also seemed to be rich, for within half an hour of conversing with him, he asked me to help arrange a full programme of music and dancing for the *Yankee* crew, and anything which cost money that the others did wish to share in, he would himself gladly underwrite. This seemed a heaven-sent opportunity for testing out our ideas on a good cross-section of American opinion, and so the next day, as a start, we drove Jim and two of his friends up to the colour-splashed mountain garden of

McConnell to meet both McConnell and Luce. There, so fast had the cooler weather helped Luce's hands and feet, and so stimulating did we both find Jim, that within another few days Luce was home and looking after herself more easily, while Jim and his friends were in our guest house. Rantun, in her own kitchen once more, was cooking in such quantities as she had never cooked before. I made one sad mistake, however. I underestimated Jim's capacity, and with rash generosity told him that the household provided free *arak* and *brum*— for of the former a toughened Balinese toper could drink but half a bottle a day, and I thought that a few noggins of its vitriolic quality would suffice for our guests. Jim was able, however, to consume and control with complete sangfroid two whole bottles each day, thereby earning the everlasting admiration of Sampih and all Balinese who were aware of this feat.

Perhaps no foreigner has stayed in Bali for four weeks who got more enjoyment out of it than Jim Ford. Each single thing he saw interested him. First he wanted to know: "Why is each house and village surrounded by mud walls? Why these narrow gateways? Are all the villages like this—are they all afraid of something?"

"They say it's to keep out the evil spirits," we replied, "who can move only in straight lines and can't climb over walls or through shut gates. But it's also perhaps a safety measure left over from the days of absolute feudalism when the Rajas were always fighting one another and looking for soldiers from among the people. There's certainly not a village in Bali without its walls."

Then we drove him up to Batuan, to see a Balinese village from the inside. The jeep scraped along narrow lanes, its roof grazing the thatch on the mud walls, till we pulled up among the pi-dogs and children outside the house of Kakul, the dancer and teacher. We showed Jim that there was far more to a village than the strip of it seen bordering a main road, for here we had travelled half a mile down lanes and paths under the shade of mango and breadfruit trees, beneath rare durians and the inevitable coconut palms, passing patches of banana trees and vegetables, all of which were quite out of sight of the main road.

Kakul sent one of his sons up a palm to cut us down a green coconut so that we might drink its milk, and we watched him hurriedly hanging out to dry the tattered costume that he wore for the Masked Dance. He kept shouting over to us, apologizing for not sitting with us immediately:

"A moment, Tuan—a small moment. Last night I was dancing again in Klungkung. Dawan my daughter is still there."

And I told Jim that for some quite original reason Kakul was teaching his children to dance the Baris with squinting eyes.

"But what a life!" said Jim. "These people have got the answer to it all. For food they have pigs and chickens and these wonderful white-bottomed cattle who look as if they had all sat down in pools of cream; fruits and vegetables grow in every village; salt they get from the nearby sea; and there's running water, coconut milk and *arak* to drink."

"But that's not all," I added. "They spin, weave and design their own cloth to make their *kains* and sarongs. They have great sport with fighting cocks and crickets; they gamble nightly with cards and dice; their religion is one that happily embraces their every thought and action, and only economics prevents a man from having any number of wives he desires."

"I don't know how good this life is for the women, but it sounds just the stuff for the men. I think I'll build me a house here, too."

In Kaliungu he struck up immediate friendships with Sampih and Kusti; and in the guest house the three of them were waited on as if it were all a game by Kusti and his young brother, Tompel, who had just joined our household and was now going to school in Denpasar with his slightly patronising brother. Tompel had a mole on his upper lip and had been nicknamed by Theo Meier "Hitla".

One afternoon after coming back from school Kusti came into the front house, where Luce and I were talking about our difficulties with Jim, telling him how the cost of the transportation seemed an almost insuperable obstacle to our ever getting to Europe or the States. Kusti stood scratching his head with embarrassment, half grinning, half ashamed. We could hear the infectious chortling of Rantun's laugh in the kitchen, and could see Ketut and Sugandi, her children, peeping around the kitchen door, looking up the passageway into our living room.

"Well, Wayan, what is it?"

"It's like this, Tuan. Perhaps it sounds very strange, Tuan, but I want to change my name again."

"But you changed it only a few months ago! What's wrong with Kusti as a name?"

"It is a good name, Tuan—but I think the name Wayan Pudja would be even better. Don't be angry, Tuan, but I ask to be known as Wayan Pudja. And next term in school I shall change to Wayan Pudja, also."

Just as I was slowly agreeing to this, mystified, and unable to find out why Wayan really wanted to change his name again, Rantun came in from the kitchen, her eyes tearful with laughter, holding an old knife in her hand. She wiped her nose on her sleeve and blurted out, "Would the Tuan like to know why Wayan is changing his name once more?" Here fresh guffaws shook her, and then, as the spasms came under control: "It is the children at school, Tuan. At first Wayan was very proud of his new name, Kusti. He even preferred to be called Kusti rather than just plain Wayan. And then one of the boys found out that if they called 'Kus-ti! Kus-ti! Kus-ti! Kus-ti!' very quickly, Tuan, just like that, it sounded as if they were calling '*Ti-kus! Ti-kus! Ti-kus! Ti-kus!*' So they started to call him Wayan Tikus, and *tikus*, as the Tuan knows, means 'rat'. Now, Tuan, it seems that Wayan does not like to be known as the First-Born Rat!"

And here Rantun ran back into the kitchen again, where, judging from the noise, we imagined her rolling about the floor in her mirth. Wayan, however, during this recital, grinned at us with extraordinary good nature, saying hopefully at the last, "Is it good, Tuan—you will call me Wayan Pudja now?"

"It is better so, Wayan Pudja," I replied gravely.

When we interpreted this for Jim he was full of admiration for Wayan. "What a kid!" he kept exclaiming, "God! what a life you lead here."

"He is a delightful child, Jim. But heaven knows how long it will last. I'll let you into a secret." I broke off and shouted something to Wayan. "I've asked him to bring us his school drawing book."

Wayan brought the blue exercise book and handed it me in silence, and as we turned the pages he stood on one leg, nervously, sometimes stooping with broad grin to explain what some drawing was meant to be.

"And what are these?" I asked him.

Wayan continued to grin, but clearly he was ashamed, for he had forgotten about these drawings and had not known that I had come across them some weeks ago after helping him one evening with his homework. I handed the book back to the child, and turning to Jim, said, "That's what I meant by saying I don't know how long kids such as these will remain delightful—from *our* point of view. I'll tell you what those drawings meant. Those were figures of bandits, or robbers, which are only too frequent in Bali these days. They always wear black masks and carry pistols. So far, perhaps, so good. Many children at home go to the movies and draw just the same things. But on each page you saw the word '*Merdeka!*' written? That is the modern Indonesian slogan meaning 'Freedom!' And this all means, I'm afraid, that at the age of eleven Balinese children are being taught to confuse banditry with patriotism by their schoolteachers who are indoctrinated from Java. Wayan's teacher, incidentally, is a young woman."

"You mean you think that I had better postpone building my house here after all?" said Jim, and shouted for more *arak*. Then, returning to where our conversation had been interrupted by Kusti, he asked, "This transportation for your group—what do you reckon it would cost?"

"Well, Jim, the group will have to go by air, because if we tried to arrange a tour by ship it would add two or three months to the length of our stay abroad, and I'm not at all sure how long the Balinese will want to stay outside Bali once the novelty wears off. I've warned them it'll be hard work, but I realize they can't be expected to visualize what they'll be in for. I've calculated we can get forty people, the gamelan and costumes complete, in one Skymaster. We'd have to have the round trip money in our pockets before we could get American visas, and that would come to about half a million *rupiahs*, or $45,000. To us this sounds astronomical."

"And nobody will take that risk? Who have you actually got working for you in the States?"

I told him that so far no American or European impresario had volunteered to risk so much money on an unknown, unseen company.

"But the most irritating thing is this. Some months ago when we

120

were flat broke, I had to sell our camera—that was at a time when Luce once had to borrow back from Rantun twenty *rupiahs* of the wages we had paid her! And now we simply can't afford to make publicity photographs. Two Danes, the Nielsens, made us some, and Dick Tregaskis, the Guadalcanal man, who came here with a cameraman in tow, had our group filmed when collecting colour material for a movie called *Fair Wind to Java*, and he sent us some prints, too. But they've all been used. However, Hollywood is still one hope. Tregaskis said there was a faint chance that a theatrical tour might be combined with being used in his film, and a friend of ours called Mal Sibley, who works in Bel Air, wrote and told us that Bring Crosby and Bob Hope are about to make another "Road" film, this time called *Road to Bali*. Mal thought we might get a Djanger sequence in that. But nothing has matured so far and we just have to face it—we're too risky an investment to be brought to America or Europe before we're tried out."

"So what now—you're not going to give up?"

"I shan't give up. For some inscrutable reason, partly personal desire, partly a balletomane's wish to show our Legong to people like Margot Fonteyn and Markova, partly a belief that such a group as ours would make a powerful, because nonpolitical, link between east and west, this thing has become what you might call "my life's ambition". Does that sound a little crazy? Well, anyhow, I've recently had another idea. A little while ago there was a charming young Dutchman here who was as mad about Balinese painting as we are about the dancing. His name was Ben Joppe, and his firm were transferring him to Kuala Lumpur, in Malaya, where he knew nobody. So I gave him an introduction to my old friend, Noel Ross, who is the British Adviser in Selangor State and very keen on Balinese and Indonesian art. These two now want me to bring the group to Malaya. If they can arrange it, they want me to fly over to Singapore and Kuala Lumpur to settle the details, and from Kuala Lumpur I'd continue on up to Bangkok and Hongkong to see what could be done there. Then, if we could bring off a tour of southeast Asia, maybe somewhere along the line a confidant of a big impresario could see us and recommend us, and off we'd go to Europe or America."

"Ye gods, what a complicated affair! But that does sound a bit more practical."

121

"Oh, comparatively speaking it would be easy. We'd have to be prepared only to cover our expenses, of course, but we'd get experience and lots of publicity, with photographs that we could use for impressing managers in the western world."

"Is there anything I can possibly do to help?"

"Yes, Jim. Just pat me on the shoulder occasionally when you see my eye looking wild and tell me I'm sane. Sometimes I can see nothing but troubles ahead. I need a little encouragement."

The *Yankee* crew travelled all over Bali, spending a day or two with Theo Meier at Iseh and seeing festivals and music all over the island, but it was the Temple Festival in Pliatan and the Barong Play at Intaran, near Sanur, that most pleased Jim. One of his friends, on the other hand, was most delighted with a mask that he bought in Mas from Ida Bagus Ketut, and which he wore all the way down to Denpasar, sitting in the front of the jeep with me, leering out at the villagers we passed. This mask was of a hirsute, protruding-lipped being, clearly but recently emerged from the jungle and very hideous. Though children were quick to recognize that this was a foreigner playing with a mask, and jeered and shouted with raised arms as we went by, and though sometimes a villager whom we passed too closely might jump into the ditch in astonishment, there was a large percentage of Balinese who looked straight at the mask and remarked it with perfect indifference, doubtless thinking to themselves that this was just another of those hideous Europeans to whom they still could not get really accustomed. It was the least flattering reaction to the white people that I ever witnessed.

The Temple Festival in Pliatan we first watched sitting on the grassy bank of the gorge above Tjampuang, near Ubud, together with the former doctor of the *Yankee*, Ted Lucas, for the whole procession would come to this place where the two rivers met, and here the Gods would be given their ceremonial bathing. The rock-bedded river streamed but a hundred feet below us, and immediately opposite was the fragile, swinging bridge of bamboo which joined the path and road to Tjampuang Temple on the gorge's farther cliff.

At last we could hear the sound of music from afar, and very soon we saw the head of the mile-long procession appearing round the bend of the road. First came four men carrying great ceremonial spears with splendid red tassels, and immediately behind them in single file a long line of the prettiest young girls, all dressed in yellow-and-green cloth of gold, their faces painted white and their heads garlanded with sweet-smelling flowers, white, golden-yellow and scarlet. The first child was perhaps five years old, and the tallest were the most beautiful virgins of the village. Somewhere about the middle of the line were our three Legongs, who looked like emeralds thrown on to a sleeve of warm brown velvet. Then came a company of young men, also dressed in brilliant colours, and behind them the Pliatan gamelan, banging away with all their might to give the greatest happiness to their temple's Gods. The metallophones were slung on bamboo poles, carried by other men, but all the heavier instruments had been left at home. The players strolled behind their bearers, playing with as great ease and verve as if they'd been seated on the verandah floor. Lebah and Kompiang had their drums slung round their waists, but the Anak Agung, in a gorgeous new *kain* woven by his sister, padded along barefoot, not feeling it necessary for himself to play in this greatly lightened and simplified version of the orchestra.

Next to the gamelan, borne shoulder high, came the first shrine, shaped like a throne but in miniature, and here the deity sat invisible, enjoying with his people the festivities given that day in his honour. Glittering gold and white umbrellas on long poles shaded the various shrines and the Gods enthroned upon them, and men ran beside them with streaming white banners and more red and gilt spears as a guard of honour. And behind them came, spread out for almost a mile, a phalanx of villagers, cheerfully dressed, flowers in their hair, small children marching along with their mothers, the whole community joining together to give pleasure to their Gods. Almost at the back of the procession came the *angklung* orchestra from the *bandjar*, or village district, of Madé Lebah, and this four-toned gamelan had a higher pitched, singing quality, and its weary bearers wiped themselves constantly with their towels, for they were horribly hot.

And after we had seen the procession break off and descend to the holy place at the rivers' junction, we drove back into Pliatan to observe in the flower- and matting-strewn courtyard of the temple itself the immense variety of the offerings that had been placed there on bamboo altars early that same morning. Everywhere there hung in the atmosphere the perfume of the acrid-sweet *tjampak*, mixed with the heavy sweetness of the frangipani and *sundat* flowers. Coconut oil was wafted to us from all sides—from the hair of the people, from the cooking in the *warongs*. From the altars and offerings arose the musky smell of burning incense, the reek of pork fat and fried chicken; and a tinge of sour sweat and clove-tinted cigarettes still hung in the humid air. As for the offerings, these varied from humble wooden platters on which were placed cones of glutinous rice, some crisp rice cakes, a splash of fruits and a lacy pattern cut from young palm leaf for pure decoration; up to tall, elegant bowls with long stems, painted yellow and red, on top of which were piled in absolute symmetry pyramids of fruits and meats and flowers and cakes, up to five or six feet high, each gaily coloured cake facing outward, like pink, white, red and saffron wheels of sugar, and between each of which, on a wooden splinter, there was mounted a single blossom; and these cakes, being light, were piled on top of layers of purple mangosteens and hairy, red rambutan fruits, on thorny, stinking durians, on limes, mountain oranges, yams, on the brown, lizard-skinned *salaks*, all balanced on a base made from six bunches of bananas and two great jackfruit. At the very tip of the pyramid were whole clusters of pink and white frangipani blossoms and deep orange heads of marigolds threaded on to a delicate bamboo frame shaped like a fan, and round the lowest layer of bananas were squeezed in bunches of pork *saté*, with joints of fried duck and chicken.

"If only I could paint," said Jim. "Truly, Tahiti has never had such colours as these. I simply can't believe what I'm seeing."

The Festival at Intaran, however, we visited only at night. Sampih had heard the news that there was to be a Sanghyang, or trance dance of small girls; an unknown dance called Baris China, and on the second afternoon there was to be a Barong Play with kris dancers.

These festivities took place before the village temple, on an open piece of grey and dusty ground, where the usual coconut frond awning had been erected, and round which there were more *warongs* than usual because Intaran was only seven kilometres from Denpasar, and many visitors on bicycle and by horse cart were expected. The temple in the background, the great banyan tree and the solid throng of villagers, made a superb stage setting.

On the first night, then we watched the Sanghyang. But although the choruses of men and women sat apart on the ground, chanting in turn, and showed us how clearly the Monkey Dance had borrowed its music from this source, the two young dancers dressed in white Legong-style costumes performed quite prettily but did not even pretend to go into trance. As for the Baris China, whose name had intrigued us, it was a dull strutting up and down of a dozen youths behind a leader, all of them wearing soft black hats pulled down over their eyes, black cotton coats and trousers, with long and straggling false moustaches, while the leader himself wore also an enormous bushy beard. Altogether, they looked like caricature bandits.

So energetically curious were the crowd that we all of us gravitated towards a *warong*, having first looked around to see which *warong* had the prettiest owner. There we had a pleasant hour or so of drinking, while the girl, a certain Nyoman, smiled invitingly at us and forced on us her cakes and *lawar* as well as *arak* and *brum*. And as anybody who has been to Bali understands, it is conversations such as these at a *warong*, with much laughter and innuendo, where Balinese keep drinking and eating alongside you, joining in the talk with absolute unself-consciousness, which constitutes so large a part of the charm of living in the place.

"That was one hell of an attractive girl," Jim kept saying hopefully in the jeep as we drove slowly home so as not to spray dust over the gaily dressed crowds.

"She was decidedly provocative, Jim. But one of the men at the *warong* mentioned that her husband is in jail at the moment for being concerned in a gang murder."

"I don't believe it." He turned to Sampih. "Well, young brother Sampih, what about fixing me up with a date tonight?"

"Jim wants you to help him replace those shadowy and luscious figures that we sometimes see flitting in and out of the back gate of our compound after dark—the ones that seem always to be moving in the direction of the guest house, Pih."

"Hell!" said Jim. "Let's talk about something else. But anyhow, you're bringing us down again tomorrow afternoon to this village to see the Barong Play, aren't you?"

At four o'clock the following afternoon we drove down again, but

125

the *warongs* and their women had not yet been set up. Seated in the dust of a broad village lane was a Semar Pegulingan, an Orchestra of the God of Love, the more minor-keyed gamelan which should correctly accompany both Barong and Legong, but which is too gentle and ethereal to play music for the Kebiar or warlike Baris. It was an ancient orchestra, out of tune and ill-balanced, but it played with a flowing rhythm and the tunes of the Barong Play are among the most simple and beautiful that there are.

For more than an hour the music played intermittently, and the sun began to go down so that I feared there would be no Kris dance in the dusk. But at last four figures appeared, the Sandaran, strange in their bell-like headdresses and white masks with enigmatically smiling lips, and swaying and cautious they advanced to the music, soon to be followed by four Djauk dancers, with masks that were red and wrathful and bulging eyed, and together these two oddly assorted quartets danced their prelude, vanishing as inexplicably as they had come.

Then the music for the entry of the Barong started, repetitive, insistent, throbbing, and at the far end of the spear-flanked lane, where two boys stood supporting the traditional gilt umbrellas, we saw the two Barong dancers climbing inside the bamboo-framed monster, whose coat was of long and shaggy *duk*, that hairy fibre which grows at the base of the sugar-palm's fronds.

The dancers twitched the monster's frame comfortably on to their shoulders, and advanced toward the umbrellas. The Barong's mask was of scarlet and had a long black beard of human hair, in which had been threaded white frangipani blossoms; his eyes were round and staring, his teeth were dazzling white. Above the mask was a great shoulder piece of gilded buffalo leather, surmounted by two long-stemmed golden flowers, all of which topped the mobile head and bristly black ears. The body was more than a fathom in length, ending in a great arched tail of painted hide, from which there hung a small and sparkling mirror; indeed, the whole Barong was as if armoured with gold-painted leatherwork studded and flashing with encrusted glass. The men inside wore brightly striped cotton trousers, of red, white and black, which gave to the body a bizarre four legs.

Now, as the brute stood between his umbrellas, he tentatively lifted his forefeet, while his jaws chattered and his teeth snicked at possible enemies, for the front dancer within held two wooden handles which governed the motions of the puppet head and controlled the gnashing or humorous jaws.

Around the ring of spectators advanced the Barong. Hesitating, its forefeet pawed and stamped uncertainly, then the great animal tripped and scampered in with surprising lightness and speed, while the whole body seemed to come to life. First its head reared up on high, tilted questioningly to one side, next it crouched down, alert, jaws clacking and savagely defensive. Sometimes, as it capered around in a most undignified gait, the body would be stretched out to its full length, looking huge, but a moment later the men inside it would concertina up, the man in the tail squatting sideways on the ground so that the Barong looked like a dragon reluctant to move, its vast rump hugging the floor, its scarlet-masked head peering round and looking down suspiciously. In happier moods the whole of its hind quarters shimmied and shivered in an ecstasy of anticipation.

When it was almost dark, and when the atmosphere was thick with the dust stirred up by the cavorting, skittish Barong, a throaty, ghastly, choking voice was heard, followed by a torrent of the high, neighing laughter of an idiot. Rangda was coming! Out on to the floor she presently stamped, strutting and shaking, one hand on hip, one hand waving her death-dealing weapon, a piece of white cloth, which alternatively could make her invisible. Her fierce, tusked mask with its great mop of bristling white hair and rolling red and flame-flecked tongue, was affixed to a body equally awe-inspiring, and the small children shrank, laughing nervously, from her path. Pendulous black and white striped breasts hung down in front of her body, which was entirely covered in coarse, long hair, and her hands ended in jagged claws six inches long.

Round and round each other in the gloom the two monsters circled, the good Barong's jaws chattering with rage like castanets, the evil Rangda challenging him, shrieking out her maniac laughter, leaning over backwards with hands outstretched, leaning over forward again, hands on her knees, shaking with her terrifying mirth. And as we watched, all at once Rangda's body seemed to stiffen, and she fell to the ground in a dead trance.

Murmuring voices arose on all sides of us, and a *pemangku* priest strode forward, white-robed, for this, though not so rare an occurrence, nevertheless meant that the play could not go on to its normal finish. Suddenly a ring of near-naked men ran up, crazed brown creatures flourishing their bright krises, furious and screaming, surrounding the prostrate Rangda, shouting at the priest, threatening the close-packed spectators: for they were the Kris dancers and they had been baulked of their prey. They had been on the verge of going into trance themselves, after which they would have flown to the aid of the Barong and hurled themselves against the Rangda, whose magic power would have turned their krises against their own bodies.

And urged on to hysteria by the argument and noise and confusion and darkness, some of the more eager kris dancers, although Rangda their enemy lay flat at their feet, started jumping up and down, plunging their krises into their chests, groaning and shrieking as they repeatedly, viciously, tried to stab themselves. Their eyes were mad and tortured and the crowd broke away, for this was not a usual thing, and therefore unpredictable.

Then the *pemangku* and his followers seized the men who had thus vainly gone into trance, it being necessary for four or five of them to grip and subdue the twitching, convulsive body of one kris dancer. Into the face of each man the *pemangku* flicked liberal splashes of holy water, and incense from the sacred fire was held to their noses by the *pemangku's* wife. There was a chaos of noise, for the whole village seemed now to be present, shouting out advice, milling around in the dust, seeking with their priest for the correct formula to solve a peculiar situation.

Our guests were mightily puzzled by what they had seen, but impressed by its obvious sincerity.

"It's probably a very good omen for the village," I hazarded. "The Barong, their protector, was so magically strong that he did not need the Kris dancers' help to demolish Rangda. It would seem that the balance of good over evil in Intaran is certain."

A day or so later the *Yankee* set sail. All the crew members gave us encouragement by saying that our dancers would be an inevitable success in their country, and on the evening before they left Benoa, the whole Pliatan club was invited on board to have their first experience of American food such as hot-dogs and ice cream. The

Balinese were very impressed by the *Yankee*, and as we watched Skipper Johnson manoeuvre out of the harbour, handling his more than a hundred-foot craft with as much ease as if it had been a rowing boat, the Anak Agung turned to us and said heavily, "A great shame, this sailing of the *Yankee*. Why could not Jim have arranged that we all signed on as deck-hands so that we could get to America that way?"

"Don't worry, Agung Adji," I replied. "We'll go abroad if you are patient. But we'll go in a four-engined airplane."

"*Beh!* Very *atom*," he said. For the word atom had just entered the Balinese vocabulary, meaning the very latest thing in modernity and up-to-dateness.

7

Invitation to Malaya

*

In the month of November a light rainy season came upon us again after seven months of warm and dry weather. The club was busy building a high thatched shelter in front of the *puri*, when a letter came from Kuala Lumpur, signed by Noel Ross and Ben Joppe, asking for a date when I could fly over to Singapore in order to discuss all the artistic and financial details connected with a tour of Malaya. They seemed to be planning at the highest level, for they mentioned that both Sir Henry Gurney—later ambushed by Chinese Communists and murdered—and Mr. Malcolm Macdonald, had signified their willingness to sponsor such a good-will visit, while Mr. Loke Wan Tho, the rich Chinese owner of the Cathay Building in Singapore and a generous patron of the arts, was showing some readiness to discuss underwriting the tour's preliminary costs.

This invitation could not have come at a better time for us, for the Colombo Exhibition was being held soon in Ceylon, to which it was also proposed to send Balinese dancers. And to date Pliatan, a village considered outside the artistic control of Denpasar's officialdom, had been ignored, and the group that had been chosen to go to Colombo was the centre of much political wrangling, in the very vociferous heart of which was our acquaintance, Nyoman Kaler and a transient Sumatran journalist. To keep the peace in Denpasar, these two had been forced to ask Lotring's rival group to join them, and we heard that extraordinary hybrid rehearsals were even now taking place, with dancers trying to fit their steps to one another's quite different styles, and with a composite gamelan being joined together under Lotring and Kaler, picked form diverse villages and "parties." Under the circumstances it was not surprising that only a very unenviable standard was reached.

Our Anak Agung, however, proud of what Pliatan had achieved in the past year, was offended and disappointed that he had not been approached about Colombo at all. To my counsel that this was a good thing and to let them go without resentment, he simply could not agree.

"Does John not think that Pliatan has a fine Legong and gamelan?" he had asked. "And have not we brought Mario from Tabanan to create a new dance? It is not good that they ignore us completely, these men from Denpasar!"

But I had replied, perhaps seeing more long-sightedly than he the difficulties that lay ahead, "Let them go, Agung Adji. I am *glad* that these people are always the ones to be called to Djakarta, to dance for the Army in Java, or to go to this Colombo Exhibition. For if we go abroad think of all the jealousy which we shall meet. Now, at the very least we shall be able to point out to the Denpasar people that it is our turn—that so far they have monopolized all the trips outside Bali."

"That is perhaps true," he answered. But then he wagged his head again sadly, saying, "But my mouth tastes bitter."

And it was while the Colombo people were still rehearsing, and while the club was building their wet-weather shelter, and Anom, the gentlest and largest-eyed of the three Legongs, was learning a new Legong story in which she had to don the horrific mask of Rangda in the story of Tjalonarang the Witch, and was able to become in the most uncanny way the aged, doddering, gibbering female monster, that the inquiry from Singapore came. I was jubilant, for now my face, together with the club's, was saved.

"It is very fitting, Agung Adji," I laughed. "The Denpasar group wins one point, and we win one, also. Neither should be jealous of the other."

While Bali thus hummed with artistic rivalry, which we regarded secretly as an admirable thing and were proud to stir up, the President came again on a short rest visit, and he called dancers from the two opposing camps. The Pliatan club, though, actually danced in Gianjar, using the *puri* gamelan which was of inferior quality, and here once again I was to observe the struggle between the so-called New and the Old. The Raja of Gianjar, Anak Agung Gdé Oka, was a pleasant and straightforward young man whom we had grown to like more than his ambitious elder brother. But both of them were the offspring of a father who had belonged to another era, a picturesque old man who still drove restlessly around Bali in a plum-coloured sedan, his fighting cocks in their cages up on the seat beside him, his human servants squatting on the floor beneath. It always fascinated me to see Gdé Oka genuinely struggling with himself to be liberal in a way that all his traditions rebelled against.

During the last year I had consistently fought with him. In this, probably, I had lacked understanding, but it had infuriated me to see the casual way in which the club would be summoned like cattle to dance before distinguished political guests from Java. They would be fetched in trucks, very early, and would be kept waiting hours and hours, getting little or no food, seldom receiving anything at all for their labours, while the gamelan leaders would not even be introduced to the people before whom they played. I would then be unable to stop myself rocking with fury at this active feudalism—which admittedly chance alone had eradicated from my own country but a few hundreds of years earlier.

Luce and I, then, to embarrass Gdé Oka, had often sat with the club on the ground in one of his *puri's* outer courtyards, declining to come in and sit with the guests, for in this way we tried to impress upon him that we disliked his using our friends as his serfs. The Balinese, of course, to whom this was all quite *biasa*, usual, saw nothing more than an inevitable evil in such things and accepted them with perfect placidity; yet they were vaguely pleased and puzzled at the strength of the rebel emotions they sensed in us.

When the President visited Bali, he always made his own little antifeudal demonstration. He would insist that the ordinary people, bare-breasted mothers, old men and women of the lowest caste, the poor and the far from clean, should sit with him and by him, taking precedence over even his own entourage. This example caused much embarrassment in the feudal Balinese heart, and both people and Raja slipped automatically back into their old accustomed ways as soon as he had left the island.

But as we had come to see more closely how Balinese society

functioned, we tended more and more to become its observers only. We instinctively regretted, perhaps, that the caste system made our friends subservient before their Rajas, and we believed that no Rajas were essential to the continued existence of what we loved best in Balinese culture; but we had found, though, that Balinese politics, as in many other lands, were often largely matters of family history or family feuds among the various rulers, and that the modern political catchcries which we understood, were mostly weapons used by one grouping of families against traditional opponents.

By the time of this Presidential visit, therefore, though we still sat with the gamelan, we had also reached an amicable agreement with Gdé Oka. As a man we liked him, and we recognized that he tried hard to look after his people in his naturally feudal way. He, on the other hand, irritated and suspicious as he must have been when he saw our leavening of his feudal bread, was glad nevertheless to see us helping the name of Gianjar by forcing the attention of outside Indonesia on Pliatan, which lay in the centre of his country.

This time the Legong danced in the morning and the President and his party of officials and correspondents drove off into the mountains to have their lunch with Theo Meier, who was finishing a painting for the Palace in Djakarta. Gdé Oka accompanied them. And then there followed an interminable delay for the club, who waited and waited with empty bellies, squatting in one of the courtyards, and, as so often happened, no trucks came.

For Luce and myself, however, the whole of this performance was made remarkable by Raka. She had fallen off a bicycle which she was learning to ride only the previous day, and she danced before Sukarno with a large piece of plaster over the tendon on her heel, where she had an already infected wound. Before coming out of the *balé* where Luce and Gusti Kompiang, as usual, had been attending to all the dancers' make-up, the child had been silently weeping, her eyes wide with misery and hurt. Yet she had such an instinctive artistic sincerity that she insisted on going through with her dance, which she performed flawlessly.

Directly after the performance we raced her over in the jeep, together with Oka and Anom, to the house of Dr. Lucas in Tjampuang, and here her wound was firmly cleaned and gently dressed. And when the pain was over—and she sat on a big bamboo bench, I remember, crouching up against me in her fear of the unknown doctor, while her friends at first grimaced at her and then carefully looked away when they saw how agonizing the wound must be—when it was over she at once became her happy small self again. In fact, she was delighted to be the centre of so much attention, and maybe she sensed, too, that these crazy people, Luce and John, really did look upon her and her two friends as their own children. Anyhow, she chatted and joked in her lilting little voice all the way back to the *puri*, while we pleaded with her not to try riding a bicycle again for a few days.

And these, of course, were the incidents which brought us very close to Bali and these three children of ours in particular—compared with them, nothing else that happened was significant.

While we were waiting for a reply to my letter, in which I had suggested flying to Singapore in the first week of December, we had a visit from our friend Count Carl Douglas, the Swedish Chargé d'Affaires, who brought with him the family Ahrenberg, who had been leading a Swedish industrial mission to Indonesia.

"Take us around. Talk Bali at us. Show us your dancers in Pliatan," they commanded.

So Sampih and I straightaway went round to the garage in Denpasar, for that aged warrior, our jeep, was once more being patched up with wire and local ingenuity And by four-thirty it was ready again for the road, as gallant as ever.

That night, for a start, we took them to see the rehearsal of the new Legong story, with Anom being taught by old Gusti Biang her witch's role; and after this Sampih and Raka ran through the Tumulilingan, which we were in the process of remoulding a little

"This is astounding music," said Ahrenberg. "Do you plan to come to Stockholm? You would be a great success in Scandinavia."

"If we could play there in the summer, we'd love to."

"On how many people have you tested your programme? Have you been able to try it out on a varied public opinion?"

"We reckon we've brought up to Pliatan about two hundred and fifty Americans or Europeans. We've learned from our audiences that we're on the right lines, but we've only had one theatrical expert here, an American named Martin Flavin. He thought the material terrific."

"But how about the Balinese? Do they want to leave Bali?"

"They want to go abroad all right. They want to see what foreign countries are like, and they want this as an honour for their club. Also, they are all poor people and they hope to make some money."

Ahrenberg pointed to the gamelan.

"Will you take a complete orchestra with you?"

"We couldn't go otherwise."

"Could you tell us how the gamelan works, John?" asked Carl Douglas.

"You mean—how does the music fit together, how is it controlled, and so on?"

"Exactly that."

"Well, I'll ask the Anak Agung to help me, but I must warn you that there are many Balinese words which don't exist in Indonesian or English, and their musical concepts are quite different. However, we can try."

And at length, with the Anak Agung pointing and with me talking, I tried to explain.

"This gamelan is known as a Gong Gdé—a great orchestra, and it's the equivalent of our symphony orchestra. We don't use a *suling* in it, which is a bamboo flute, and we don't use the *rebab*, which is a devilish two-stringed fiddle, perpetually off tone, and which I nicknamed the Cat's Voice when they once used it to see if I liked it. That means every instrument in this gamelan is percussive. Now the principles of Balinese orchestration and percussion, according to an inexpert Coast,[1] are these.

"First, most of the instruments are arranged in echoing pairs. And a piece of music is built up contrapuntally through *polos* and *sangsi*, which are two ingenious and *interlocking* patterns of music which fill in a composition."

"Have those two words—what were they, *polos* and *sangsi*? Have they any meaning?"

"Yes. I'll come back to that in a moment. Now I want to tell you about the second, connected principle. This is what I call the echo

[1] With the New York subsequent aid of Colin McPhee.

FULL BALINESE ORCHESTRA: GONG GDÉ

1 and 2.   KENDANG, WADON & LANANG: drums, female and male.

3 and 4.   G'YING: leading metallophones.

5 and 6.   GANGSA POLOS: "simple" metallophones.

7 and 8.   GANGSA SANGSI: "complex" metallophones.

9 and 10. KANTILAN: "flower-parts" metallophones.

11 and 12. TJALUNG: cello metallophones.

13 and 14. DJEGOGAN: double-bass metallophones.

15.   KEMPLI: tempo gong.

16.   REYONG: battery of 12 syncopation gongs.

17 and 18. TJENG-TJENG: cymbals.

19.   KEMPUR: small gong.

20.   GONG: large gong.

principle. A metallophone player strikes a true note on his instrument, and that is called the *pengumbang* note, the round, full note, and this is echoed by the answering note, called the *pengisap*, struck out almost simultaneously on the second metallophone of the pair. The two metallophones are tuned a quarter tone different, and hit the smallest fraction of a second after one another. In Bali, therefore, the sound *ping!* does not exist; a doubled sound exists instead—a sort of *pi-ying!*"

"John, John—give us some examples. This is not at all easy to follow. The principles are quite strange to us."

"Maybe I'd best begin again. Let's take the drums. There are two, the male and the female, one slightly larger than the other and of slightly different pitch. When you hear them played, you will observe that they beat out their rhythms in an interlocking pattern which makes the two drums become one drum. It is impossible to separate one drum from the other when they play. The Balinese word for drum, incidentally, is *gupakan*, and to drum is to *gupak*. This is purely onomatopoeic. *Gu* is the deep noise of the flat hand hitting the centre of the large end of the drum, and *pak* is the light noise that the tips of the fingers make when they flip the edge of the smaller drum skin."

I looked around, but they all nodded intelligently, so I continued.

"Now the drums control the tempo of the gamelan. The two of them together are the conductors. But almost equally important is the leading metallophone player—he's far more important than a first violin, for example. In this gamelan Madé Lebah plays the leading metallophone, which is known as the *g'ying*. But with it he not only leads the melody—he can also influence the tempo if he thinks the drummers are going too fast or too slow; and since the metallophone section quite often plays when the drums are silent, the *g'ying* player then becomes the conductor. You could even say it was a matter of personality. A brilliant *g'ying* player could always, through his *tabuh*, or style of playing, dominate and lead a mediocre drummer."

"That seems clear so far," said Douglas, tipping experimentally with his fingers on the end of a small Legong drum.

"It's clear so far," I replied, "because this is the easy part to explain. But let's go a little further. The tempo is also underlined or shaded by the two cymbals players, whose *tjeng-tjeng* chatter and

137

clash and sometimes nearly drown the melodious metallophones; by the big *gong* and the smaller gong, called *kumpur*, and lastly, in our gamelan, by the *kempli*, which is a single gong, small and held on the knee of the boy who sits next to Madé Lebah, and who pounds it with as regular a beat as any westerner could desire. That's all for the tempo section."

I paused a moment. Then:

"Now we come to the counterpoint, and this is where I wish I were a musician. Let's look at the metallophones first. Lebah's *g'ying* is the slightly larger metallophone in the centre of the front row. He, on the echo principle, is at one with the *g'ying* exactly behind him. All the metallophones, incidentally, have ten leaves, or keys, of brass alloyed with silver, and the scale is one of five tones peculiar to the Balinese; but each pair is tuned that fraction of a tone apart."

"You mean, then," interjected Douglas, "that this echo comes a fraction of a second *behind* the playing of the first metallophone in a pair, *and*, say, a fraction of a tone *below* the first metallophone?"

"Exactly that. To come back to the counterpoint, though. On Lebah's right sits Bregeg, and he plays the counterpoint part known as *polos*, which means "the simple"; and on Lebah's left is the fat Kuwus, who plays the second counterpoint part called *sangsi*, which means "the complex". But in order that all the tones of the metallophones blend and become reverberatingly one, the player sitting behind Bregeg echoes Kuwus, and the man behind Kuwus echoes Bregeg, all on diagonals. The four metallophones that play this simple and complex counterpoint (both equally tricky to follow for me), are known as *gangsas*. At the back you will see the *kantilans*, two smaller *gangsas*, which fit into the counterpoint patterns, too, but which perform the highly ornamental "flower parts". They play very, very fast, putting in those highly elusive and cascading arabesques of sound which give the enchanting surface colouration to Balinese music."

Our friends had now reached the stage of pulling out their handkerchiefs to wipe surreptitiously at their brows, but I was nearing the end, so I plunged on.

"You see the two pairs of heavier, taller metallophones, played by men seated on stools, and with only five keys each? The deeper-voiced pair are the *djegogan* and might be compared to the western double bass; the smaller pair are the *tjalung*, and are something of cello, viola and second violin. Their tones are nearer to those of a cello, but they are often given the main melody to hold, though in simplified forms.

And lastly there is the magnificent *reyong*. That's it—that long battery of a dozen gongs of diminishing size with the four men seated on the floor behind it. Whereas the metallophones are played with wooden hammers like tiny ice picks, the *reyong* is hit by two stubby batons in the hands of each player, and can make two types of sound. If the player hits the edges of his gongs, they make a harsh *ke-tjek ke-tjek ke-tjek* noise; but if he hits them throbbingly and square on the inch-high knobs you see sticking up an inch from each gong's centre, then the *reyong* brings forth a full and thrilling sound, deeply melodious and rich and warm. The gongs vibrate superbly because they are all threaded on hide strings, and don't touch the wooden frame at all."

"But how does it fit into the gamelan?" they asked me.

"I just don't know! I recognize it as the most explosive instrument of them all, but its syncopations, after living with them for a year or so, are still a mystery to me. Sometimes it seems merely a great battery of syncopated gongs; sometimes it out-clacks the cymbals; yet it can alternate with the metallophones and take the melody and the counterpoint parts away from them. It's the most baffling instrument—and only few Balinese can master it."

At this stage, when my own head was beginning to feel a little woolly, and when my friends' faces were assuming frozen looks to conceal their throbbing heads, I shouted suddenly to the Anak Agung, "*Adoh, Agung Adji! Bingung sekali kita!* We are all in one hell of a muddle!" And the rehearsal swept on again, bringing escape and relief in its wake.

On the following day we crowded into the jeep and drove to Klung-kung, the seat of Bali's first Raja, the Dewa Agung, the Great God, whose dynasty dated from the time his Hindu ancestors fled from Java in the fifteenth century when it was being swept by the Moslem tide. But Klungkung is also the centre of the silver industry, and the area produces almost all the smiths who make the gamelan instruments, except for the big gongs which come from Java, and the Ahrenbergs wanted to buy a silver bowl from a man whom they could watch working.

It was on the way home that we stopped near the house of Madé Lebah, and I dragged them to the site which we had selected for the Pliatan "guest house for foreign artists" which we contemplated if we ever had any money to build it with.

It was a broad corner of grassy land beneath coconut palms, which backed on to Pliatan itself, and was separated from the wood-carving village of Mas by several kilometres of slowly descending terraced rice-fields. The boundary between the site and the *sawahs* was an irrigation stream one long stride across, cool and rapid flowing. In the distance could be seen the blue sea, and breezes off the Indian ocean blew up off the water-filled rice-fields at all seasons, so it was never too hot.

"This land would be perfect for us," I told them. "The Anak Agung has offered us his own Gamelan of the God of Love to keep here if we ever do build; Madé Lebah's family owns part of the land; it is in Pliatan but not too much in the public eye, and there is a building club in the village which would do all the work for us, since we would build in real Balinese fashion. Our food would come from that princess of cooks, our own Rantun; Madé Lebah has even sworn to keep down the *leyak*-spotting dogs! At its rowdiest, in the morning we would wake to the crowing of the fighting cocks, and when Rantun came back from the market there would be the pounding noise of her fourteen or fifteen spices being prepared for blending with her tingling yet infinitely varied food. On the hottest of afternoons we would always have that cooling and quite universal Balinese music—the sound of fresh water trickling and falling from one rice-field's terrace to the next. In the evening we could dip and pour in a bathroom, or lie in the stream which flows from the mountains. And at night the club would be rehearsing on the most gentle and heavenly of gamelans, the *Semar Pegulingan* . . ."

Our Swedish visitors left only one day before the letter from Singapore arrived, asking me to fly there as soon as a plane vacancy could be found. On December 8th I left Bali, swearing to Luce that I would be home before Christmas, leaving her to the care of the Anak Agung, Sampih and Rantun, and, more distantly, our good friend Islam Salim. At all costs we would dine in Pliatan and know our Malayan fate by Christmas, and at mid-day our entire household would eat with us together for this family festival.

140

I arrived in Djakarta after a five hours' flight via Surabaya and stayed at the Hotel des Indes, where I learned that I was to call on the President and the Foreign Ministry. They both asked me the same question: was I still their public-relations official, or had I consciously allowed my appointment to lapse? And to both of them I answered that I considered myself now a free individual, responsible to, and drawing a salary from, no official source. Difficulties arose only when the President asked me my present plans.

"I am off to Singapore, sir," I said. "I have friends there who want to bring over a group of Balinese dancers for a tour. I'm flying there tomorrow to arrange all the details."

"Splendid!" said he. "Your old idea still, I see. And which dancers are you taking?"

"Why—our people from Pliatan, of course! We've been working like madmen for over a year for this very thing. If all goes well, I was hoping to ask for the honour of your patronage."

Then came his gentle bombshell.

"But please, *please*, John, do not take the three little girls from Pliatan."

He looked at me with his orator's eyes, even raised his hands in an imploring gesture toward me. But the steel in the Indonesian velvet was there. I felt it, and began to perspire freely. For an extra half hour the next visitors waited while I tried to plead, argue, reason, wriggle.

"But we need this experience, sir. This is the only way we can find it. We just hope this preliminary thing will lead to an offer from Europe or America. Our sponsors are waiting for me, are paying for my fare. I feel committed to them."

But to all my words he turned a charming smile and a deaf ear. His mind was made up. His asking me not to take these three children of ours was as concrete an order as he cared to give.

"What shall I tell my friends in Malaya?" I asked. "And how shall I ever face the Pliatan club again? Sir, you are cutting the very earth away from under all my work."

He answered, "You may take any other group you like. Take the group here in Djakarta, or take Saba—but those three small girls in your club in Pliatan are Bali's best. In my mind there is again that old plan we discussed before. You go to Singapore now, try to excuse yourself to your friends, use my name if it helps, see if they would accept another group—and then come back here and we will talk together again."

And hoping the doors were still open, I left.

On the flight to Singapore I tried to think out how best to explain the strange dilemma I was in, for it was clear to me that there existed only the slenderest chance of changing the President's mind. If I discovered that the desire in Malaya to see Balinese dancers was great, I thought that it might be appeased if we were to send over some other village group—though Luce and I would not dream of associating with any except Pliatan.

Both Noel Ross and Ben Joppe met me at the airport, and when I sat talking with them I at once had the feeling of a betrayer; for my friends here had everything ready for us and were so embarrassingly enthusiastic. As I watched Noel's animated face beaming behind horn-rimmed glasses, and heard how he planned not only to play in Singapore and Kuala Lumpur, but to get out into Kelantan and play to some Malay villages, I saw that I might have to let down an excellent and prepared plan.

Percy McNeice, in whose house we all stayed, was not only the overworked chairman of Singapore's Municipal Council, but his wife, an elegant and distinguished Chinese girl, was the sister of the Loke Wan Tho who was to help float the project financially.

So that very evening I outlined bluntly to Noel and Ben, to McNeice and Loke Wan Tho, exactly how things had developed in Djakarta. And when we went on later to the house of the head of the broadcasting station, and I showed there a film of our Legong and Kebiar made long ago in colour by the Nielsens, I had to tell Malcolm Macdonald, who was present, that the dancers he had just seen might not be able to come in the flesh, but could perhaps be represented by another group. This he accepted with surprise, for it seemed that the reception committee was formed already and that under his chairmanship leading personalities of the Malay, Chinese and British communities were sitting on it.

Yet worse coals were heaped on my head late the next night. After an official engagement, Macdonald met us half an hour before midnight in the stadium of the Happy World Amusement Park. This was a great concrete arena that could hold nine thousand people, and George Lee, its owner, generously offered us its use for two nights in February free of charge, giving us this help as a gesture of good will. When I said tactfully to Macdonald that this would be a cold and gigantic place for our group to dance in, he laughed at me with most practical arguments. The arena, he said, could sell five thousand seats to the local population at very cheap prices indeed—then the ordinary man in the street would be able to see it; and the remaining four thousand seats could be sold for high prices, and in these two nights we would be able to cover all our financial outlay, so that for the rest of our tour we could travel and play to the real people of Malaya as much as we all wished. The thoughtfulness of these sponsors of ours was increasingly shaming.

Then we left for Kuala Lumpur in a very British manner. This city lay about two hundred and fifty miles north up the Malay peninsula. The road generally ran through rubber plantations and low-lying villages, though nearer Kuala Lumpur itself dense jungle descended from the hills steeply to the very border of the twisting, rising road. And Noel, who was one of Malaya's senior civil servants, had a shining black Humber limousine for his use. Instead of carrying an ordinary number, its plates advertised it as "B.A. SEL."—British Adviser, Selangor State. And fixed at the radiator cap I saw two short masts, paired like a V, for flying standards. Somewhat hesitantly I asked Noel about the road up, for this was only a few weeks after Sir Henry Gurney, the High Commissioner in Kuala Lumpur, had been ambushed and assassinated on a jungly road in spite of an armoured-car escort. Things were not going well at this time in Malaya.

"Do you carry a gun, Noel?" I asked.

"I used to, but now I've given it up. If we were ambushed what could we do with a pistol? I don't like firearms."

"How is the road we are travelling? Doesn't it seem a little crazy for the British Advisers all to label their number-plates with "B.A. SEL." or "B.A. some other state" stuck out in front of them as an encouragement to snipers?"

Noel laughed.

143

"Don't worry, John. It's not as bad as people think. We believe that we have to show the flag otherwise all the villagers we pass will think the British are afraid of the damn bandits."

"Hell's bells! Do you literally fly a flag as well?"

"Of course. Two. The Union Jack and the Selangor State flags."

"If I were a senior civil servant I'd use a small Morris and change its numbers every day."

"We'll be all right. There's only one bad stretch just south of K.L. itself. Last week there was a nasty incident there. They ambushed a car and stabbed its passengers to death through the windows with bamboo spears."

And off we went up the hot west coast road, both flags flying merrily, the white-uniformed Malay driver smiling happily. And because we were late, we crossed the pass well after dark; and because it was dark, we couldn't be bothered to lower the flags. I felt that this was magnificently foolish, and probably quite right psychologically, proclaiming the only spirit with which to encourage the village people against the jungle-infesting Communists. In fact, Bali's petty and insular murders paled away and I found a great admiration for the stoicism of all Malaya's nationalities, who carried on as usual under tense and brutal strains.

Kuala Lumpur was as ready for us as Singapore. The *Straits Times* even published a news item about the coming of the dancers while I was staying at Noel's Residency, and though I did try again to paint a faithful picture of conditions in Djakarta to him, he could not believe that the trip would be cancelled at this stage. I promised him at any rate to try to send another group if the edict on Pliatan stood firm.

From K.L. I flew to Penang, and in Penang changed to a Siamese Airways Dakota and went on to Bangkok, my former home. Here I stayed with friends, and for three blissful days imbibed again the atmosphere of the one traditionally independent kingdom in this part of Asia. It was the cool month, and the city was gay with the equivalent of Balinese temple festivals. And though the smells of Bangkok's *klongs*, those pink lotus-covered waterways, and the yellow robes of the shaven-headed Buddhist monks, and the glittering tiles of the gold, green, blue and russet-brown roofs of their *naga*-gabled temples were as attractive to me as ever, I also found out very soon that the visit of a group of dancers to Siam could never pay its way. Bangkok is too cinema conscious a city, and Bali is too kindred. And exquisitely petite though the girls of Bangkok still were, I found my mind straying more and more concentratedly toward Kaliungu and my very dear partner, Luce.

Quickly I left Siam and spent one night only in Singapore where I learnt that Malcolm Macdonald had sent a letter to Sukarno about the dance group, and next morning I was bunched up between Chinese businessmen on a Catalina flying boat, headed for Djakarta through the Rhiouw Archipelago of smugglers' islands and via the isle of solid tin, Bangka. That evening I telephoned my old foe, the Palace Secretary, and contrived to get an appointment with the President before the weekend when he would leave for his palace in the mountains of West Java.

Sukarno welcomed me calmly, offering me coffee, and I began to explain to him the embarrassments I had met with. But very soon he interrupted me with: "But you did manage to cancel the trip?"

"I thought, sir, I was to find out what had been prepared first, and then ask for your ruling? If you will forgive my saying so, I am in grave trouble with my friends in both Malaya and Bali."

"I must ask you to cancel the Malayan trip," he said. "But later on we will send there another group—perhaps the group that goes to Colombo can visit Singapore on its return."

"That is a clear order, sir," I said, and sighed deeply, for in one sentence he was not only dooming Pliatan but handing the fruits of our work over to this very mediocre Colombo company. "I don't know how to face my friends in Bali," I added.

"Wait here five minutes," said he, and left the room without a further word.

Presently he came back again, a pen still in his hand, waving a sheet of paper in the air to dry it, and this he handed me, smiling, but again without comment. I read what he had written, and a conflicting flood of emotions poured over me. For what I read was an official letter in the President's own hand, recommending the Ministers of Foreign Affairs and Education to give me their full and immediate help in sending a group of Balinese dancers abroad to Europe and America.

"You understand the last paragraph, John? I have said that besides you there must also be one 'fellow impresario' of Indonesian race. You know how Indonesian sentiment is these days. Do you have any objection to that?"

"Not only do I have no objection, I would prefer it that way. And sir—thank you a million times for this confidence you are showing in me."

"Good! That's settled then. Now you had better take up once more that matter of an appointment with the Foreign Ministry. This will mean full-time work. Go and discuss the whole idea with Dr. Subardjo, the Foreign Minister."

"Excuse me, sir—I swore I'd be back in Bali before Christmas. May I come back again to Djakarta soon after Christmas when I've told this momentous news to the Pliatan club?"

And again I thanked him for his kindness, and promised to send him a copy of the letter of cancellation that I would have to send to Noel and to Malcolm Macdonald, and in which I would tell them the compromise solution which meant that the Colombo group would probably soon visit Singapore. With powerful, yet very mixed feelings, I booked my passage for Bali on December 24th.

As the plane flew in over Kuta Bay, our former hut was easily visible, and as we bumped down onto the grass strip, I could see the staunch old jeep, D.K. 1682, waiting in the small car park. I could hardly suppress my many excitements when Luce and Sampih met me at the immigration barrier, but in oriental fashion we all waited until we were in the jeep and on the way home, while I sucked in deep breaths of Balinese sea air once more.

"Well, the Malayan trip is cancelled," I told them at last. "The President himself would not permit it." A tangible silence of despair filled the jeep. "But—he proposed something else. He has offered Government help to send our group to Europe and America."

From Sampih came a deep and explosive "*Beh!*" and an ear-splitting grin; he was as eager and excited as a human being could be. Luce, however, reacted as I had done, and was thoughtful. Then she said, "Is this really good or bad news, Johnnie? I don't know. How free are we going to be artistically now? How many ties will official-dom tag on to us?"

"That, dear Luce, is exactly the question. But don't you see—I was caught! I *had* to accept. He stopped our going privately to look for our own contacts, but he's had the vision and confidence in our taste to back my old, old plan which has already been torpedoed once. So of course I accepted—and cheerfully, too. Heaven knows there'll be hurdles galore to trip us, but let's take them when we come to them. Next month I'll be going back to Djakarta to arrange an appointment once more at the Foreign Ministry and we'll be solvent again."

"What will the club say, Pih?" asked Luce.

"What will they say? *Beh!* They will be crazy with joy. This is the biggest victory for Pliatan. Who would want to go to Colombo now?" He crowed in his own delight.

"All right, Pih," I said. "Here is your lesson number one from your elder brother. Don't even talk about this outside the club. Don't arouse jealousy now—there'll be enough later on. Just say that some such possibility exists, if people ask you, but insist that nothing is certain at all."

Sampih, quick on the uptake, at once saw the point and agreed. His eyes gleamed, though. And then we were back in Denpasar's one street of wooden shops, passing the Bali Hotel, bumping along the Kaliungu lane, and running up the steep bank into our garage. Here, according to a pleasant Indonesian custom, I at once opened my bags and produced the *oleh-oleh* I had brought home, little presents for every member of the household from Luce to Rantun's Ketut.

And that evening the club did go mad with delight; but I made them swear not to brag with loud mouths in front of even Pliatan villagers, and over and over again we cautioned them against inviting envy.

Then alone together at last that night I spoke with Luce of another great problem that had finally presented itself to me. Partnership in our venture, I told her, was not enough; for in Bangkok I had known my dependence on her. Suddenly and to my indignation this had been made very clear to me. I now asked her to marry me according to the complicated Moslem-Christian, Indonesian-British regulations: which would make it doubly binding, doubly certain. And never knowing which way she would jump, I waited with a vast anxiety for her reply. But she looked at me very calmly and rather tearfully, but said coolly, "Yes." For the period when we had fought violently together, neither willing to give up our equally prized independence, was past; and

147

already we had discussed and inspected and faced the difficulties that would arise from a finalising of our mixed marriage, and we had decided that for us it would be workable, though children we might not dare to have.

So Christmas, 1951, was a most excellent day for us all, and the Legong was given in honour of the two of us, and we were all very happy together.

8

Enter our Impresario

*

The New Year of 1952 fell quickly upon us. I explained to the club that we would now have to work out a programme timed to the minute and suitable for western ears and eyes, and I was also writing reports for the Government in Djakarta, offering them the fruits of our experience during the last fourteen months, and outlining precisely the nature of the subsidy we would require. In the first week of January the Indonesian Cultural Attaché in Washington, Suwanto, a soft-spoken, oblique-glancing young man, with pink cheeks to his brown face, happened to arrive in Denpasar, and since he was then mentioned as my possible "fellow impresario of Indonesian race", we journeyed together to Pliatan and the other villages where our dancers came from, so that he could begin to know the people whom later he might be directing jointly with me.

And then it was time to brief our household and the club concerning their work while we went away to Java to beard the Government and get doubly married. Sampih was left in charge of the jeep. We promised to try to send them paying guests, and left them enough money for food and wages for six weeks. We asked the Anak Agung to start rehearsing the two Balinese ceremonials, a marriage and a New Year's Day celebration, which we wanted to include in the programme, but which I had so far avoided as being too complicated for handling in a theatre.

In the middle of January we left for Djakarta, I to stay at the Des Indes, Luce with her mother. The ordeal of meeting Luce's mother had loomed rather large, for she was the widow of the Pangeran Ario Sujono who had died at the Athenaeum in London when a member of the Netherlands War Cabinet. But this lady, now living in very modest circumstances, I found easy to get on with, and our first evening together we spent learning from her about the technicalities of our weddings. It appeared that Luce would have to bring me before a *penghulu*, a Moslem priest, who would invite me to be married by the Moslem law; and when I declined, we would be able to apply to a magistrate for a civil ceremony. To make the marriage binding according to British law, a British consul would have to be present as a witness, and after the ceremony he would present us with a Lex Loci certificate.

We fixed February 4th as the date, and Haji Agus Salim, a very old and respected protector of mine, was to act as my father for the day. In the meantime, while Luce looked for some clothes, I concentrated on obtaining a letter of authority to start negotiating with American and European impresarios, since the President's letter had expressed merely a wish, and was not a valid executive order. On January 23rd Foreign Minister Subardjo gave me such a letter, and immediately I wrote off to Sol Hurok and Columbia Artists Management in America, detailing the whole proposal. In London I wrote to Joan White, my actress cousin. Then I called on K.L.M. and B.O.A.C., and later on Philippine Airlines and T.O.A., to inquire about pay-loads and charter fees, and found that a four-engined plane could in fact transport forty-five persons with gamelan and costumes complete. And lastly I had time to see my old colleague, Ruslan Abdulgani, at the Ministry of Information, who looked carefully through my files and said that since this was the first orderly and competent plan to send dancers abroad that he had inspected, he would try to bring his Ministry in also to support us. An article in *The New York Times* at about this time, written by Tillman Durdin, who had visited us in Bali before any Government interest was assured, particularly caught the eye of both the President and the Governmental authorities.

On February 4th, thanks to old Haji Agus Salim playing patience and telling me soothingly not to fret, while the clock in his house ticked on fifteen minutes slow, I was late for the ceremony and found a svelte tigress waiting to devour me. It was a most strange ritual performed under a glaring Coca-Cola advertisement. The Dutch Protestant service, translated into Indonesian, became a stilted oddity and obviously baffled the charming official who legally joined us. However, the forms which Consul Harcourt held out to us all for our signatures looked more normal and made me feel that at last this highly complicated marriage of ours was real. Our reception was amusing and curious, too, for in a flower-packed lounge we were honoured by usually internecine political opponents among our guests. When it was all over we spent an amusing night in the house of our friend, Willard Hanna, the head of the American Information Service, swatting mosquitoes. On the next day we left for Singapore and stayed with some more friends who had spent a week with us in Bali, and together with them we were invited to lunch with Malcolm Macdonald at Bukit Serene, in Johore, where we were able to explain and apologize in person about the cancelled tour of Malaya.

From Singapore we flew up over the dark green jungly hills of the Malay Peninsula, nine hundred miles to Bangkok, where a waiting car of our friends brought us swiftly into the town, which was still enjoying its brief cool season. Our visit was Siamese and concentrated, for I had always determined that my wife must like Bangkok. Our hosts were of the family of the late Prince Regent, Rangsit of Chainat, who was the last surviving son of the great King Chulalongkorn. The Prince Regent had married a witty German lady, and their younger son was our host, Mom Chao Sanidh Rangsit. Sanidh in turn had married an Italian-Swiss girl of great beauty, with brooding and troubling eyes, the Mom Amelia. At times Sanidh was a Siamese Prince to the tips of his fingers; at other times he was a gourmet from his beloved Ascona. During the latter periods his branch of the family was nicknamed the "Swiss family Rangsit". They and Luce each spoke fluently at least four languages, making me feel uncomfortably peasant.

Though Luce was taken to meet Rhambai and her infant, who was my one Buddhist goddaughter; to Jim Thompson's shop, which had supplied the cloth for *The King and I*; to the Thieves Market, where you could sometimes buy back an article missing recently from your own house; to eat Szechaun duck at the Tein Hoi restaurant; to Sanidh's floating house up the broad, turgid river of Bangkok; and to the house of the Oxonian editor of *Standard*, Prince Prem—two things stood out from the whole visit.

151

The first was our rail trip up to Chiengmai, the capital of mountainous north Siam, where we lived in a log cabin built near the top of the Doi Suthep mountain by Sanidh. Here we ate my favourite *mu som*, orange meat, a delectable Siamese pork fermented with oranges and packed into long sausage-like leaf sheaths, and which is correctly eaten with salted peanuts, coriander leaves, ginger and green onions.

The second was our trip to the Temple of the Reclining Buddha, accompanied this time by my friend, Kukrit Pramoj, editor of the capital's most successful newspapers.

We were strolling, then, through the spacious, stone-flagged courtyard of the temple (the reclining Buddha is forty-nine metres long, a figure lying on one side, whose giant toes are engraved and decorated exquisitely with mother-of-pearl), when Kukrit said to us quietly, "Don't look for a moment, but over there there's a photographer who's meant to be doing a book about Bangkok. He's staying with Prince Chula, who brought him out. His name is Baron or something."

At which my head fairly spun around and, miracle of all miracles, Baron in person it was—Baron the prince of ballet photographers, an old friend from the days of the Press Bar at Covent Garden Opera House, and who had photographed my "Javanese Dancers" of 1946.

"Baron—maestro!" I shouted. "This is an act of God. You must come at once to Bali and make publicity shots of my dancers there." And the rest of our days in Bangkok we spent with the Rangsits, Baron and Kukrit.

On the day before we left, we went to the Temple of the Emerald Buddha, the glittering pagodaed compound being part of the Royal Palace, and before the great stone walls we bought two cages of little birds from vendors, since the Siamese idea is that birds thus freed make merit for their benefactors, and fly away bringing luck to those who have freed them, as well as bearing their liberators' sins away on their backs.

Sadly, yet eagerly, we left Siam, heading back to Djakarta where so many problems awaited us. We arrived there on February 25th, and from that day the tempo of our work changed, heading for a crescendo and pace that would drain the energy from my body as surely as the water was drained from the ancient battery of my brave old jeep.

On our first morning in Djakarta I sped down to the Ministry to see what replies might have come in from America. To my delight, both Hurok and Columbia Artists had cabled interested replies, while Mr. F. C. Schang, President of the latter organization, had sent also a four-page letter setting out the financial and theatrical details of a tour of the United States, saying how he and his partner, Coppicus, had been eager to bring some Balinese to America ever since catching a glimpse of them at the Colonial Exhibition in Paris in 1931. These replies I showed to Dr. Subardjo, and we decided to carry on negotiating in parallel with Hurok and Columbia until something definite was offered.

Ruslan Abdulgani, meanwhile, had already brought his Information Ministry into the support of our group, and was now asking what practical help we needed. I replied simply, "We need publicity stills, some coloured movie film with sound, or at least some tape recordings; then a little cash in a Denpasar bank on which we can draw to start making new musical instruments and ordering costumes, and also for office expenses."

He was the ideal partner. He and the Foreign Ministry agreed to bring Baron down from Bangkok in exchange for free publicity stills, and it was Baron who had to refuse because of the death of King George VI, which necessitated his instant return to London. But during the next days I received some tape recordings, while two photographers were detailed to accompany me when I returned to Bali; and since I had been given another Rolleiflex as a wedding present, it at last looked as though we would get the publicity material which we had so long needed.

To the Ministries assisting me I sent in a preliminary report concerning the subsidy needed. I was still in the midst of negotiating, I said, but at the moment I wanted about five thousand *rupiahs* to start things moving in Bali, where the final budget for costumes, instruments and office cables would be not much over forty thousand *rupiahs* (£1,250. 0. 0). Then there would be the outfitting of the company at a good but inexpensive Djakarta tailor, which would mean, I reckoned, another sixty thousand *rupiahs*, and abroad more clothing would be necessary for our Balinese who found 65 degrees a very cold day— about eight thousand U.S. dollars, I guessed, in foreign currency,

153

would cover second warm suits, woollen underclothes, overcoats and raincoats, which could be bought in big stores in London or New York. The major item, however, was the transportation. My requirements, I explained, were being worked out by several airlines who had offices in Djakarta, and it had been confirmed that the whole group could be lifted in one Constellation or Skymaster. A return charter was being very roughly estimated at about six hundred thousand *rupiahs*, and this meant that the total Government subsidy for a round the world tour for the forty-four of us would be in the region of about eight hundred and fifty thousand *rupiahs*, or just under £26,500. 0. 0.

The one thing delaying my return to Bali was my personal contract. At this time, all Indonesian ministries were very wary of employing foreigners for reasons of racial sentiment and for fear of resultant criticisms in Parliament. Understanding this, I agreed to less favourable terms than in earlier political contracts given me during the revolutionary period. I hoped to be able to run my establishment in Bali, look after my own expenses when I came to Djakarta, even pay my own postage, all on about one hundred and fifteen pounds a month. The ministry would look after my Djakarta hotel bills and plane fares between Bali and Java. It was just enough. Yet in order to protect themselves, the Administration Service worried and trembled about unsuspected angles from which they might be vulnerable, until they hit upon the idea of making clause one in my contract a reference to the President's original letter of recommendation, which not only let them out neatly, but which pleased me in that it proved I had never asked for this employment. I was given the sonorous title of Technical Expert on Cultural Relations and Information for Countries Abroad, and on March 14th the document of it was formally handed to me, together with a month's salary and a letter of reference to the head of Bali's Local Government in Denpasar.

Our last weekend in Java we spent in the Puntjak mountain home of Bill Palmer, the most hospitable American in this part of Asia, where we met Ted Smith of the Motion Picture Association, who had just returned with his wife Tudie from a second honeymoon in our Kaliungu house. They both had been enchanted with Bali and the dancing in Pliatan, but reported that the roof of my jeep had been knife-slashed right across by some vandal, unknown, at night. It sounded like a first active spasm of jealousy. When I mentioned it to Islam Salim (who had been transferred from the command of Bali and was now week-ending also with Bill Palmer prior to taking up his appointment as Military Attaché in Peking), he grinned, showing no surprise at all, and said, "You surely expected things like that, didn't you, John? The bigger your success and the nearer your departure, the worse it will probably get, too."

Not exactly encouraged by this realistic reply, we set off for Bali with two official photographers, but when we bumped along the Kaliungu lane all seemed serenely quiet and normal. We asked Sampih about the jeep roof, but he did not know who had slashed it or why, and otherwise our household were so elated to see us and so pleased with the *oleh-oleh* we brought them that it felt thoroughly good to be home. The photographers were staying at the Bali Hotel, where they would use their bathroom for developing, and for days on end we photographed the grinning, sweltering dancers posing in the sun-light. We made some colour movie shots and selected the best of our rough proofs run off in the hotel bathroom for taking back to Djakarta and mass producing and sending abroad.

When the photographers had left I began to think about making a courtesy call on the local authorities. At this stage I knew Sutedja, the head of the Government, only by sight, and had heard little of him beyond a rumour that he disliked a white skin, but in a country just emerging from colonization this is a far from rare condition. To look at he was young, bespectacled, wavy haired, eyes close set together, well built. I asked for an interview and he gave me one. Perhaps appropriately it was ten o'clock on the morning of April 1st that I sat at a table with him in his office, in company of one Gusti Bagus Sugriwa, a man almost bald and goatee bearded, an intimate of Sutedja's and his official adviser on religious affairs. I handed over my letter from the Foreign Ministry and allowed them to read the terms of my contract, and then told them politely the history of my old idea concerning the dancers. Equally politely they listened. I left them after an hour, pursued by smiles but with no idea as to whether I had pleased or offended. But Denpasar is a tiny place, and soon one of the officials began talking to a friend outside, and this friend moved on to gossip with an ally of ours, and one evening this last man rode up to

Pliatan, where in whispers he told us, "Denpasar feels that it has been by-passed by Djakarta. You are a foreigner and therefore suspect. And if that were not enough, the men who have just returned with big mouths from dancing in Colombo are urging the Denpasar government to order *them* to go to America. They are the *official* artists, they say."

"I am sorry, very," I replied. "I only hope they will take this out on Djakarta and not on us."

"You see, they feel also that Pliatan belongs to reactionary Gianjar, and is therefore in territory *politically* opposed to them."

I said, "I can see that this thing is going to end in a sickening struggle of wits. It will be a miracle if we come through."

"John—may I ask you one question?"

I nodded.

"Well—this thing, as it grows, will indeed cause jealousies. If you want to go on living in Bali, why not give the whole idea up, or at the least seek a compromise with the Denpasar people?"

I answered slowly, watching the Anak Agung's face, which had become a set, plump mask.

"Who knows what will be left in Bali twenty years from now? I know we are running risks, but, quite simply, my heart is set on showing this Balinese Legong to the western world. To Luce and me, all the rest of the programme we are devising is but a setting to the Legong jewel. What we are doing, we feel, rightly or wrongly, is important. We will help broaden just a little the horizons of European and American art.

"And secondly, there's my pride. I won't be beaten by this handful of little people who are merely jealous and who don't care about the arts of Bali at all. Mark you, I don't blame them in the least for being suspicious of a foreigner. If my throat is cut it will be sad and ironic— and just an ugly item in Indonesia's evolution from being a subject country. But stop I cannot. And as for a compromise, it would be like blackmail—without end. We have worked together a year and a half like a family. One alien official forced on us, stuffed with self-import-ance and half-baked political ideas, could ruin the spirit of our group. In any collection of human beings of this size, there are bound to be troublemakers—especially among artists. But we know ours and, if left alone, can control them easily. Lastly, as you know, we are only interested in Pliatan and our other dancers because they are the best we have been able to find. Compromise would mean lowering our standards. I want little Raka to mingle with ballerinas of international fame; I want the Anak Agung and Sampih to meet Serge Lifar and Youskevitch. So—on we shall go, but as inoffensively as possible."

"In that case," said our ally, "I can only wish you good luck." And he drove off noisily into the blue-black night on his motorcycle.

I turned to the Anak Agung:

"And you, Agung Adji—what do you say?"

"*Terserah!*" he replied with a shrug. "It is surrendered to you."

Going home that night, Luce and I talked over our position. To both of us it was clear that we were now in a state of cold war with a powerful, but small, clique in Denpasar, which was using national or racial sentiment against us to appeal to Sutedja. We imagined that irresponsible people might bribe or persuade some thugs to kill us or burn down our house, or, if the Denpasar officials did genuinely feel that the central Government had by-passed them, and resented my foreign role besides, we could anticipate a web of intrigue stretching from Denpasar to Djakarta. So I decided, as one addicted to the game of chess, to play out this contest coolly and patiently, endeavouring to anticipate and block my adversaries' moves, unwilling to sacrifice a single pawn on the board unnecessarily, a single musician or dancer in my team. As to our good friend the Anak Agung, it would be unfair to count on his active support. He had to live in Bali; he was not young, his ideas were fixed and his philosophy resigned. For us it was enough that he was the most inspiring musician in the island; he and all our other Balinese friends would have to shelter behind our strategies.

The theatrical preparations then really got under way. We called to Kaliungu the Anak Agung and the Pliatan club leaders, with Tjokorda Oka of Singapadu village, a new member of our Masked Dance quintet and according to the Anak Agung quite the best designer of dance costumes in Bali, as well as a fine maker of Barongs and carver of Rangda masks.

Our time limit, I told them, was Indonesian Independence Day, August 17th, for on that day we had been called to Djakarta to dance at the palace. We would leave Bali by ship about ten days before then.

"But how large can the group be—finally?" asked the Anak Agung. "The gamelan club alone has twenty-eight members, and there is ill feeling already because some of them know that they will have to stay behind."

"Agung Adji—we have talked this over many times. You know that twenty-three is enough for the gamelan. We will have to make a system of fines for non-attendance at rehearsal and the most hard-working and valuable men will go with us."

Then we came to the programme. First I no longer found Tabuh Telu the ideal overture. It was too evenly balanced, with not enough light and shade. So I played them the Benjamin Britten *Young Persons' Guide to the Orchestra* on our gramophone, asking them whether they could not find some lively North Bali melody which could be treated in such a way. Western audiences could then begin by hearing Balinese music broken down into instruments and sections. Instantly Lebah replied. "Kapi Radja!" he snapped. "The very piece for such an idea. A Kebiar from the north—we will rehearse it tonight."

And though the programme kept its original core, I now wanted a Barong story for our finale, so I asked Tjokorda Oka to commence at once on making a Barong for us.

"The black *duk* fibre is already collected for the Barong's coat," said the Tjokorda. "Also the hides. If the Tuan has money for me I can put ten men to work at once on preparing the hides, carving the smooth skin, encrusting the glass gems and preparing the gold paint. I myself will carve the masks."

"Wonderful, Tjokorda. Begin this very day, for the money is in the People's Bank here in Denpasar now."

And then we wrangled over the Djanger and our need for two Oleg dancers who could double with the Djanger, too. For of the original proud Djanger, only two girls remained, and they were the least attractive.

The Oleg was a lively modern dance brought down to Denpasar from the north before the war, and there refined and softened. It was performed by girls in male or female costumes according to taste, and in Sayan village, two thirteen-year-olds who had learned it from

Sampih, danced it with absolute precision and very feminine smiles. For borrowing these two children we were to pay the Sayan club five hundred *rupiahs* a month while abroad. But still we needed two more adult Oleg dancers who could play in the Djanger, and who would not ask for wasteful chaperones to accompany them.

Also, no reserve had been found for Sampih's Kebiar and Bumblebee roles. The Anak Agung hankered after Gusti Ngurah Raka, who was his friend and had been Mario's first brilliant pupil in the thirties; but this man was chained to his wife and her fifty hectares of rice-fields.

Then there were the costumes. Here Luce and Tjokorda Oka were in charge and faced a most complicated labour. Luce had to reckon how many yards of cloth, some silk, some cotton, would be needed for this company of over forty persons. Then she had to select the yarn, choose the dyes, distribute the hanks of dyed yarn among weavers in several villages, and collect the finished cloth on time. With the Tjokorda she examined and picked out the most decorative traditional patterns for each *kain*, and then the Tjokorda had to trace these patterns on each *kain* with chalk and then gold-paint them. He had to buy *antjur*—a fish-glue base—with red Chinese paint for the first coat, and then white of eggs to mix with the gold paint for the outer glittering layer. This mixing of the gold paint with egg-white made the gold gleam as if it were real and delighted the Balinese; the idea, of course, was ancient, and we had borrowed it from the painters of the Renaissance at the suggestion of Jim Ford. Each yard of cloth was painted by hand.

Next the Anak Agung wanted a second gamelan. And thinking of our payload, we worked out a variation on an *angklung* orchestra, a cheerful, singing-toned gamelan of only four notes. This involved many trips over to distant Klungkung, and during a period of six weeks we watched a set of new gongs for a small, light *reyong* emerge from a hand furnace; and rows of new metallophone "leaves" we saw hammered and scraped and forged and tuned in the mud yard of a famous smith. While the smith fashioned the metal parts, Rantun's former husband, the overfruitful Pagah, carved simple wooden stands for the new metallophones and *klengtangan*, the latter, an all-bamboo xylophone, played with two long-handled vibrant hammers. Three more highly skilled craftsmen worked in a *balé* near the Anak Agung's

159

kitchen for five weeks, while they carved four delicate and intricate frames for two pairs of Shadow Play metallophones—the soft and infinitely melodious Gender Wayang. And without ceasing, the jeep travelled around and around, pushing, pleading, and paying out wages to our teams of workers.

As the news of our impending departure spread around, idle people flocked to see us and ate away our little time. Each prominent figure from Java that came to Bali fell into the Gianjar family propaganda net and was swept up to a command performance in Pliatan, until I protested that the dancers belonged to Indonesia and not to Gianjar, and suggested that these notables would surely be equally interested to see us rehearsing, without being given special performances that wasted our time. Then in Kaliungu, smiling and ambitious young men visited us, smoking our cigarettes and drinking our coffee, complimenting us on our orchids and languidly strumming on our metallophones, seeking under any pretext to honour us with their company abroad; and when, inevitably, we told them this was most regrettably, almost certainly, impossible, they smiled again and drifted away into the ranks of our enemies.

Encouragement, however, continued to arrive from abroad. From Paris there dropped in a M. Cocqué, of the *Figaro*, dry, shrewd and experienced. He predicted a storm of appreciation for us in Paris. From London came the Macmillans, the younger generation of the publishing house of that name, who were equally confident of our reception there, though so far my cousin had found us no London manager.

About the middle of April—my correspondence, meanwhile, with America and Europe, with tailors and air-line companies in Djakarta, with Consuls, with the Ministries now interested in us, and my books of accounts, were already a full-time job—about this middle of April, then, there came word from Suwanto in Washington to say that his other work forced him to withdraw from the role of "fellow impresario"; and by this same mail came a long cable from Columbia Artists stating that in triangular fashion they, Suwanto and I seemed to have come to a basis for agreement. Mr. Schang, their President, would shortly be flying to Bali in person to witness my production with his own eyes. I urged the acceptance of the Columbia offer,

29. The Pliatan Gamelan orchestra on stage at the Winter Garden Theatre in London, led by the mayor of Pliatan village, Anak Agung Gde Mandera, who was the conductor and artistic director. On August 26, 1952, the troupe opened a two-week season at the Winter Garden Theatre before leaving for New York and a 13-week tour of American cities.

30. The three Legongs photographed from the wings of the Winter Garden Theatre, London, August 1952.

31. Sampih performing the Kebiar Duduk at the Winter Garden Theatre, London, August 1952.

32. The warrior Ardjuna, in the foreground with his bow, is about to do battle with the wild boar sent by the god Shiva to test his prowess. In this condensed play, based on the epic *Mahabharata*, Ardjuna triumphs over all the temptations to try him, and then is chosen by the Gods as champion against the King of the Demons.

33. In the programme's Finale, the Barong, a mythical animal who protects the Balinese against evil, triumphs over all its adversaries, in particular Rangda, Queen of the Witches, who brings the imbalance of illness and death.

COLUMBIA ARTISTS' MANAGEMENT INC.

by arrangement with

The Cultural Department of the Republic of Indonesia

presents

Dancers of Bali

and

PLIATAN GAMELAN
ANAK AGUNG GDE NGURAH MANDERA, Director

COMPANY OF 45
Direct from Bali, Indonesia

Produced by **JOHN COAST**
Scenery and Lighting by **RICHARD HARRISON SENIE**

Exclusive Management: COLUMBIA ARTISTS' MANAGEMENT, INC.
Tour Direction: COPPICUS, SCHANG & BROWN, INC.
113 West 57th Street, New York City

Company Director-General Representing Indonesian Cultural Department: R. M. INDROSUGONDO
Assistant Director-General: R. SUTARJO

34. Publicity from Columbia Artists' Management, which presented the American cross–country tour of "The Dancers of Bali". From the opening night in New York until their last night in Miami, the dancers and musicians were greeted by enthusiastic audiences and reviews. The drawing is by the Mexican artist Miguel Covarrubias, and is reproduced from his classic account of Bali published in 1937, *The Island of Bali*.

35. The "Dancers of Bali" reach Broadway. In New York, the Balinese occupied four floors in a midtown hotel. In between rehearsals, the dancers whiled away their time riding up and down in the hotel's elevators and lolling in the hotel's bathtubs. Sitting in the tubs, they would pull the plug and say that the sound of gurgling water reminded them of their native streams.

36. John Coast directing a rehearsal for the premiere at the Fulton Theater on Broadway. The group had rarely experienced professional theatre lighting prior to the tour.

37. The Djanger ensemble in their US debut at the Fulton.

38. Rangda, Queen of the Witches (left), representing evil, and the Barong (centre), protector of the good. The Barong costume is supported by two men inside, whose remarkable teamwork and footwork in the front and hindquarters delighted audiences throughout the tour.

39. Sampih performing the Baris. Baris is the idealized warrior figure which, in turn, is dangerous and dauntless, vulnerable and frightened, wary and aggressive. It has become the test piece for all male Balinese dancers. Sampih's acting and mime for this intensely concentrated work were memorable. The Baris hero is often accompanied by one or more clown-warriors. Five clowns were among the members of the troupe: Serog, Tjokorda Oka (who also designed and made the costumes and masks for the tour), Kakul, Rinda and Anak Agung Raka.

40. Male star Sampih in the Kebiar Duduk, interacting with his director and lead drummer, Anak Agung Gde Mandera.

41. A sequence of photographs of Ni Gusti Raka in the work Tumililangan (the Bumblebee Dance), specially created for her and Sampih by Mario. Ni Gusti Raka, in the role of a bumblebee, wriggles and flits in childlike delight as she sees her first flower garden. Too young to flirt, she spurns the male bumblebee who comes buzzing around. It was the performance of this role that gained for her acclaim and stardom.

Opposite: 43. Ketjak, originally a section of a trance dance-drama based on the Indonesian epic *Ramayana*, was enlarged and developed by Bali resident artist Walter Spies and dance critic Beryl de Zoete in 1932. It quickly became a separate and popular piece. Here is Serog, the clown, with some of his hissing, grunting and chanting army of monkeys, in a spectacular scene from the work.

42. The Djanger dance being performed at the Thunderbird Hotel in Las Vegas.

44. Dancers Oka and Raka sipping orange pop in the Fulton Theater, New York. Orange pop and ice cream were the only American foods which appealed to the Balinese. Often they looked in vain for a Chinese restaurant which could approximate the Balinese diet of rice with a little boiled chicken, shrimp or pork, a green vegetable and their own highly seasoned sambal which they had brought with them from Bali.

45. A new delight for the Balinese dancers in America was ice cream. Here they are enjoying their favourite flavour—vanilla—in Manhattan.

46. While the group was in Los Angeles, they visited several movie studios. Here the three Legongs pose with the legendary Walt Disney.

47. The troupe visited the Paramount Studios in Hollywood, where Bing Crosby and Bob Hope happened to be shooting some TV commercials for their new film, *The Road to Bali*. The Legongs were highly amused when the comedians started dancing à la Balinese. They attended a special preview of the film in San Francisco, and insisted on seeing it several times before they left the US, claiming they would see it yet again in the new cinema recently built in Bali.

48. The three Legongs meeting prima ballerina assoluta Alicia Markova.

49. The three bemused Legongs and Luce Coast looking over a leading American magazine which featured the troupe. The Balinese dance company received widespread coverage in leading British and American media of the time, including the *Illustrated London News*, *London Telegraph*, *Life*, *New Yorker*, *New York Times*, *New York Herald Tribune*, *New York Post*, *New York Daily News*, *Time* and *Newsweek*.

50. A farewell picture taken with John and Luce Coast in Miami before the group left without the Coasts for Brussels, Bonn, Paris and Rome. John Coast is at far right. Next to him is Frederick C. Schang Jr., President of Columbia Artists' Management, and standing between them is Sampih. Second from left is Luce with the three little Legongs in front, flanking Anak Agung Gde Mandera. Problems with excess luggage increased as the tour progressed. When the troupe left Miami on January 8, 1953, 500 gallons of gas had to be offloaded from the plane because of the extra weight and space taken up by the group's luggage.

51. On their first return visit to Indonesia in 1966, John and Luce Coast had an emotional reunion with members of the "Dancers of Bali" troupe. Ni Gusti Raka, at the age of 25, was a widow with four young children, living on the outskirts of Denpasar. She is shown here with her youngest child, a son called Gde. At a dance competition held during their stay, the Coasts saw Raka dance the Tumulilingan, this time with Bagus, the 17-year-old son of Anak Agung Gde Mandera.

52. Ni Gusti Raka in a publicity shot for the 1971 Australian tour, led by Anak Agung Gde Mandera. The troupe performed in Sydney, Canberra and Melbourne.

53. John Coast in his London office, 1981. He had established his own Concert Artists' Management business. Behind him are photographs of some of his famous clients: Mario Lanza, Luciano Pavarotti (whom Coast had discovered as a young unknown singer at a vocal competition in Modena, Italy), Montserrat Caballé, "Dancers of India", and high over his left shoulder his beloved "Dancers of Bali".

54. Reunion dinner in Pliatan, August 1983. Left to right: Belge (Sampih's son), John Coast, Anak Agung Gde Mandera, Ni Gusti Raka and Anak Agung Anom. Belge's un-Balinese name was bestowed on him when on the day he was born his mother received a letter from Sampih in Brussels postmarked "Belge" (Belgium).

55. Pegil, Belge and John Coast in Iseh, Bali, August 2, 1983. Pegil was a boy of ten when he joined the Coast household in 1950.

56. Ni Gusti Raka, in January 2004, teaching a child during a class at the Agung Rai Museum of Art (ARMA) in Pengosekan, Ubud.

for the other impresario had lapsed into a so far unaccountable silence.

The Galungan season now came again and passed agonizingly slowly, but at this festive time we escorted a Javanese doctor around our villages, where he made a first medical inspection. And also during Galungan, Dr. Subardjo himself, no longer Foreign Minister after a disagreement with the Parliament about American Aid, arrived in Denpasar; we looked after him gladly, for he, more than any other Minister, had helped us forward.

By the beginning of May we were progressing fast. Our Barong, from a pile of raw hides, bamboo, paint and fibre, was being rapidly moulded into the gleaming and shaggy-haired monster in gold, black and scarlet who would be our protective spirit. The two young Olegs from Sayan were as pretty as paint and learning to interchange roles with the Legongs; the Masked Dance comedies were shaping, and when I had suggested the gamelan club forming a 'Tjak, or Monkey Dance chorus, the Anak Agung was inspired to put Serog, Bali's greatest clown, to mime as a buffoon in its centre.

Then Mario came over from Tabanan again to train our Bumblebee Dance understudy, Desak Putu from Sayan village. But Raka complained angrily and secretly to us, chanting, "But I shan't *be* sick, I tell you; I shan't *be* sick." And having taken some lucky photographs of Mario, I dashed off an article for the London periodical, *Ballet*, describing the conception of the Bumblebee Dance, and risking telling Richard Buckle that we hoped to be in London by late August.

Just when I was toying with another new idea—one which appalled the club—of taking with us two fascinating, undulating-bodied old crones to dance the Mendet, a true temple dance performed by older women with smoking braziers of holy fire held on the palms of their hands, came the news that the Barong was ready.

And well I remember the Barong driving from Singapadu to Pliatan, spread out like a gigantic black bear rug on the roof of a small bus, with the Anak Agung beaming beside me in the respectfully attendant jeep, while Tjokorda Oka, its creator, looked solemn with pride seated at the back of the bus. At the boundary of the village, the club and the gamelan formed into a jubilant procession, and the Barong entered Pliatan in noisy triumph. That night the Anak Agung's younger cousin, the Anak Agung Gdé Raka, who was both *pemangku* priest and *balean* doctor, and who was to dance the part of the Barong's front legs, performed a mysterious rite in the little temple of Gunung Sari. I stumbled there barefoot behind the Legongs, splashing through a river behind them, who tittered like birds and guided me with pushes and pulls in the unaccustomed dark. And in the temple court, beneath a hissing lamp, the *pemangku* recited his magic formulae while special offerings were prepared, after which he cut a small, deep hole in the Barong's forehead, burying therein a small river ruby, a little gold and I know not what besides, thus giving the Barong its *djiwa*, its *kesaktian*—its soul, its magical power for good. Kneeling demurely in a neighbouring courtyard, before their own shrine, the little Legongs were solemnly offering their own devotions.

Every evening, and throughout the whole of each Sunday, when the entire cast assembled, I took my rehearsals. The earth of the *puri* compound we marked out to designate a stage, and I explained to them how a great curtain would open and close, how lights would blaze down upon them and blaze up at them, how the audience would only be seated in front of them and not on all sides, so that they would have to try to face in that direction most of the time, and how they must not be surprised by applause. We had to build a fence to keep the villagers off our stage, so interested in the lunacy of the producer did they become.

We were just timing the Masked Dance story of the Fasting Ardjuna, which I had selected from Hindu myth because of its popularity and because it demonstrated Sampih's warrior Baris in the character of Ardjuna, and we were working on the grand finale, a comical Barong story lasting only six minutes, when once again I was summoned to Djakarta, this time to meet Mr. Schang, who was due before the middle of May from New York.

With my head still swimming with details yet to be thought out, I handed everything over to Luce and the Anak Agung as I grudgingly boarded the plane to Java. On arriving at the Des Indes, I found our friend Suprapto waiting for me, the radio station official who had made us the tape recordings, and whom Dr. Subardjo had agreed might be the group's manager, since we had all liked this hard-working young man, who was so sympathetic to Balinese art. But his face now, behind the thick lenses of his glasses, seemed troubled.

"Have you seen the press attack on you?" he asked, pushing a notorious gossip column under my nose. I was criticized, I read, for taking only Balinese dancers abroad—was not the Candle Dance of Sumatra also Indonesian art, asked the writer?

"Forget it, 'Prapto," I laughed. "Those lunatics are friends of mine. I've even written for their rag of a paper. If it goes on I'll run down and explain everything to them."

Suprapto, however, was still very much tied to his radio station, and in that no successor had yet been agreed upon to take over from Suwanto, it was left to me to run around finding out about American and British visa requirements, about transit visas, about Indonesian exit permits and re-entry permits, and to check on all the airline companies and their estimates, as well as sending off a Dutch tailor posthaste by air to Bali to take the measurements for suits for all the group. But most wearying of all was the universal hesitation on the part of officialdom to commit itself over the financial subsidy. In the end, on the very day before Schang was due, I tried to hurry the matter by promising to try to pay back part of the subsidy from the profits. This pleased everyone; but the men from the Finance Ministry at once wanted to know how much we could expect to pay back.

"Gentlemen," I said, "I am willing to put in writing now that in a good week we will pay back to the Government 40 per cent of the profits, and in a bad week 20 per cent. But as to whether that will amount to one dollar or a million depends on how big a hit the Balinese are, on how long they want to stay abroad, and on whether or not we have any lucrative film and television offers. Let me say now, though, that if we're the hit I think we shall be, and I make millions of dollars worth of good-will for Indonesia, I shall regard you as soulless bureaucrats if you *accept* one cent from us."

At which these officials, old colleagues of mine, grinned evasively and protested against the need for putting anything in writing yet. But they made me uneasy. I felt that they already regarded the group as their purchasable property to be used under some official heading for the purpose of exploiting their young country's name—to them a quite logical development. But I, though a foreigner, thought of our group as separate human beings, with whom Luce and I had eaten rice,

163

and some of whom, in our days of poverty had quietly and anonymously left rice at Rantun's kitchen door for us.

The last man out of the K.L.M. Constellation next noon was Mr. Frederick C. Schang, Jr. He wore a blue Palm Beach suit, smoked a newly lighted cigar ten inches long, was short and sturdy, with a square jaw and steely blue eyes. He was, I judged, in his late fifties, tough, fit, alert. I introduced myself and we went over to the Des Indes together. And Schang quickly turned out to be an original character. Before Bali was even mentioned he was talking about his collection of forty-eight Paul Klees and putting a Klee booklet into my hand. When he heard the plane for Bali left in two days time, he disappeared in a flash and snatched some rounds of tropical golf. At the Capitol Restaurant he personally superintended the mixing of a Dry Martini to the proportions of one in twelve, and he brushed his teeth in soda water, shouting over to me, "I start drinking water again when we reach Rome on the way home."

Though we made one or two official calls of an introductory nature, he wanted only to get to Bali; and having arrived in our guest house he was too polite to say so if he was uncomfortable, while Sampih raced off to buy a crate of soda water. With Luce and myself he was reserved, but friendly enough, for he wanted to inspect the programme before committing himself in any way at all. So we quickly collected the whole company in Pliatan, and on three different nights played through the programme in slightly varying orders.

We were anxious about Schang, terribly. We feared he might call for a buxom Djanger chorus and like all the wrong things. We had determined under no circumstances to cut the Legong to less than seventeen minutes, and we bristled with defensiveness. But Freddie Schang had the right stuff in him. His start in the world with Nijinsky and his forty years on Broadway helped him to get easily to the heart of the matter. He sat with a watch in one hand, perched on the edge of his bamboo chair, while the entire village of Pliatan surged curiously about two inches behind his shirt collar, and directly Raka entered in her bumblebee role, his eyes glistened, and he kept repeating to nobody in particular, "The little darling—oh, the little *darling!*" He was enslaved and our friend henceforth. At the end he summed up, "Those ceremonials are too hard to handle. They look like a mob scene. Unless you're very keen, cut 'em out would be my advice. That Djanger is weak—*very* weak. Maybe two pretty girls would stiffen it enough so as it'd get by. It's padding, though. The Monkey Dance is a knockout. It'll remind them at home of a cheering section at the Yale Bowl. The little Olegs would be winners if it weren't for the Legongs. Sampih is terrific—that boy's got the technique. But Ni Gusti Raka—there's your star! She's everything you wrote and told me and then some more. She's *great*. She's so sweet I could eat her with a spoon. *All* the little girls are darlings—the American public will go crazy about 'em. They're terrific kids. You—you—you've got together here a galaxy of talent that's going to make even Broadway blink. But what gets me is to think I come twelve thousand miles to this little mud-walled village under its coconut palms and find *great art!*"

Our views, in fact, were near enough the same. So next morning he was in the Wisnu Store, buying the best *kains* and cloth as presents for the little girls. There remained only the terms and our signatures.

On our return to Djakarta we went our rounds in search of official blessing on the contract. At the Foreign and Information Ministries all went well, but when we called at the Education Ministry we received a shock. We went in together, but Schang was at once ushered out again to kick his heels very audibly just outside: and I was left face to face with the Secretary-General and a couple of Denpasar officials, together with Indrosugondho, the official from this Ministry who had headed the dance-group which had gone to Colombo. Without preamble they tried to force me to accept Indrosugondho as my "fellow impresario", while I protested it was not in my competency to do so and disturbed them by saying that I knew other Ministries had other candidates. Then they, excited, perhaps, or plainly threatening, said that the present state of affairs might lead to the breakdown of law and order in Bali! But all I would, or could, do was agree to talk with Indrosugondho later, for I had heard pleasant things about him. This whole move I regarded as an attempt at a *fait accompli*, an attempt at a checkmate without enough strength being there to back it up.

Then Schang entered, and for fifteen awkward minutes I became translator between them.

The key figure, however, was the Minister of Finance, Dr. Sumitro, without whose prior signature mine would be worthless. He not only had to approve the contract, but he had to sign a transportation guarantee appended to it. But Sumitro, who had lived four years in New York and had known me since 1945, had long seen the value of such a tour, and had agreed to sign. We actually overtook his car on our way to his house, he taking his children for an airing; and forthwith he stopped and scrawled his signature to the latest draft which I held against the dashboard. This further baffled Freddie Schang in his appreciation of Indonesian officialdom. That evening we both signed, too, and thenceforward the Balinese were due to open in New York on September 15th, after a short tryout in London.

After dinner we went to the house of the Subardjo family, where a programme of Javanese and Sumatran dancing was being arranged, for the idea had always been that if this first Balinese trip was a success, in the following years other groups should go out from other Indonesian islands. It therefore seemed a good idea to show Schang some dancing other than Balinese.

Very late that night at the hotel a boy brought me round a fat envelope, the contents of which purported to explain the curious incident at the Ministry of Education that morning. Enclosed was a copy of a so-called Letter of Protest, signed by the Sumatran journalist in Denpasar, together with a Balinese who had recently come to my house, I thought as a friend, and whom I had helped seek contacts in Singapore where he said he wished to take his own group of dancers. These two, in the name of one defunct and one moribund dance club in Denpasar, demanded the right to inspect and control all dancers who left Bali to go abroad. They used much of racial sentiment, and warned that the contract which their Finance Minister had just witnessed could only enrich "one person". My informant added that this libellous concoction had been officially handed on to the Palace Secretary. Copies of this charming document, I was to observe, had been sent not only to the President, but to the Parliament and Students' Association, as well as to the thirteen toughest young nationalists in Bali. The signatories hoped, quite clearly, that one or other of the latter would stop me in a manner that they themselves did not dare.

I sighed loudly and read the thing out to Schang.

166

"Just a couple of boys who want to go along, too," he commented with a grin. And then: "Is it serious? D'you want to tear the contract up? *Can* you push it through? I've got to lay out tens of thousands of dollars, don't forget—better for me to know now."

"It'll go through. This effusion stems from about half a dozen people only—but one of them, I'm afraid, is highly placed. I'm up against a noisy and very unscrupulous little clique. Fortunately the President and most of the people who count are on our side."

And next morning early, when I saw him off, he said, "This project is going to die another thousand deaths—I feel it."

"Perhaps I shall be one of them, Freddie."

"You'll pull it through, as I said last night. See you in New York September 8th. Good Luck!"

And he was off on his way to drinking water again, to his Paul Klees and his New York.

9

Preparations and Politics

*

My own overwhelming desire now was to rush back to Bali,
because the threats being made in Denpasar might as
easily be directed against Luce as myself; but first I had
to attend a somewhat comical meeting of the no less than five
Secretaries-General interested in us at this stage. The meeting was
presided over by a jumpy Palace Secretary, who seemed honestly convinced that bloody murder was about to flare up in Bali, and more
particularly in my compound in Kaliungu.

He handed me first a letter he intended sending to the Denpasar
Government, suggesting pacifically that since conditions were so
critical there, it might indeed be better for representatives of Denpasar's cultural organisations to accompany us abroad.

I replied: "*If* things in Bali are as bad as you think, I want to get
on a plane at once and go to my wife, who is now alone there. And if
things remain bad, I could perhaps agree to taking with us *one* trouble-
maker from Denpasar. With all respect, though, I believe it is a long
way from Denpasar to Djakarta and this threat is very largely a
bluff."

To which the Palace Secretary replied: "There have been one hundred and eighty murders reported officially in Bali during the last
year. They were not in bluff." He was genuinely a very worried man.

The letter, therefore, was sent. But since the intrusion of even one
of our Denpasar enemies could disrupt entirely the spirit of family
which governed our group, I resolved to fight this solution up to the
point of actually risking my neck. So, since the Palace Secretary had
no constitutional authority, I determined to visit at the earliest

opportunity the Ministry of the Interior, whose proper concern all law and order was, and whose Minister was a very old friend, Dr. Rum.

Meanwhile, some steps forward were taken at this high-level gathering. The office of Ruslan Abdulgani was made my one channel for operations, and would disburse all the money we needed. This would avoid struggling for the impossible: a joint and unanimous decision of five Indonesian Ministries. Then the Ministry of Education put forward their candidate to be my fellow-impresario, and the Ministry of Information countered with theirs. Here complete deadlock occurred. So, hoping to squeeze one official out of our budget, and one more dancer in, I suggested that national sentiment would surely be happier still if I went abroad with *two* Indonesian chaperones —and added that I hoped that *both* the candidates mentioned would go with me—but as Government "Directors-General" on behalf of their respective Ministries, and therefore outside our group's budget.

Finally, these eminent officials decided that I must fly back to Bali in an Indonesian Air Force Dakota with a top priority: and I was given two escorts. These were Suprapto, who was excused from his radio station for a few days, and a certain Balinese student who had formerly represented in Djakarta two Denpasar cultural organisations, and who had no respect at all for the signatories of the notorious Letter of Protest.

But in the day or so before the next Air Force plane left, I found time to call on Indrosugondho, with whom I had a most cordial talk, for to my delight it turned out that he was a dancer, musician and painter, and only most reluctantly an official. He was soon to leave for Bali himself, to "test the atmosphere" there; so I told him briefly that I thought Denpasar was trying out a most unpleasant bluff on the Palace Secretary and all of us.

Lastly, I went round to see Dr. Rum at his Ministry, and when he heard our difficulties he wrote out a most lucid letter, which he addressed to the Governor in Singaradja, with a copy to Denpasar, giving me his fullest support. In my eyes, (taking a correct official view for once), this letter was a valid order, whereas the Palace Secretary's note of compromise was well-meant, but irregular.

Islam Salim, who was hard at work in Djakarta learning Mandarin and now expecting to leave for Peking very soon, wrote me one final letter of recommendation to Lieutenant Tantra, at present an officer in the Indonesian Army, but formerly the most feared and active nationalist in Bali's resistance to the Dutch. I then felt fairly well armed.

But on arriving home, so far from finding a desolate compound, I found Luce sitting safely and peacefully in our open house, sewing and stitching while she chatted with Rantun and Budal, a young girl who had succeeded Agung as our laundryman, Luce with her own skilled hands sewing on the hundreds of sequins of many colours to the velvet collar of Raka's Legong costume.

So first we went to see the acting police chief for the whole of Bali, and a younger officer, commanding the police in Denpasar alone. But both these men said confidently, indeed somewhat indignantly, that law and order were being easily maintained.

Next, we drove to Singaradja in the north, up eighty kilometres of rutted, mountainous road, zigzagging and sliding around bends over a surface buried in inches of soft, silent dust, passing through tall forests and ragged coffee plantations, till we dropped abruptly down past unbelievable rice terraces into the hot sea plain around Singaradja. We called on the Governor, a Javanese, on the Resident, a Balinese, and when they had listened to our tale, the Governor, a handsome and gentle man with grey, curling hair, commented dryly, "But surely this sort of thing is quite normal. Human beings are always jealous of one another. Here it is much more explosive, perhaps, because we still have our colonial experiences in mind."

Then on the way south again, our student escort asked us to stop on the mountain road and led us off through a vegetable patch to a simple wooden hut, where we found the renowned leader of Balinese resistance, Lieutenant Tantra himself, popularly known as Pa' Poleng, the Piebald Father, his former revolutionary *nom de guerre*.

He read Islam Salim's letter. Then he smiled and promised us that "he would rub the head a bit" of one of the signatories of the protest letter and use his influence to see that all went quietly and well. This group could do much for Bali and Indonesia, he said. But then he added, in a serious voice:

"But remember—the head of our Government in Denpasar, friend

Sutedja, feels just the same way about Gianjar as I do." He looked at us all in turn, with unblinking eyes. "None of us must ever forget what we suffered at the hands of the former regime—and even now we must always be on our guard against their machinations."

We saw Pa' Poleng again several times before leaving Bali, finding him the type of young revolutionary who compelled respect by his sincerity. He had wide-open, uncompromising, straight eyes; was wiry and thin; rode in no comfortable car but was content to lead a Spartan life in the Army, using an older jeep than mine, and setting an austere example to his men.

The other group of nationalists we met through the manager of the People's Bank, Ida Bagus Pedada. Their leaders were two intelligent, subtle men, named Widja and Mantik.

Though Widja used his influence in Denpasar, Mantik quickly became our adviser and friend, driving up to Pliatan most Sundays to eat with us and watch the rehearsals. We were sorry not to have met him before, for his brain was acute and fearless, while his tongue could cut like the spur of a fighting cock.

Indrosugondho arrived in Bali a day or two later, and after drinking tea with us in Kaliungu, and after we had watched him talking with the Pliatan club and strumming on their metallophones, comparing their scales with the Javanese, we saw how fortunate we would be were an artist such as this to accompany us on behalf of the Government. He told us, though, that nothing had yet been settled.

Before he went back to Java I told him the results of our political delvings, hinting that reports exposing this little bluff would soon be on their way to Djakarta. Indrosugondho listened quietly and was silent; but from the amused expression in his eyes I knew that he had already come to the same conclusions.

We now became too busy to heed any politics or intrigues, too everlastingly at work to have time to reflect on any role played unconsciously against a backdrop of the drama of Bali's social evolution. And though we were becoming more and more tired, and daily summoning the old Javanese woman from behind the village barber's hut to come and massage us, we were so impregnated with the music, so gladly feeling the responsibility of building up and dovetailing and

171

concentrating the loveliest of the dances for Western eyes, that in our isolated world we were thoroughly, if ephemerally, happy.

We now had exactly the forty-four dancers and musicians to which our contract limited us. Our gamelan had been cut to twenty-three, but, as we had feared, the Kebiar reserve for Sampih, Gusti Ngurah Raka, failed us. After fetching him and losing him again several times as soon as he had returned home, the Anak Agung and I drove over once more to his distant village, walked far down muddied precipices and with a guide clambered across a fast-flowing torrent by stepping-stones that were invisible and treacherously smooth under the muddy water, and for which our feet groped prehensilely. After this little adventure we ascended a high, vertical bank, and entered a spacious but empty compound, where a child told us in a thin, piping voice to wait while she sought her father.

At length the dancer came, and we asked his wife to join us as we sat talking in a small *balé* of wood painted blue. And for the last time we related to both of them our need for a Kebiar dancer. He answered, saying he would come. Then I turned to his sullen wife, who owned the rice-fields and had borne him five children, and she answered sourly, "I bow always to my husband, Tuan."

So, for three more days he rehearsed with us, and his melancholy face warmed a little. Then again he went home, and after a week, a classic letter reached us through the post.

"Respected Tuan," it read. "On account of the disease of madness which sometimes affects my father, and because there is need for a man in this house, with this letter I hereby cancel the going abroad of my husband to dance." And that was the end of him.

Another younger pupil of Mario's danced once or twice in Pliatan but our doctor found that his lungs were tubercular. The important Kebiar and Bumblebee roles were thus still without a reserve for them.

As to the programme, it was now as full of action and entertainment as was legitimate, and so condensed that in a normal month's living in Bali you would not see such varied and good dancing. I was sad only because time forbade my including Kakul's Djauk dance. In it, Kakul, on feet as light as air, faced a solo drummer and did a quite incredibly rapid, feinting dance *at* the drummer. It was breathtaking, but an inseparable part of a long Djauk entry.

The Kaliungu "office", meanwhile, quivered with life, too. We sent London and New York painted sketches of the set we required, a Balinese gateway, pencilling in the exact proportions. We wrote and sent out notes for the script to be used by a mistress of ceremonies on the stage apron. We sent programme notes concerning each dance. We made a plan stating the room accommodation required for us all, including kitchens, utensils for cooking, rice, meat, vegetables and exotic spices. Columbia Artists were undertaking all this for us. And then, more than a month after our contract had been signed, came the long-delayed offer from Sol Hurok, whose secretary had mistakenly sent it by sea mail. The stamped envelope I sent back to his office to prove that we had not deliberately done this to him. We felt sorry for the secretary. . . .

The costumes were coming along well. Luce was now, with the help of friends in "Perti," a very awake Balinese firm in Denpasar which made fine *kains* and sarongs, supervising the final tailoring of traditional Balinese jackets, like high-necked black mess jackets, one of which was being made from warm material, one from thin cotton, for each of the thirty-three men in the group.

Only one clothing drama arose, but Tjokorda Oka survived it, though for a time he feared he had lost eight hundred *rupiahs* of money to pay his workmen. The Tjokorda, a most honest man, apparently lived in torment for two days after losing this money, and prayed to the village Barong to help him find it. He suspected the thief to be a man who had wandered suspiciously near him while he bathed in the river one evening; he searched this villager's house violently and in vain, but in order to scare him kept uttering publicly the most horrible threats of vengeance. Two nights after his loss, he awoke to hear a dreamlike voice bidding him go down to the river and look by the bole of the tree where he had left his clothes while bathing that day. He dressed himself hurriedly, lit resin torches, took his servants to the river's bank with him: and there the money was! Next morning he came to us, mightily relieved, to tell us his story, and he added, "*Beh!* Our's is a powerful Barong in Singapadu. I prayed for its help, and it helped me. Now I shall make special offerings for it and give the village a Barong Play."

On yet another level we were travelling round to all the *Punggawa's* offices and police stations, getting letters of good conduct for each man and woman in the group, while the Denpasar Immigration Office was preparing the passports, and the whole group had come down in instalments to be photographed in the town. On a table in my house was a pile of American visa application forms nearly a foot high, for every one of us had to fill out a three-page questionnaire, and all this naturally became our task, too.

In Denpasar, too, we had discovered Dr. Angsar, a young and modern physician, who cured Luce's old complaint after discovering her allergy. He now inoculated and vaccinated all of us, and coped with our two casualties. For Serog, our invaluable old clown, had a horny growth creeping over his eyes, and this old peasant dared to enter the hospital and have both his eyes operated upon, not even losing his humour—which kept his ward in a state of quite dangerous laughter—when his eyes were bandaged and he was blind for four days. His was an example of courage and trust; and when he had recovered, he confided to us that his ambition abroad was to buy a set of false teeth—he owned but one stump and could not chew his *sireh*.

Then one day the Anak Agung said to us, "This Gusti Oka—according to our Balinese custom she should not go with us. She will defile the company."

"What's the matter with her, Agung Adji?" I asked in surprise, for Gusti Oka was the pretty leader of our Djanger.

"She is *sebel*—unclean. She is more than twenty years old and has never menstruated. Often she looks swollen and sick. She may not enter a temple, strictly speaking, for fear of desecrating it; and of course no man would think of marrying her."

But Dr. Angsar injected hormones into her, and in about a month she had soiled her *kain* for the first time to the amazed delight of her whole family.

It was outside Bali, however, that my main worries were now centred. In the first place, the London try-out date just didn't materialize. Since the K.L.M. charter had to be paid three weeks in advance, and its date had to fit in precisely with the London run, we were faced either with losing our charter or arriving in London to find no theatre ready for us—for we could not finalize the charter's date

174

till the London theatre was found for us. This was a situation that was driving me frantically to telephone Djakarta in the two half-hours a week when such phone connection existed—at a time when all good officials were taking their afternoon nap.

Then, just when things were moving to their climax in Bali, another press campaign started up in Djakarta. This time three papers in the political group opposed to President Sukarno were sniping from their gutters at us, and I was sickened and furious and quite unable to do anything about them from Denpasar.

So, when once again I was called to Djakarta this time to meet my Directors-General finally elect, Indrosugondho and Sutarjo, I was only too glad to jump into the first plane, intending to visit these foul newspapers as well as settle the K.L.M. charter. But, as I said to Luce, the first night I was at the Des Indes I would put through a long-distance call and I would speak to Anthony Hawtrey, the director of the small, artistic Embassy Theatre in London, who had had experience of the Javanese Dancers in 1946. It was already July 7th when I left Bali. . . .

Directly I had dropped my bag in the Des Indes I booked the call to London for the following evening, and then jumped into a Ministry car and drove to Indrosugondho's small bungalow, where I found him with Sutarjo, a tall, heavily-built man who wore spectacles and a black Moslem *pitji* hat. Sutarjo told me he was then trying to help Suprapto escape from his radio station so that he could get on with handling the group's insurance and baggage. Indrosugondho, as the senior of the two, would sign the K.L.M. charter agreement, and early next morning the three of us called on the K.L.M. office, asking them to wait patiently for a final charter date till I had spoken to London.

That evening the English voice of Anthony Hawtrey, made tinny by the great distance, came through clearly. First I told him of the project, adding that my cousin Joan could show him all the publicity material he needed; this group was 100 per cent better than the students' troupe of 1946: was he interested? Yes, said Hawtrey; and if he could get a West End theatre, since the little Embassy Theatre was being repaired anyway, wouldn't I prefer that? Obviously, I replied—but don't get too big a theatre—this is an intimate show. How long could you play in London? he asked. We were wanting a week in

Paris and a week in London, but Paris is hopeless in August; so we want two weeks between August 25th and September 6th. Good! came his voice shrilly. I'm pretty sure I can get either the Princes or the Winter Garden Theatre. Anyhow, confirm by cable and keep in touch, said he: but it's a deal.

So I walked out of the booth on air, stopping on the dining verandah at the table of an ECA friend, where I said, "Andy, I've hooked a deal in London with six minutes' telephoning. I can't believe it."

On the following morning it so happened that the newspapers smearing me quite excelled themselves. One of them published a filched copy of my Foreign Ministry contract, protesting at such "enormous" wages being paid to a foreigner. Another predicted that all the profits would disappear into my pockets. Yet another hinted darkly that it was incredible how this one miserable white man could twiddle the Indonesian President and three Ministries round his little finger.

I therefore went in search of some of my Secretaries-General to ask them to explain publicly that two Indonesians would now be going with, and over, me to save national face; and I also wanted it made clear that the Balinese venture was merely a first experiment, which, if successful, would lead to Javanese and Sumatran groups going abroad in subsequent years.

There then followed one of the most extraordinary weeks of my life. Though I realised that this was more than a mere personal attack on me, being rather a tragic and unpleasant symptom of Indonesia's social evolution—which in turn was but one facet of all Asia's nationalist revolt—I had never felt more frustrated and sick at heart.

For my one "official channel" now dried up on me! During four critical days I tried to speak with Ruslan Abdulgani, to ask him to make the statement I needed. And for four whole days he either locked himself up in his house or held himself incommunicado in his Ministry, mysteriously refusing to see me. Meanwhile, more jealous officials from Denpasar arrived in Djakarta, where they again started whispering in the ear of the Palace Secretary. . . .

On the fourth evening, when Abdulgani was still in his retreat, in desperation I called late at night at the private house of the Palace

Secretary himself, who then and there hissed at me that I had misled the President about the situation in Bali; that no *one* official channel had ever been agreed upon, and that each and every step I took must be taken with the full concurrence of all the five Ministries; that I must never presume to darken the Presidential Palace again.

So I went at once to the Secretary-General of my own Foreign Ministry, Dr. Darma. It was then eleven o'clock at night, and Dr. Darma, a most industrious man, I found lying in his pyjamas on the floor of his living room, reading the current *Economist*. I told him my dilemma—that I needed a statement made by the Government, that Ruslan Abdulgani was invisible, that the Palace Secretary had forbidden me to go to the Palace. But he replied: "You must see the President, obviously. Try to get an appointment at the Palace tomorrow and say that I support you." Having said which he rolled over onto his stomach again and continued his reading.

But next morning, while once more I lay in wait at the Ministry of Information, Ruslan Abdulgani suddenly manifested himself.

He was cordiality and normality itself. And from his office we telephoned to the President and I was actually in his presence an hour later. In a most embarrassing interview the Palace Secretary, specially summoned, was informed by the President that he understood nothing of these underground, artistic Balinese politics. But any public statement—well, that was in the province of Ruslan Abdulgani.

But when I returned to the Information Ministry, Ruslan said: "Later on, when the whole group is in Djakarta en route abroad, we will make a full statement."

I said: "And what of my name being dragged in the mud day after day in the mean time?"

"Ignore it," said Ruslan. "It is a compliment to be attacked by such people."

"But you are a Secretary-General and racial sentiment can't be used against *you*."

"Ignore it," he repeated.

I said, "*You* know the truth of the matter; the ordinary reader doesn't. It's always me, the foreigner, who gets it in the neck. The

Government says nothing because it's beneath its dignity, and my enemies in Bali only see what is published in the papers. Even Izak Mahdi, my closest Indonesian friend, was puzzled and spent hours discussing the whole problem with me last night."

"I can't forbid you to call on these men," said Ruslan, "but my advice remains the same: ignore them."

I went that afternoon to the office of one of the gang against us. "I'm sorry, friend Ruslan," I had said, "but I want just *once* to attempt to tell them about what we're doing."

But the interview I found tragic in its racial implications. The columnist was a tall youth, handsome and neurotic, and he asked to hear the whole story. He listened, his head jerking nervously up and down, then said, almost hysterically, "The President has absolutely no right to meddle in things like this—he has acted quite wrongly. And you yourself are now associating with such contemptible political figures that you are automatically suspect—muddied with their dirt."

"Leaving aside your malicious abuse," I replied, "the President only *recommended* this project, and hasn't it struck you that if I'm working for an objective I *must* work with the persons who are in the Government?"

He changed his ground.

"Anyhow, you're being paid far too much—and we object to your calling yourself an expert on Indonesian culture."

I answered quietly, "I am receiving about the same pay as a Second Secretary at the British Embassy. As to the word 'expert' I loathe it, never use it, and am not responsible for the Foreign Ministry's nomenclatures. But they don't describe me as an expert on Indonesian culture."

With disdain in his eyes he strode lankily to a filing cabinet and flung a photostatted copy of my contract on the table.

"Read it!" he said.

I read out, "'Technical Expert on Cultural Relations and Information for Countries Abroad.' That means I'm called an expert on *channelling* this country's culture to countries abroad."

He snatched the purloined document from me, furious and ashamed, for he had published my contract in his column without properly reading it. But reasoning with him, alas, was hopeless; he was

178

tormented with suspicions that might not disappear until his grand-children's time.

I reported this interview to Ruslan, who, seeing at last that I was serious—for after all, if no-one in the Government had the moral courage to defend me merely because I had a white skin, it was as good as inviting one of Bali's hoodlums to add me to his list of "enemies of the Republic" to be patriotically shot in the back—seeing this, then, Ruslan did now agree to allow his Information offices in Bali to publish a statement to protect me. But, on talking this over with Indrosugondho and Sutarjo as we flew the length of Java on our way to Denpasar, a day or so later, they said simply, "We're now a political football between the President's group and the group who hate him. *Ja, sudah!* That's all there is to it!"

Arrived in Bali they paid their respects to all the local authorities, and calming statements went out through the local Information offices and over the radio. Then we all went to Pliatan, watched the rehearsals and the last costumes being made, and within three days the two Directors-General had returned to Java, where their families awaited their news anxiously.

Soon after they had gone, the Speaker of the Indonesian Parliament came to Bali and asked to see our dancers. But with him came not only Anak Agung Gdé Oka of Gianjar, but Sutedja, too. After the dances Sutedja came forward cheerfully, smiling and misleadingly friendly as always when we met in person, and together we discussed the Bumblebee Dance. He, like many of the young moderns, was curiously Puritan.

"Don't you think that during the flirtation the male dancer comes just a *little too close* to the girl?" he asked.

"How many centimetres apart would you like them? We'll measure 'em with a yardstick if you like," I replied. And we both laughed.

Yet seriously I was perplexed how best to explain to him that people abroad might find it strange were two bees to flirt with several yards between them; nor could I usefully inform him that the one part I had contemplated cutting from the Kebiar was that where Sampih flirted with the drummers—this short sequence, of humour to the Balinese, had caused more than one spectator to ask me whether Sampih was not, perhaps, just a little bit—er—queer? Yet Sampih

179

was the most natural of young men and such a suspicion could never have entered a Balinese head.

Every Sunday the Nationalist leader, Mantik, with his friend Nyoman Oka, came and ate with us in Pliatan and watched the training and packing and costuming and filling-in of forms with friendly admiration. Nyoman Oka, had we had the fortune to have met him earlier on, we would have tried hard to take with us as our manager, for he spoke admirable English.

It was the forms, though, that nearly defeated us. Though the Immigration Office moved en bloc one day to Pliatan and worked right through the entire group until each passport was filled in and ready, the three-page American visa application forms were our nightmare. An idea of our difficulties can be gathered from considering just one question.

"How old are you, Agung Adji? What was the date of your birth?"

He thinks solemnly for a while, turning to his brother for assistance, trying to calculate by asking his brother how old *he* was at the time of the *puputan*, the mass suicide, in Denpasar in 1906. Then: "I must have been born in 1902."

I start to fill this in, but glance at his passport and see there the year 1897 given as his year of birth.

"But Agung Adji—your passport says you were born in 1897!"

"*Masa!* But that cannot be true. I do not feel that old today. Truly, it must have been 1902.

"Oh, all right. Maybe they won't notice anything. Or maybe we can change the passport later. Now, what month and what day?"

"*Adoh!* Is the day of the month necessary, too? How should I know? How should any of us know? Who keeps such dates in Bali?"

And when we started composing dates, we found that eight out of the first twelve men said that they had been born on December 12th for this was a lucky month and a date of good omen. . . .

On July 25th Luce and I moved up quietly to Pliatan, this being part of my "end play", my strategic withdrawal. We had sold our house in Kaliungu; we had found a buyer for the jeep, who would receive it on the day we left; we had rented the garage for another year, and the furnished room at the end of it we made over to young Pudja and Tompel, leaving money for them in the bank so that they could clothe themselves and continue their schooling; to each of the servants we gave four months wages and presents, but our dear Rantun and Budal came with us to the *puri* in Pliatan. It was sad, this sale of our house. But in our absence we feared for its safety.

The group, too, now concentrated more and more inside the *puri* walls. One of the metallophone players had reported an armed band near his house at night, and though I thought this a wild story and most improbable, I suggested that the outlying club members sleep in the *puri* if they wished, and this they did, gossiping on the rehearsal verandah floor till the small hours nightly, wrapped up in their blankets. They thus acted as guards for the costumes, which would have been irreplaceable had anyone destroyed them at this stage; Luce and I, in fact, slept in a well-roofed shack with all the costumes beside us, sharing our room with some gigantic rats, and delighted with the Anak Agung's gift to us of a new cement lavatory, so modern as to possess everything except a door. Ten crowded days among the men and women of the *puri* we spent, waking as the cocks crew immediately outside our windows, hearing the rhythmic pounding of the rice each morning, and on our porch daily were the three little girls, chattering and squealing and joking, while Luce helped them fit their costumes, sew their smart new *kebaya* blouses, and fold their *kains* tidily in the Javanese way for travelling.

On the last day of July Suprapto arrived to take over. The group were to sail on August 7th, though we had carefully spread the tale in Denpasar of a later date; and they would go on board in Singaradja, being taken north in Indonesian Army trucks up the Kintamani mountain road, thus avoiding enemy territory, Denpasar. Luce and I were flying a day or two earlier to Djakarta, for the K.L.M. charter was still not synchronized, and I was almost ill with worry about it.

For three final days we rehearsed in Pliatan, and then it was finished. The show then ran one hour and forty minutes precisely, or two hours with the one intermission. If they rehearsed any more, they would be in danger of becoming stale. They were ready for the Djakarta palace, ready for London.

On our last day, while the club packed their costumes and the gamelan, and we our own belongings, a young Frenchman, Louis Guerin, walked into the *puri*. He was from the *France Soir*, he informed us, and could he take some colour film for television use in Paris? Alas,

M. Guerin, we replied, you see that we are packing up. But we sent him to Saba to take his pictures there, and he gave us some Paris addresses of impresarios, for we hoped to meet there.

Then we handed over to Suprapto, urging him always to work through the Anak Agung, pointing out the few troublemakers whom we knew of in the club, asking him to watch over the masked dancers with special care, for they all were older men and came from outside Pliatan itself. And hating to go, already depressed at the thought of missing the music of water in the rice-fields and the everyday beauty of this richly-blessed island, we tore up our Balinese roots on August 4th, 1952, after two years and three months of living there, taking with us two of the Anak Agung's *bebek tutu*, the smoked duck, to eat with Luce's family in Djakarta.

At the President's palace, the arrangements for our dancers were simple. On Independence Day, in an all-Indonesian programme, they would perform two dances on a stage built around the base of a giant tree on the palace lawn; and if the President so desired, a full dress rehearsal would be given on the night after. As I left the palace one day, the eye of the Palace Secretary lit upon me.

"And is it settled—who goes along with you?" he purred.

"Why, Indrosugondho and Sutarjo, *two* persons of Indonesian race," I said. "Not *one* as the President's original letter suggested."

"Hah! But what of my letter permitting one or two of those others from Denpasar to go along too?"

"I don't know. I know only that we have the forty-four dancers and musicians required by the contract. We found no lack of law and order in Bali, so maybe it wasn't necessary for those others to come along. They never approached us."

And "Check!" I whispered, under my breath. But the next move would have to be 'Mate.

Then I telephoned Hawtrey in London again, and he told me that the Winter Garden Theatre was available and that the decor was coming along nicely, designed from our sketch. Couldn't I come on ahead, he asked? Impossible, I replied. Well, never mind, everything looked all right, but nobody in the Indonesian Embassy knew anything about the theatre or Balinese dancing.

182

On my last trip it had been decided that I must look after the group in Djakarta, and I had sent an authority to the Embassy in London to carry on the negotiations with Hawtrey, based on our previous correspondence. I had even phoned the Embassy and gratefully heard that they would guarantee to look after us, although the notice was indeed rather short. We had sent cables setting out our accommodation and food needs, asking primarily for the whole group to be in one warm hotel near the theatre, and for two large rice meals a day. Now, suddenly, we received news that the Indonesian Embassy possessed their own impresario, one de Marney, and that Hawtrey had withdrawn.

"What can this mean?" everybody seemed to be asking me.

I told them that I'd spoken to Hawtrey only the previous evening, and he'd said all was going well. De Marney must be one Derrick de Marney, who was making films, when I last knew him, from an office in Bond Street. I advised doing nothing that could embarrass the Embassy at this late stage, saying that in London we'd soon find out what was wrong.

On August 12th Luce and I were at Tandjong Priok harbour, waiting on the baking hot docks amid the garbage and bustle of the Javanese labourers for the ship from Bali to come in. Not till well after midday did we climb up the gangplank, running into the arms of the Anak Agung, who shouted with pleasure and told us that all was well, the gamelan, the costumes, the baggage, all safe thanks to our excellent manager, Suprapto. With the Anak Agung and the little girls squeezed into a jeep from the Ministry, we led the way to their hotel, whose garden actually adjoined the front drive of the American Embassy. Amid great excitement they settled in, sitting out at first on chairs on the lawn, not yet daring to walk out in the traffic-jammed streets of so great a city.

The British visas were a modest labour compared with the American. But thanks to the personal interest of the ambassador and the patience of Vice-Consul Josephs, after two whole days of interpreting, fingerprinting and signing, the forty-four American visas were safe in the fat dispatch case of Suprapto. Then the tailor who had earlier flown to Bali came in with their suits, fitting and altering where necessary; then came the suitcases ordered by Suprapto; and then came, too, my opportunity for handing over my accounts of the Bali work of the last months.

But though all went well with the group's expenditures in Bali, my own Ministry now vexed me by again becoming cautious vis-à-vis the Parliament. They asked me to relinquish my salary while abroad, for it would prevent press attacks (it didn't!) and make their position impregnable in the face of aggressive members of the House. I agreed; but had I known that they would have desired this, I would surely have added another clause to our contract with Columbia Artists, for in communal Balinese style and as a member of our Pliatan family, I had rashly allowed for no producer's fee at all. And *then* they asked me to sign a note to the effect that I would try to pay back the whole Government subsidy. I reminded them of my former offer, but they said no, this was a better plan, for it would again guard *their* position from criticism. I signed, therefore, with a resigned shrug; for as I pointed out, what could I do if the Balinese were to ask to come home after the first few months, or if no fat fees came our way from films or television?

Then came the palace performance before the whole Diplomatic Corps and all Indonesian officialdom on Independence Day; and on the next evening, before the President, the American Ambassador, Ruslan Abdulgani and other staunch allies, we played the programme through exactly as planned for the theatre. At the end of the performance, the President wished the group God speed, complimenting and thanking us graciously for our long-suffering work.

However, there was already reason for our backers to show confidence. Not only had I heard from Freddie Schang that the sale of tickets was building up very encouragingly, but *The New York Times* had devoted an editorial to us, hailing our advent as an historic landmark, as the first east-west cultural mission. And Colin McPhee had risked his reputation by backing us indirectly through a long article that had appeared under his name in the *Times*, also.

Then came the last minute rush. Only now did our Directors-General receive their appointments which would guarantee their financial independence while on tour; and we were helped, in this contradictory Djakarta arena, in a score of ways by friends who were members of the same party of people as the newspapers which were vilifying us! At the very last moment we collected the hundreds and hundreds of artificial frangipani, hibiscus and *tjampak* blossoms, made by some Djakarta Chinese especially for us. And at five o'clock on our last afternoon a tea party was given for the whole company in the palace gardens, where the President allowed himself to be photographed with the three Legongs, his adopted daughters. After the tea, Luce and I tried to express our thanks to the President for his help, and for the encouragement he had given us all along, standing behind our idea like a rock.

Came the dawn of August 21st, and we were all at Kemayoran Airport, sitting, waiting, gazing out at our chartered Skymaster which yesterday we had carefully helped load with our own hands. With us were our oldest allies, Ruslan Abdulgani, Dr. Subardjo, Harjoto from the Information Ministry, Tjokro from my own Ministry. The Anak Agung gave me a nudge.

"I trust that Hanuman is now content," he said. For in the last months the club had nicknamed me Hanuman, after the heroic White Monkey prince who came to the aid of Rama in the Ramayana epic, and who always achieved the impossible in a flash of time.

At 7.45 a.m. we filed slowly into the plane, followed up the steps by a microphone from the Djakarta radio. The stewards explained to the Balinese how to fasten their seat belts. They were offered peppermints. The little girls sat just in front of us, solemn-eyed and for once almost too excited to chatter. They stared out of one window, waving to Anom's father, Dewa Gdé Putu, who was watching the take-off. He was staying behind to guard the families of the group in Bali while we were away. The plane door clanged to. As if on a reflex, the Anak Agung, Luce, Sampih and I looked at one another; Indrosugondho and Sutarjo, too, smiled their relief. And the plane, piled high with gamelan instruments and costumes in crates and our noble protective Barong, lumbered thunderously down the runway.

The mouths of the Balinese formed silent "Peace on your Stayings." I turned to Luce with fingers crossed. "Checkmate!" I said.

10

London Interlude

*

When Schang had originally insisted that we try the company out in London, Luce and I had been delighted. For London is my city and I wanted to introduce my Javanese wife to my friends and show her, not the Tower of London or Westminster Abbey, perhaps, but the ballet at Covent Garden and the restaurants of Soho. She, now, had to meet my family. As for the Anak Agung, on hearing the news he had said, *"Pantas sekali*—just as it should be. Now I shall have the pleasure of seeing John's country, too."

The four days flight from Djakarta was very tiring indeed. Suprapto and I were soon weary performing the impossible feat of disentangling more than forty Balinese at each night stop and finding them their hotel rooms, while they waited in the lobbies with infinite patience and a trusting helplessness. And arriving in Damascus on the third evening, hot though it was and gale-tossed over the desert though our plane had been, we made each man dress up in his European clothes, for the tying of ties and the use of braces and waistcoats were all quite new to them. Tjokorda Oka fussed noisily around old Serog, grinning, saying to us, "When Serog went to Paris in 1931, Tuan, nobody showed him how to untie his tie; so he kept it on, night and day, for over two weeks."

But it was the air sickness that was defeating us, and as I looked at the children, my heart quailed at the thought of having to ask them to rehearse the very day after they arrived—but our opening night was to be only one day later. They had become a wan, miserable collection, unused as yet to the poor imitation of Balinese food which the K.L.M.

stewards tried hard to supply. And our flight over the burning hot desert before Damascus, where for hours the plane had sideslipped and shuddered and swooped aloft like a drunken feather, had vanquished practically all of us. Little Raka had lain pale and quiet, her head in Luce's lap; Sangayu, the Oleg from Sayan, had bandaged her eyes so that she should see nothing; the big-eyed Anom had been unable to eat anything at all, looking very pathetic, and Oka, the strongest character of the three, had sat with me and we had been quietly sick together. If adversity sometimes unites, it can also, if air sickness be its form, disintegrate, and especially if the victims are Balinese dancers.

Touching down for an hour in Rome, we had a most cordial and friendly welcome from the Indonesian younger generation from the Embassy there, and later that same evening the Balinese managed to rouse themselves a little when the red-roofed rash of London suburbia began to reveal itself below, and from the men the expletive *Beh!* kept exploding forth, as mile after mile of endless city rolled into view.

It was seven o'clock on the evening of this fourth day when our plane came to rest at London Airport. One or two photographers clicked agilely around the children as we carried our handbags across the asphalt to the waiting room; and after a while they filed off through the immigration offices, dragging themselves along with apathy, their stomachs still queasy, the ground treacherously unlike the feel of the warm wet soil of Bali. In between peering over official shoulders, interpreting, there was time to exchange a few words with de Marney, who with a handful of officials from the Embassy, was there to meet us. An hour or so later, still in a daze, the whole party of us were seated outside in two long buses.

"All aboard, Suprapto?"

"All aboard."

And the buses drove off through an endless succession of suburban shopping streets. I was quite lost, and moving up to the driver asked him where our hotel was. Was it far from our theatre, I asked him?

"Far from which theatre, would that be?"

"The Winter Garden—in Drury Lane."

He laughed out loud.

"You'll be a little matter, I should reckon, of about thirteen miles

187

outside of Drury Lane," he said, capping this with the news we were to live in some students' settlement in Surrey, just outside the fringe of greater London. I had an awful foreboding, yet rather than say anything to depress the Balinese further—they were now silent, hungry, feeling as lost as if on another planet—I just whispered this news to Indrosugondho.

He threw his hands up, exclaiming beneath his breath,

"Who can have chosen such a place? But perhaps it's good there. Let us wait and see."

It was about nine o'clock and the late summer dusk was falling when the buses came to a halt in what seemed in the gathering gloom to be a little red-brick street at the back of nowhere, and I felt something akin to panic rising in me. But at once a friendly, energetic man with a wide smile of welcome on his face, came out to meet us.

"Ah—that's fine," said he. "*Here* you are at last! The food's all waiting ready for you. Should they go to their rooms first, d'you think, or would they prefer to eat straight away?"

Numbly, trying to suspend judgment, I asked the Anak Agung which would be best. Some of the group still felt sick, he said, and they all were dirty and wanted to bathe.

"They'd prefer to go to their rooms first," I said.

Now our welcomer was that type of man who is full of honest enthusiasm and the scoutmaster instincts. He was frighteningly well meaning. But his establishment, as I soon remarked with black despair, though admirably suited to impecunious students of foreign races who were already acclimatized to the weirdities of the humbler British way of living, repelled and drove the Balinese back into themselves, so that dumbly, hopefully, they looked to us, to anyone who might help them. In this strange new world they asked but two things: that they sleep and live warmly and all as closely together as possible, and that their bellies be swiftly filled with good rice.

Instead, quite innocent of the rebellion he was rousing in their peasant hearts, this cheerful fellow started off to show them to their rooms. He managed, he said pleasantly, some dozen or so houses around this neighbourhood, only the dining room and club rooms being in the house outside which the buses had stopped. The Balinese, who only with difficulty had become inured to the good hotels along the K.L.M. route, were now to be split up, two men on the ground floor of one house, three men in a room on the third floor front in a house a hundred yards away, four in another room three streets off, and so on. The nine girls were all in one room.

It took two rebellious, darkening hours, ourselves carrying their bags, to persuade most of them to walk to their rooms; and when they had been brought back again at about eleven o'clock to the dining hall by a now freely perspiring host, none of them could swallow a mouthful of this, to them, strange-tasting food. The Anak Agung shook his head gloomily.

"John, we've got to find rice for them," he said, "If it goes on like this . . . *adoh!*"

None of us ate that night. It was long after midnight when we stopped trying to sort out the last unclaimed suitcases left on the pavement outside, and drove a last insistent photographer from troubling the sleep of the small girls. Then we searched till we found the room of Indrosugondho. He was sitting on the edge of his bed, smoking, running his hands through his rather long, thickly wavy hair. There was little enough that needed saying.

"Tomorrow," he said. "Tomorrow I shall go to the Embassy."

We bade him a good night, Luce and I climbing two or three flights of uncarpeted stairs to our own sparsely furnished quarters. We talked, going over our situation over and over again, till well after five, and rose at seven: and again there was no eatable rice.

The buses came and a hungry collection of Balinese were driven in to London, right up to the stage door of the Winter Garden. Indrosugondho, with a strained face, left at once in a taxi for the Embassy, and when de Marney arrived we told him that we had no idea who was responsible for our feeding arrangements, but that we simply must get rice, lots of hot rice with the vegetables and meat and chilis we had cabled for, and within a few hours. He went out to look for help.

That whole day we spent in the theatre. An outfitter came around and sat efficiently in a gangway seat, measuring the men for their raincoats; and before the rehearsal could start, the cast mooched round the stage, looked in at their dressing rooms, sat with hands in pockets in the front stalls, examined the curtain, quietly discussed the decor, which was a fair reproduction of the gateway design we had sent Hawtrey to copy.

After a while de Marney returned with the tidings that only fifty yards down the street there was a Greek restaurant that would have a hot rice meal ready by three o'clock. So, while we waited for the girls to come back from an expedition with Luce to search for umbrellas, raincoats and strong shoes, he and I sat down for a technical discussion.

The contract I was unable to see because it was at the lawyers'. But I learned that we were to play eight times a week, including two matinées. I asked whether we could play only seven times, and cut one matinée, as we were doing in New York, but in London eight times was normal and the children would have to go through with it.

There had not been time to locate Hamish Wilson, who had lit the "Javanese Dancers" in 1946, so de Marney himself was going to do the lighting. He had a plan in his head, he told me. He wanted to start off in bright sunshine, and because the last item in the programme was a Barong, (which according to the books he had read, always took place in the evening), the last scene would be almost dark. Thus the performance would pass through a Balinese day, from sunlight to dusk.

I pointed out that this production was set exactly according to the programme viewed by Freddie Schang in Bali. The second dance, for example, the Monkey Dance, had to be done in near-darkness. The Barong finale used a comic and noisy story for which I wanted the lights full up.

Next I asked about the script for the Storyteller. Had they found a suitable Indonesian girl, I enquired? No—Mrs. Subandrio had been able to find us no pretty or charming girl, he said. But they had improved my script—they'd cut it around a lot and it was much better now. Remember, I said to myself, de Marney only heard about our dancers a few weeks ago. Be patient with him. How could he have any inkling of the sweat and blood that had gone into the making of this thing?

It was a strangely unreal day. The stage crew arrived, and two amiable young women moved up into the girls' dressing room to learn to help Luce. The wings were filled with irritating Indonesian shadows who flitted they knew not where, save certainly in our way.

And confident in all white villainy, they slipped into dressing-rooms and appeared on the stage, whispering into the ears of our friends rumours of anticipated foreign trickery and exploitation.

Meanwhile, I asked the Anak Agung where north was, for otherwise we could never have orientated and directed the dancers; to the Balinese dancer, left and right do not exist, only west or east, nor is there an upstage or downstage, only a north and south. Then we placed the gamelan on the stage. The acoustics were fine and I ran the programme through, myself running about the auditorium, from back of the stalls to the balcony, listening, observing, positioning, explaining. The crew were good, picking up the lighting cues quickly, and on the curtain calls de Marney helped me with advice. For more than two hours we worked. By then the Balinese were muttering about eating, and the restaurant owner came in just at the right time to tell them that their food was ready.

I looked around the auditorium, conscious again. I found two ballet critics, old friends, Lionel Bradley and A. V. Coton. I discovered Peggy van Praagh and Maggie Dale, who had run around from Sadler's Wells to see what new exoticism had been brought to town; Baron, our photographer from Bangkok, with an elegant redhead, was enthusing over the show as I counted the dancers off the stage on their way to the restaurant. I was still preoccupied, so that when a shadowy figure came up to introduce himself I nodded vaguely at him and said, "Twenty-eight," still counting.

The figure pounded a stick on the floor.

"Perhaps you did not hear my name," it said, very distinctly. "I am Sol Hurok."

"Oh God—I'm so sorry about your offer, Mr. Hurok. Please stay for the afternoon. Let us talk of the tragedy of your delayed letter."

The Balinese ate and came back rather more happily. The rehearsal went on again. De Marney complained bitterly that he had no time to fix the lighting, which was only too true. We were walking through the whole show for his cues this second time, and we were trying out the male Storyteller. The Balinese only half understood what was being done, and there were frequent checks. Critics, correspondents, the curious, meandered in and out in the back stalls.

The Storyteller was put into Balinese costume and looked soft and apologetic. In place of my script, sentimental phrases such as "our three precious maidens" tumbled from his lips. There was no time as yet to remodel it. Let it go on. Later, perhaps, we could inject something of Bali into him, something earthy and real. After arriving only a day and a half before an opening night, who could be blamed? On, on, on, till the buses honked outside as dusk approached, waiting impatiently to take us away again.

It was quiet, ominously so, in the bus that night. Indrosugondho sat silently near us. The little girls were slumped over, asleep. Whenever we caught a Balinese eye, we smiled back feebly, for their appeal was so obvious and heartrending. In the dining room the children sat wretchedly before the table. Anom had to be shaken gently to keep her awake. And again none of the little ones could eat. Anom started to cry quietly. Her face taut, Luce led the children and girls up to their room, two streets away, where she stayed with them, herself on the verge of tears.

The Anak Agung and I sat once more in Indrosugondho's room. I said, speaking slowly in careful Indonesian, and near mad with thinly controlled rage: "Brother Indro and Father Agung—it would be without use to criticize or complain. Maybe we should never have been encouraged to come to London. Maybe we'd have done better to have stayed longer in Djakarta and flown straight to New York. All I want to ask of you now is this: *if* I can find a hotel near the theatre and move all the girls out of here tomorrow as a *fait accompli*, will you support me?"

"Allah! If you can but do it!" said Indrosugondho, "I was myself weeping just now when I saw Anom in the dining room tonight."

"Then things *might* start improving tomorrow—but back me up! This insult to our people, I will stand no longer. Nor do I believe that all the hotels are full up and too expensive."

Before the midday meal next day thirteen places had been found in the Grand Hotel in Southampton Row for all the girls, for the Anak Agung and Sampih, for Luce and myself. On the following day we would look for rooms for the rest of the group. And at once the news spread like fire among the Balinese, whose faces again became happy, so that we were no longer so ashamed. Hanuman was up to his tricks again, they told one another.

That afternoon de Marney worked steadily at his lighting cues and I continued to shudder at the un-Balinese, romantic lines of our Storyteller. Backstage, the artificial flowers were being fixed by Luce and Gusti Kompiang, as in Bali, into the headdresses; the windows were sealed to prevent draughts; the crew were jumpy and worried. Already our First Night was upon us.

But the Balinese, who have natural theatrical instincts, played up gallantly at their opening performance. The gamelan cascaded its fugal tones out into the auditorium, loud and magnificent. Not a mistake was made, and not a seat was empty. And after the show the ambassador gave a reception and champagne buffet on the stage.

There, for the first time little Raka, with Sampih and the Anak Agung—the latter had developed on an instant a warm and dominating stage personality—sipped at the cup of fame. But they accepted it coolly and easily, with their intrinsic dignity and charm. But below the surface enthusiasm of our guests and friends on the stage that evening, and beneath the loud voices of the pompous and the glitter of the socially minded and the gorgeously dressed, the small hand of a Legong caught at Luce's arm, and a little singsong voice chanted up at her, "Ibu Luce! Mother Luce! We go home soon, yes? Home to our new hotel? Tonight, yes?" And indeed that night saw the beginning of a happier era for the children.

They were delighted with the Grand Hotel. The nine girls had four rooms, the Legongs closest to us. They fitted two in a single bed with ease, explored their tiled bathroom, squealed with delight at the hot and cold running water, so that nightly Luce and I had to listen before going to sleep, for as like as not the children would be all three playing and chattering and shouting in their bath after the show at one o'clock in the morning, waking up the other guests. They loved the flow of the water running over them, for it reminded them of the streams in which they bathed at home.

On their first morning they started to snare the hearts of the hotel servants and management. They "Oooh-ed" with delight as the lift sank downward, and "Ooosh-ed" with mock consternation as they were swept up again afterwards. They carried little umbrellas, wore black velveteen-collared grey coats over their Indonesian *kains*, with always a tiny blossom or two in their well-brushed hair. Everywhere they went arm-in-arm, commenting, discussing, laughing, asking us questions all the time. In the dining room they were soon at their ease, after the second morning ordering their own breakfast by pointing to the menu and giggling. This all-important part of our family was happy again.

But most of the men dancers and the gamelan club were doomed to disappointment. Though Indrosugondho and I, accompanied by Madé Lebah to represent the club, found rooms for them all in Bayswater, they were never permitted to move. Only now we were told, defensively, evasively, that the other rooms had been paid for two weeks in advance. It would be too expensive to move everybody. So now the club was divided into the privileged and the unprivileged, and for the first time in over two years they saw my hands tied in such a way that I could do nothing to relieve their distress.

One day we came down to the theatre to find Freddie Schang sitting in one of the dressing-rooms, a wad of press cuttings in his hands. He had flown over from New York to see the production on a real stage. He jumped up and we greeted one another warmly; but then he stood back and looked at me. "For heaven's sake, Johnnie, what's wrong? You've a fine success on your hands—I've been reading your reviews —but you look about as happy as a ghost."

Over a table in Soho our troubles came out reluctantly, one by one.

"I've always loathed officials, Freddie, even when I was one myself. But the worst of the breed I've found yet are the pompous little creatures who think they know something about art."

"Come down to hard cases—I don't get you."

"*I* don't get it. We've been here a week and I'm damned if I could tell you who is even meant to be responsible for what. Tony Hawtrey, with whom I was negotiating till a couple of weeks ago, is nowhere on the scene. De Marney, in addition to acting as our local manager with no previous briefing, is also having to help out with food and heaven knows what besides. He's trying to do the work of three blind men. But there are these bevies of helpful officials to trip over in every conceivable corner. *No one* could produce theatre discipline on this stage. Why—d'you know what one of the leading metallophone players said to me last night? He said, '*Never mind, Tuan John—in another few days we'll be on our way to America.' They*, my dear Freddie, are pitying *me* in my own country!"

"Well, don't let it get you down, boy. We'll soon have 'em all right when they get to New York. Tell you what—I'm going to propose a toast—that the three of us work together and pledge ourselves to remember always that this company is only as strong as the three little girls." We drank, and felt better.

That same afternoon my father came up from the country to meet his daughter-in-law, and before the performance he came backstage and greeted the Anak Agung as a kinsman, too, and with old-fashioned manners, shook the hand of each member of the cast. Though he knew little of my troubles, this simple act of his helped to bring another family motif into the club, who were impressed at this courteous, white-haired old gentleman.

In the second week things improved a little. De Marney helped practically by arranging two rice meals a day at the nearby Greek restaurant and by preparing a list of salaries, strictly according to Equity rules, and though the original gamelan members objected to dancers who had only recently joined us being paid more than them, who had worked for two years, they were all now able to go around the shops, looking for things to buy, with their eyes especially out for gold sovereigns and for bicycles to send home.

Then the leading dancers of Sadler's Wells came to see the Balinese dance, and the Balinese were invited to Covent Garden to watch a dress rehearsal of *Sylvia*. When we brought little Raka down onto the vast Covent Garden stage to be photographed with Margot Fonteyn and Frederick Ashton, they asked the Anak Agung what he thought of the *Sylvia* ballet.

"Please tell them," said he, "that we are so happy to see that people in the West use stories of ancient gods and goddesses and spirits of the woods for their dancing, just as we Balinese do. This ballet reminds me of the tale of our Raja Pala—the Raja who went down to bathe in the river and found some heavenly nymphs swimming in his own pool."

"And then what happened?"

"He fell in love with one of the nymphs and stole her *kain*. When he revealed himself, all the other nymphs snatched up their *kains* and flew up into the heavens. But the one whose *kain* he had stolen cowered down into the water, hiding her nakedness. And he wouldn't give it back to her till she consented to take him as her lover."

"Charming," they both said. "Please tell him we find his Raja Pala story quite delightful."

Though time did not permit any of the Balinese to travel outside London, we were able to hear some of their views on this city. They couldn't begin to understand what English people lived on—where were their rice-fields and coconut palms, they kept asking? They went to the zoo and hated it—it was tiring to walk and the animals smelled horrible. They grabbed at their own photographs in the newspapers, and condemned all save the few which portrayed them with modest smiles not showing their teeth, or in perfect dance poses. They were happy when Mrs. Churchill came to see the show and wished them well on their tour, but the Anak Agung was crestfallen to learn that the Royal Family was in Scotland, and that he therefore would not be able to shake hands with Queen Elizabeth.

On one of our last afternoons there was a coming together of officials from Indonesian Embassies throughout Europe, who wanted us to bring the dancers to their capitals on the way home. But when we were pressed by these eager young men for dates, our replies were diplomatic. If the Balinese were not homesick—and some of them wanted to go home already!—and if spring in Europe coincided with the end of the American tour in the warm South, there was nothing that we personally would prefer than to bring them to Paris, Rome, Copenhagen, Brussels and Amsterdam—where the best dance audiences were. But November to March were out of the question.

"You'll let us know by November?" they kept insisting.

"Everything depends on the timing," we replied. "Midwinter weather in northern Europe would endanger the health of old Serog, to say nothing of the children." And with that they had to be content.

On the last night in London, while packers were taking down the scenery in the theatre and putting the costumes into theatrical costume baskets, ready for our take-off next morning, two of the younger dancers came up to me, clearing their throats, smiling, intimating that they had been a month now from home, and—well, hadn't seen a woman for a long time. As their elder brother, was it not my English duty to do something about this for them?

So, after tramping the streets for hours while they stared and commented *dadong*, grandmother, or *djegegeg*, not pretty, till I was walking almost on my knees, we at last bumped into a pair of buxom and expensively-dressed wenches who stopped the Balinese open-mouthed in their tracks. Some little while later, as I sat drinking the girls' champagne in a kitchen, while two bedroom doors were left slightly ajar, I was called upon to carry out my most intimate role of interpreter yet. And thanks to this satisfying interlude, two of the Balinese who still lived out in the wilds of Surrey, left England with feelings of rather more warmth.

When the plane was flying over the Irish Sea next day, I made them a brief speech.

"Don't blame anyone for the chaos in London," I said. "They had only six weeks to prepare for us, and in America they've had three months. Tuan Schang asked me to promise you that there will be no photographers in New York at all for two days; no rehearsals for five days; that the hotel is near the theatre, and warm; and that there are sacks of rice there awaiting you."

And with that we tried to compose ourselves to sleep.

11

Balinese in America

*

To the casual pedestrian walking along the pavement of West 45th Street, the old Hotel Schuyler wore its habitual chromium-entranced air; but to its normal theatrical clientele, the entire building seemed to have been invaded and taken over by the Orient. Our group's fortress, in fact, consisted of the top five floors of the Schuyler Annex, where Balinese in sarongs and pyjamas cooked and gossiped and lazed, commenting and speculating upon the unbelievable city of New York.

During the first days they kept close to the hotel. They had found thirty sacks of specially milled rice with meats, vegetables, hot spices and cooking utensils, ready and awaiting them there; and their first days were spent in rest.

But while they stayed at home, we went swiftly to work. On the first morning I went to Freddie Schang's office, which occupied most of three specklessly sanitary floors in the Steinway Building, and where there was indeed a fine collection of Paul Klees. He took me to his room, summoned his secretary, planked down a cheque for our first week's guarantee, and said two things—that now the group were in business and I had better go around to the National City Bank on Fifth Avenue to open up an account there. Then, with his jaw coming forward a pugnacious two inches, he said that we'd find his company strict until they got their investment back—the pre-opening expenses to cover the rent of the theatre, the making of the set, union fees, bonds, salaries, publicity and heaven knows what besides came to well over thirty thousand dollars.

Next I went down to look at the Fulton Theatre, just off Times

Square, and only two blocks walk from our hotel. It was a perfect small theatre, seating just under a thousand people, intimate and admirably suited to our show. The dressing-rooms were well equipped, the building was warm, there was no orchestra pit to separate the audience from the dancers, and on the stage Dick Senie, the designer responsible for our Balinese gateway set, and for the flaming draw-curtains figured with a pair of fighting cocks battling in midair, was supervising the hoisting up of the lighting paraphernalia.

I learned here, too, something of the wages which the theatrical unions had won for their members. The forty-four of us were dividing our weekly guarantee equally, and we all received about half the wage of our unionized wardrobe mistress. . . .

Then came the work with our press agents. They were "the tops", Freddie Schang had said. They were exceedingly active, we soon found out. Life, in fact, after the first 48 hours, developed into a necessary and daily hell of photo calls and broadcasts and television appearances. But first we gave a lunch at Sardi's to the press of New York, cooked by Luce in Sardi's kitchen and served by the Anak Agung in person to the representatives of the big dailies and magazines. This was most wearying work, but it founded for us a nation-wide publicity, and the lines in front of the box office soon reflected our efforts.

Our opening night brought a packed and curious house. The public, though friendly enough, were wondering how authentic was the material they were about to see. Dr. Ali, the Indonesian ambassador, came down from Washington with his wife and a smile of officials. He showed a rather anxious hopefulness. The Balinese, though, feeling more atmosphere in the New York decor and lighting, and a greater physical nearness to their audience, and observing, too, the professional stage crew around them, led by Tom Skelton, our stage manager, who began to learn the Indonesian language within a day of meeting them, excelled themselves in a truly brilliant performance. From the first shimmering crash of the opening chord of music, we played to an audience sitting on the edge of their seats. The overture quite literally stunned them. Then the little Olegs danced to their more lightly tinkling orchestra, and before the audience could wonder much at their stylized, exotic patterns, the Olegs had vanished and the

Monkey Dance chorus was chanting raucously on a dark, moonlit stage. The utter difference and unexpectedness of the Monkey Dance won over even the most bored habitual first-nighters, and by the time Raka made her first entry as a gilded and scarlet bumblebee, her glittering antennae aquiver, the audience was solidly with us. During the intermission I wandered through the foyer, and nearly burst with internal satisfaction to hear the mixture of delight and astonishment with which New York was receiving us so far.

And it was exciting after this first night to have our stage as crowded as Times Square, with ecstatic and beaming enthusiasts congratulating us all, with officials from the embassy now proud of their countrymen's success, with ballet dancers and actors and actresses being photographed with Raka and the Anak Agung, with the ambassador, with us, while the team from Columbia Artists congratulated not only us, but themselves, for already they could sense a friendly press reception and hope that their financial outlay would be returned in due course.

At length the children escaped to remove their make-up, and bundle themselves into their new shoes and fawn-coloured socks, into Indonesian *kains* and *kebaya* coatees of silk, gaily flowered, and wrap themselves up in their neat grey overcoats. Then together we walked through intrigued crowds who smiled and waved at the Balinese, frustrated by the Tower of Babel, and climbed into buses to drive to the Park Avenue penthouse of one Matty Fox. Matty was an astute financier and friend of Indonesia, and tonight he was opening his home to the entire cast, to embassy officials, to as many dancers and persons from the kindred arts as we had cared to invite. He provided mounds of rice and curries and Chinese vegetables for everybody, and there, pecking at her plate, I was delighted to find Alicia Markova, with Lucia Chase, the director of Ballet Theatre, who had written to me long ago in Bali, asking about my work there, of which she had already heard. And then suddenly there strolled in Martin Flavin, white eyebrows ajutting, and with an elegant cane, crowing loudly over our success, which he had so long ago prophesied. To complete our family circle were three well-groomed young gentlemen, affecting crew-cuts and dark flannel suits, those hall marks of the better-known American universities, whom we with difficulty recognized as the former hands on the brigantine *Yankee*, who, in shorts and sarongs, had stayed with us in our Kaliungu house—none other than Jim Ford and his friends once again.

The Balinese, ever practical, seldom romantic, finished their food and were at once ready to leave. So, most of them departed with their full bellies to a place where they could at leisure discuss the luxuries, quite meaningless to them, of such an American penthouse.

"*Beh!* This man seems to be very rich," said one of them, stepping into the elevator. "Perhaps he would care to give us an electric generator for the club?"

It was long after midnight when we went cruising around in Jim Ford's car to look for the first editions of the morning papers. We pounced on them near our hotel, thumbing through their pages with a painful excitement. Ah! Here we were! Lots of notices! And, by all the gods, another editorial about us—this time in the *Herald Tribune!* They were wonderful reviews, all of them. That day each of New York's nine major dailies raved about us at length. Their generous acclaim was exhilarating, yet I remember that Luce and I felt a certain humility, fearing that it just could not be true, that this was just too much to expect. But perfectly true it was. When the weekly trade paper, *Variety*, with its own esoteric and incomprehensible jargon, appeared that week, the "Dancers of Bali" were proclaimed in bold black and white print, wholly comprehensible, as the first Broadway hit of the 1952 season.

Before very long, though some of them naturally worried about their families in Bali, they began to enjoy parts of their strange new existence. Jim Ford, as a start, took them on a sight-seeing bus tour. They were all speechless with surprise, I remember, when I pointed out some "Bowery bums," (echoing our guide,) who had added casually: "Look! There are two drunken women on the pavement. Drunken women are rather rare here—you are lucky to have seen them," all in tones that might be indicating some unusual specimen of the local fauna. And when we came to the Empire State Building, the Legongs, who had been taken up once already by a too energetic newspaperman, said quite simply and sincerely to Jim, who couldn't believe it, "We want to stay in the bus. We have been up already, thank you."

When they shopped they thought sensibly in terms of their family and village needs at home. Accordingly, in their never-ceasing search for gold, they continued to hunt after English sovereigns, which they assured us had a purer gold content than American dollars. They would drop mysteriously into pawnshops and jewellers, slowly articulating the formula: "I want gold money, please," while smiling and waiting. One or two of them meant to buy typewriters for relations at home who were officials or clerks; many of them wanted sewing machines for their wives or themselves, though they hastily dropped this plan when they reckoned that similar machines sold just as cheaply in Djakarta. Madé Lebah wanted to buy motor spare parts. Gusti Kompiang was saving every cent, he said, to buy a rice-field, and I only hoped his cock-fighting enthusiasms would not undermine this wise decision when he returned home. The Anak Agung quickly set his heart on a Chevrolet station-wagon.

As soon as their desires were specific, however, we found ourselves in a vicious financial circle. After our tremendous reception in the press, I had told them they were a great artistic success. This they saw to be true, for every night at the theatre, for seven solid weeks, the house was sold out, even to standing room. The Balinese, then, possessed themselves in patience for two or three weeks and then, very realistically once again asked whether they could not receive more money.

"John, we are a success, are we not?" some of our grumblers of old would ask.

"You are indeed."

"And every night the theatre is full—all the seats are sold?"

"That's quite true."

"And the seats are very expensive?"

"By our ideas, yes."

"Well, couldn't we be paid more?"

And then in the unwilling Indonesian tongue, I would have to try to explain about the $34,000 of pre-opening expenses which had to be paid off first, and about the modest cost of running our show, which at the Fulton was $14,000 a week. But, with devastatingly simple logic by their village standards, they would reply, "*Beh!* But in Pliatan we played for Americans and only for two hundred *rupiahs*."

Or, "Why should the decor cost us 75,000 *rupiahs?* In Bali we could build a large guest house for so much money."

And to relate these two standards was not possible. Trying to keep patient, I scribbled on piece after piece of paper in many a hotel-room conclave, showing them that our share of clear profit in addition to our guarantee would come in fast only after about the tenth week; while to reap the full benefit of our particular contract, we should be prepared to play for five months in America, and hope to make a film in the New Year. But the thing that silenced the grumblings a little was when Richard Rodgers came to pay a generous tribute to our visitation from the true South Pacific. When he had gone, I said to one of them:

"That man writes successful musical shows for the theatre. He is very rich."

At once they replied, "Hah! If he is a success and rich, why aren't we the same?"

"Now listen carefully. Our show could run in New York for perhaps four months to a full house. We have 970 seats to fill. Tuan Rodgers has four or five shows playing at the same time, in theatres twice this size, and some of them play for four years in New York alone, and one of them has played for ten years in America without ceasing. If you want to be rich in this country, that is how hard you must work."

They were dumbfounded, and at last, mercifully silent. Thanks to the authors of *South Pacific*, peace descended again on the island of Bali, and the Anak Agung was no longer so pestered. He had recently been so irritated by petty troublemakers that he had threatened to resign.

"In Bali these were ordinary people," he would say, "but here they are *lice*." And when really moved, he would swear at them by leprosy, the curse of the Great Sickness. "*Sakit Gdé!*" he would explode.

But he and I both knew in our hearts, that these grumblings owed part of their origin to the suspicions lisped into our dancers' ears when in London.

As the group found American friends, they began to move all over New York; and the further afield they wandered, the worse it became for Suprapto and me. It was nothing for the two of us to be dancing like dervishes at the stage door, jumping in and out to look for truants who had meandered off, watchless, and failed to think of the theatre in time. On occasions, a dancer or two would go to their hotel rooms and just sleep, and go on sleeping, only to be discovered by a perspiring manager still asleep in their rooms after the show. It was lucky that we had trained plenty of reserves.

Foremost among our friends now was Colin McPhee. Like the few others familiar with Balinese art, he had at first had natural mental reservations as to the quality of the group we were bringing over. But having seen our rehearsals from the wings, and having met so many of his former household at the Fulton Theatre, he again became a member of the Pliatan club. He, with Margaret Mead, even showed us some old movies in which we glimpsed the prewar Legong of Saba, and saw Sampih dancing Kebiar as a nine year old, before a then slender drummer, our same Anak Agung.

Every sort of invitation now came our way from friendly Americans, who could not understand how tied we were to our routine; and there were distinguished visitors galore who came to see the dancers in their dressing-rooms, only the barrier of language, in fact, preventing the Balinese from being nightly mobbed by their fans.

In the bedroom of Indrosugondho and Sutaryo we were opening the first official mail from Indonesia. We read it avidly, but in silence, then looked dumbly at one another. It contained not one word of praise, not one syllable of thanks, but a bald cable from the Foreign Ministry forbidding any lengthening of the tour in America. There were press cuttings too, sent by friends. The presidential newspapers reported our triumph; but in three papers I learned that I had treated the Balinese like my slaves in London, that I had pocketed all the profits, and that Indrosugondho and Sutaryo spent all their time on pleasure jaunts.

I asked them in weary disgust, "Who can have sent these lies to Djakarta?"

They answered tactfully, "London is full of friends of the President enemies. These newspapers all quote London sources."

There was one other yet more revealing press cutting. It reported that according to rumour a coup d'état was being plotted against the President. If this were so, our group might again become politically so "hot" that our friends in Indonesia, in their uncertainty, might not dare to defend us.

I now fell ill with a streptococcal infection, brought about, I was told, through sheer exhaustion, and was ordered to take a train with Luce soon afterward to rest for a couple of days in the New England home of the Lashar family. But though the Lashars only woke us up to feed us, I found myself so restless and irritable just before curtain time that I would phone the Fulton to be assured by Tom Skelton that all was well and the cast not lost.

When we returned to New York, the pace seemed to accelerate rather than slow down. One night our Storyteller failed to turn up. So Luce, who knew almost every note of the music and each step of the dancing, reluctantly took over at a few minutes notice. Her reception was then so warm, and so easily could she joke Balinese in faultless English, that she was pressed to continue.

Outside our theatre work we had televised in Ed Sullivan's "Toast of the Town" programme, showing parts of the Bumblebee and Monkey dances to an audience of thirty million; and all the time we kept our eyes open for a film. The *Road to Bali* was finished, we knew, and *Fair Wind to Java*, which Dick Tregaskis had spoken of in Bali, was almost complete, too. Our friends advised us to wait till we reached Hollywood on our tour, and to hope for a film in the New Year.

The Balinese, meanwhile, were each continuing to find their own experiences. The Anak Agung went to meet the timpanist of the New York Philharmonic Symphony Orchestra, and came back sniggering contentedly, saying to us, *"Kalah dia!* I beat him!" and related that the American had been staggered—as may well have been the case— at what the Anak Agung had done to his drums.

Sampih was teaching the Oleg to a class of Americans, and his pupils included Michiko, the dancer from *The King and I*, whom he and the Anak Agung referred to as Madé Michiko. Raka, having seen her photograph in countless journals, was becoming conscious of her ballerina status, and when her understudy once danced her Bumblebee role to lighten her work for her, she refused ever again to wear the golden *kain* which the other girl had sullied. Their American dressers, Mac and Kelly, were devoted to the children. Listening outside their door, one might hear a peremptory: "Big pin, Mac!" or "Kelly—slow poke! Come queek, come *queek!*" It was the dressers who established the children's much publicized taste for vanilla ice-cream, which they ate nightly in the intermission.

Old Serog had already been given a complete set of new dentures with Freddie Schang's help, but only on consideration that he never wore them on the stage, which he always wanted to do. For the old man would then simper sweetly at the audience, where before he had grinned and clowned. With his teeth in, he dared not open his jaws for fear they should leap across the footlights into the front row of the orchestra stalls.

The worst life of all was that of our harassed manager, Suprapto. His was the dreary routine work of administering the Balinese, and it drove him nearly demented. Sometimes he would mutter furiously, "What do they think I am? Am I their *budak*, their serf, perhaps?" I never tired of hearing his English which, though very efficient, often landed him, literally, in Dutch. When telephoning a Chinese restaurant, for example, he would invariably start his inquiries for food like this: "Good evening, I am Mr. Su*prrra*pto. I am the Manager of the Dancers of Bali. Have you, perhaps, some flesh . . .?" For in Dutch, the word for meat is *vleesch*. On one occasion I was overjoyed when he ran up to relate what he had just suffered at the hands of a "very brutal laundryman." *Brutaal*, in Dutch, means insolent or cheeky, But Suprapto was conscientious and invaluable to us, and his few temperamental outbursts were wholly justified.

Originally booked for four weeks in New York, our success at the Fulton caused us to extend the season by another three weeks. But between our fifth and sixth New York weeks we had to go out on tour to fulfil certain engagements that could not be cancelled, all in towns within an easy radius of New York.

We left the city in buses, heading first for Boston, and as if to speed our departure a driving blizzard of snow blew through the fiords of Manhattan and we next met the sun when approaching Boston. Accompanying us was our tour manager, Dick Skinner, a plump and gentle man, born and bred in the theatre, enjoying his exotic education.

During the bus trips the children were generally in boisterous spirits. The Anak Agung, however, sat silently, his eyes glued wistfully to the road, sighing after each station-wagon that he saw.

Boston Opera House, then, was the start of our tour, and we played to two packed and friendly houses. In our hotel I shall never forget the masked dancer, Rinda, calm and dignified, appearing in the main lobby clad only in a pair of combinations and an open overcoat, in his hand a bottle half filled with oil, seeking the stairs to the kitchen where we had permission to do our own cooking. The hotel staff straightened their smiles and courteously conducted him below.

Philadelphia was the city where Raka proved her artistic integrity. She danced her Bumblebee dance in the first half of the programme, but inexplicably refused to eat her ice-cream in the intermission while changing costume. In the second half she danced in the Legong, played her Golden Bird role, took her final curtain-calls—and burst into uncontrollable tears. At length Oka explained. The little tot had felt part of her costume coming loose in the Bumblebee Dance and was afraid it had been noticed. She had contained her weeping, however, until the whole performance was over.

In Newark the gamelan members wore flowers in their headdresses, sent them by the children of a girls' school; and in Washington we played before sixteen Ambassadors. . . . We were up the next dawn and on our way to play again in New York that same evening. The girls slept later, and Luce brought them along by a midday plane. We had played seven performances in seven days in five towns and had sampled our first "one-night stands". I sat next to the Anak Agung in the bus and said, "If you want to make money in America, Agung Adji, you would have to go on playing like this for six months. That's what the western ballet companies have to do."

Returned from this tiring week, the company were given an advance out of their future profits. I had easily persuaded Freddie Schang to do this for psychological reasons, though it was not in the contract. Touring was not only far harder work, but by the time I had paid the hotel bills, Chinese restaurant bills, doctors bills and other travelling expenses, there was less pocket money than usual left from the guarantee to divide among them: and the Balinese cared only for the cash in their pockets, grudging each superfluous cent spent on comfortable hotel rooms or on food other than rice and spices.

The Anak Agung, meanwhile, was so possessed by his innocent desire for a station-wagon, that his absent-mindedness was becoming chronic. One midnight he banged at our hotel room door in a terrible frenzy, sobbing out that he had lost his talisman rings. The stone of one came from Bali's most holy temple on the slopes of the Great Mountain, while the other came from the also sacred Peak of Tabanan. These rings held the magic power to protect them all, he stammered. Furthermore, they were only a loan. . . . I dressed at once, for this could be serious, and together we went down to the theatre. We searched for his black jacket costume in the empty dressing rooms, for the rings he usually placed in its pockets just before the curtain rose since they interfered with his drumming The jacket was nowhere to be found. We searched the corridors, groped our way over the entire floor of the stage, lifted up the musical instruments, shook out every costume. There was nothing.

Then we looked through the telephone numbers at the stage door and found our wardrobe mistress listed there. We phoned her at once. She was very sleepy, but told us that the jacket had gone to the cleaners. We phoned the cleaners. They were shut. We phoned the wardrobe mistress again, asked for the name and address of the owner of the cleaners, telephoned him, and he woke up a boy who went down to look in the black jacket's pockets, which was lying on one of his shop's shelves. A long hour later he phoned us back to report that no rings had been found. Then I told the Anak Agung that it was past three and time to sleep. On the next day we would go to the cleaners' place, which was far away, and look for ourselves.

Minutes later, it seemed, a timid but persistent knocking woke me again. I opened our door irritably, to find the round-eyed Anom smiling apologetically outside, and well behind this decoy stood the Anak Agung, still trembling with anxiety, ready for the search again. The rings, he now said, had undoubtedly been stolen by an enemy and had probably been sold already. Thank God we discovered them about one hour later, deep down in the lining of his black jacket on the cleaners' shelves.

"The soul of our club might have been destroyed," said the Anak Agung, "if those rings had been lost."

* * *

Indrosugondho was sick, so Sutaryo, the Anak Agung and I were talking with the Indonesian Foreign Minister in New York. He had come to America to attend the United Nations Assembly. He was very happy at our success. He said he would make a statement when he returned home to counteract the malicious rumours that had arisen from "certain sources".

Then he said, "It is politically important that the group come home through northern Europe and perform there under the auspices of our Embassies in January and February. How do you feel about that?"

I answered, "Didn't we agree that human and artistic contacts were the strongest and best? If you want to politicalize our tour, I think you weaken the strength of the appeal of the dancers. And if the group were ordered to return in midwinter, with all due respect, I would resign as a token of my protest. It would be risking their health."

Said the Minister, "It must be January. Sutaryo has canvassed the group, even to the little girls. They all say that they are willing to visit Europe in January if the Government asks them to."

I considered this. Then I looked at Sutaryo, whose eyes flickered away quickly. This, I could see, was the oblique, but gentle, way of dropping the alien pilot. This Minister had long been my friend and supporter, but new national pride goes far deeper than mere personal friendship. So I said, "I would prefer to resign then. My idea has already succeeded. That must be enough for me."

The Minister turned to Sutaryo—was there relief in his face? He said, merely, "Then the Foreign Ministry will assume all responsibility in Europe for the tour. And whatever you decide to do, John, I shall stand behind you." Smiling, he put his arm round my shoulder.

12

End of his Journey

*

New York was still quite warm on November 9th when we left the city, heading eventually for California. Ours was an impressive departure. Only thirty minutes before the train was due out of Grand Central, 108 pieces of unwieldy baggage were being lined up by a sweating Suprapto on the pavement outside the Schuyler Hotel. The train was as good as lost, moaned Dick Skinner. But, shouting like a drill-sergeant, I mobilized sixty male Balinese hands and the baggage went in higgledy-piggledy—but all of it was inside those buses within two minutes. The express train was only held up fifteen minutes, as the Pliatan club slouched up the long platform, humping on their shoulders sacks of rice, which they stubbornly refused to leave behind.

This was our second and last week of one- and two-night stands, and we had long distances to cover between four cities. On the eighth weary morning our trek across the continent, two thousand miles to Las Vegas in Nevada, began. Good warm weather had been guaranteed us there.

Travelling with the Balinese was seldom dull. When other passengers passed through the train, our Pullman impinged on them like an unseen glass door. They would suddenly find themselves in a brown-skinned coach, where men and girls were sprawled out asleep and snoring, or chatting with one another in an unknown language, while Kakul would probably, in a high oriental and nasal tremulo, be chanting for his friends' delectation some extract from an Ardja play.

For Luce and myself, the journey across the great plains and through the Rocky Mountains was a delight because we could open the door between our bedroom and that of the little girls, and of a morning Raka and Anom jumped into Luce's lower berth, while I joined Oka, and there we all sat wrapped up in blankets like Indians, watching America flash by. The children were so confident that we were heading for warm weather that when we looked out at vast expanses of the Middle West's gritty mountain snow, they were sure it was the hot white sand of a desert.

Our Las Vegas engagement was to last a week before we went on to Los Angeles. That we loathed cabaret work was inevitable. However, our objectives in Las Vegas had been warmth and an engagement that would pay our expensive way across America, and this much the Thunderbird Hotel helped us to do.

And what a town was Las Vegas! Young, raw, the home of the Golden Nugget gambling house of "Western" fame, it looked as if it had erupted from the pink and grey Nevada desert but a few nights ago. It existed for the gambling. In the Thunderbird alone, hundreds of thousands of dollars changed hands nightly at the green baize tables, while the pull-handle slot machines, known as "one-arm bandits," were not only in all the hotels and gambling houses, but in each shop and drugstore to tempt the buyer of a tube of Kolynos to gamble with his change. The currency of the place was silver dollars. And here the Balinese, renowned cockfighters, received official, if optimistic, orders not to gamble.

The weather, which had been promised at a steady 80° each day, was dry and blue skied, but by night very cold—so cold that before going to bed we put saucers of water outside the Motel cabins to freeze, the ice formed by morning persuading the Balinese to wear warm clothing.

California, however, lived up to its reputation. As the train rattled through orange groves and the sun shone forth in a warm sky, we peeled off one layer of clothing after another. At Los Angeles station we were met by a barrage of photographers and a tall elegant lady, blue-grey haired and chic, who carried off all the girls to the hotel in a fat Cadillac, for this was the home of Katharane Mershon, who had lived long in Bali before the war and had helped, with Walter Spies, to choreograph the original Monkey Dance.

I shall always think kindly of the people of Los Angeles for giving our Legong no less than seven curtain calls. It was our record. In New York we had started off carefully with seventeen minutes of classical Legong, and the audience had always given us a glad three curtain calls; so, gradually, I had inserted fragments of the Lasem story, till from seventeen it crept up to twenty minutes, from twenty to twenty-three, and in Los Angeles to twenty-five minutes of pure classical dancing. The children, though, as they received their applause, bowing in solemn and slow tempo together, hands and fans clasped on their breasts, little gilded bottoms of dragonfly bodies emphasized in profile by the hollowness of their backs, scowled over at us in the wings each time the curtain fell, pretending great weariness and irritation at their ovation, but secretly delighted and proud.

The Balinese were quite cinema conscious enough to be pleasantly thrilled at seeing Hollywood. This was to be *the* adventure to relate when they returned home. They clamoured for me to produce film stars on the stage for them to meet, and though Anna May Wong naturally intrigued them, the children seemed to like best the soft-spoken Olivia de Havilland. But if they were impressed by Los Angeles, the city was not without interest in them. The Anak Agung, as "mayor" of Pliatan, was invited to be the guest of honour at a mayors' convention attended by about three hundred mayors from all over the United States. In deep embarrassment, he even whispered a polite speech to them. And although Los Angeles' people claimed to be immune to sensation and accustomed to any impossible sight on their city's streets, when the Anak Agung dressed up for this occasion, putting on a cerise and gold-threaded long *kain*, a jaunty golden head-cloth and a snowy shirt, adorning himself with a kris, the gold- and gem-encrusted handle of which projected above his shoulder, all the denizens of the most modern Statler Hotel fastened their eyes upon him in fascinated silence as he passed majestically through the lobbies.

One day we went out to the Paramount studios to meet the stars of *The Road to Bali*. Having first watched Martin and Lewis for a moment making a comedy film about golf, we found Bing Crosby and Bob Hope running off some brief television publicity shots for the "Road" film which was soon to be released. In a minute the Balinese were joining in the laughter of the technicians at the unrehearsed clowning of Bob Hope, and after a while Bing and Bob looked up and saw the Legongs watching them, and came over to chat. It was a case of mutual love at first sight. The five of them posed together, first the two Americans getting into their Balinese positions, and Bob Hope almost gave Anom hiccups from laughing when he tried slowly, creakily, to make the Balinese neck movement. Then they all tried to put a sarong on Bob in the correct way, while the publicity cameras clicked again. From then on, Bing and Bob were part of the Legongs' family.

It was after this and other excursions that the Anak Agung's cousin, the *balean*, who danced inside the Barong, said to us, "Now that I know how films are made, I dare go see them and enjoy them. I used to think that real events were filmed, and I always felt so sorry for the people who got killed."

Perhaps there were too many stars around—anyhow, here Raka had her one and only real tantrum. The theatre auditorium was vast, and, knowing that the Balinese idea of make-up was that if they looked beautiful to themselves in the mirror they must look beautiful to the audience, I asked Tom to increase Raka's make-up for her, since her features just could not be seen from the back of the audience. Normally each dancer and musician did his own make-up, and Raka, though she was devoted to Tom, rebelled at his work. *"Djelek!"* she cried. "I am hideous!" and she was still weeping as she made her entry on to the stage.

When she came off at the end of the Legong, Tom was in a state of real agitation and Raka was still sobbing. The three Legongs came to our dressing room, where a frenzied Tom made up his own two eyes, one in the Balinese way, one in the modern way. He wanted to convince them. After the final curtain calls, he ran over to the far side of the stage while the Legongs and most of the cast stared at him from the opposite wings.

"Which eye looks bigger?" shouted Tom, kneeling down to face them.

"The left one," they all answered definitely. And this was the eye made up in the Balinese way.

"In that case," said Tom, "Raka is right and the whole theory of modern American dance is wrong."

Which perhaps it is.

By the time we left Los Angeles, serious booking problems faced us, for no clear instructions had yet been given concerning the group's time and route of leaving America for Europe. Indrosugondho telephoned the Indonesian embassy daily, for I told him that if we were forced to be idle, our profits, which were now just beginning to come in nicely, would all be used up paying hotel bills and food.

In San Francisco we had a week of Barong-protected and unexpected sun for our season, and here, too, the Balinese superstition that the 12th December is a lucky day—it may be remembered that eight out of the first twelve of them, when filling in their American visa forms in Pliatan, had claimed their birthday on that auspicious date—won remarkable confirmation. On this day Raka received her medallion from *Mademoiselle* magazine, for what the editor termed her superb east-west cultural exchange work. Luce received her British passport which we had applied for in New York two months ago. Suprapto ended the current "strike" in which he was indulging as a protest against being used as a "serf" again by the Balinese. And lastly, on this same day, a preview of *The Road to Bali* was arranged for us all to see. The movie had nothing of Bali in it, but everybody, and especially the little girls, loved the film. "*Itu* Bob!" they exclaimed to one another helplessly—"That Bob!" Before the end of the tour the children had stolen off to see it twice more, and Anom said, smiling happily, "And we will see it all over again at the Wisnu Cinema in Denpasar when we get home."

At last there came definite news of their return through Europe, and speedily Columbia Artists thought out a plan that would save money and earn them some more, and routed them through the South to Miami, where they could board a plane at least two thousand miles nearer to Europe.

To accustom them all to the idea of being administered by Indrosugondho, of whom they were fond, and by Sutaryo, whom they tolerated, while they all went back on a train to Los Angeles for a Christmas rest, Luce and I drove down to Pebble Beach . . . for the Flavins were at hand again, and now they were offering us their ranch in the Carmel Valley as a resting place when the tour was over. In those wild, wooded valleys and mountains, we gathered, there were no politicians or officials, only pumas, bobcats, rattlesnakes and intriguing gophers.

Christmas, though, we spent together with our family in Los Angeles. Luce and I, deep inside, already felt horribly depressed and frustrated, yet against evolutionary racial processes there was nothing we could do. So we tried to make this, their one American Christmas, a time they would remember. On Christmas Eve Vicki Baum gave them a wonderful party in her Hollywood house. But we were very un-Hollywood and sat on the floor and ate with our fingers, stuffing ourselves with rich white rice and spicy curries, and with prawn crackers which were still fresh from the tins in which Vicki had brought them sealed from Bali fifteen years ago. Then lazily from the floor we watched her films of Bali, seeing the ghost of Walter Spies moving before us as he bathed in the pool of his house at Tjampuang, the house which we knew so well.

On Christmas Day the nine girls came to our room and were given bulging Christmas stockings, each inscribed with their names.

On the following day we went with Katharane to the Walt Disney studios. After first lunching in the canteen, we went right through the various studios. When we left, Raka and Oka chose to be shy and offered limp hands with inaudible good-byes; but when the limpid-eyed Anom gave Disney her soft smile, she unexpectedly enunciated in her clear little voice: "Good-bye, and thank you very much," at which Disney swept her off her feet in delight and hugged her.

That same evening, to add to or to alleviate their frustrations, Tom and I took some of the men to a burlesque theatre in Main Street, where they saw Lily St. Cyr and their first "strippers." The resulting groans and writhings in the hotel rooms that night were pitiful to hear. *"Tjelaka duabelas!"* said old Tjokorda Oka, "Twelvefold calamity!"

By December 27th we were on the move eastward again, this time on a several-thousand-mile trip to Miami. After two last performances there, the group would board a B.O.A.C. Constellation and fly directly to Brussels. Our time with them was running out sickeningly fast.

One night we played in Phoenix, and New Year's Eve we spent playing in New Orleans. Sampih, with Tom, Luce and myself, watched 1953 come in from a restaurant window in Bourbon Street, blowing fatefully at our cardboard trumpets.

215

And so through Orlando in the heart of the beautiful orange-growing part of Florida to the end of our journey—Miami. The Balinese now felt the weather becoming more and more like home, and as we drove from Orlando to the station, we saw a great alligator (or crocodile to them) lying half out of a lake at the edge of the road. We passed endless and oceanwide miles of orange and grapefruit orchards. There were glorious bougainvilleas straggling over verandahed wooden houses, even a stunted frangipani or two, and all was at last green and luxuriant again and made them homesick. Finally, they saw coconut palms growing; and it was when the Anak Agung looked up to see coconuts high above his head once more, and when Oka had woven her first little basket from the young palm leaf, just as in Bali, that our friend smote his broad thigh and exclaimed aloud: "*Beh!* Now I admit that this really is a country!"

Our hotel was near the sea and the auditorium was new and well designed for our performance, and it was good that our tour should end with a bang and no hint of a whimper. We played to two absolutely packed houses, while in front of the box office a milling mass of people struggled to buy returned tickets. As the curtains went up and down for the last times on the tableau of Freddie Schang and our entire company, he having just presented us with a great souvenir plaque with all our names inscribed, it was the end for Luce and me. The packers poured in, old Leo Dupont, our chief carpenter, moodily knocked the scenery down, while the tour wardrobe mistress grudgingly folded away the costumes in wicker baskets that had once again been measured to fit a plane door. We had three days to go.

On one of these days we were invited out to Miami Beach to lunch at the Surf Club. As we drove back to our hotel, I asked the Anak Agung curiously why so many gamelan members were suddenly refusing to sleep in the same room with one of the metallophone players. He replied enigmatically, "Because his clothes are still alive."

After much unravelling I eventually discovered that right here in Miami they had unearthed a *leyak* in the gamelan club! They had detected the demon-in-the-man by the way the fellow snored at night —it was a rhythmic soft whistle, followed by an angry grunting, which the Anak Agung promptly demonstrated to the anxiety of our driver. This snoring had convinced his neighbours that a *leyak's* spirit

216

was escaping nightly from the sleeper's body. This man had long studied black magic, and secret formulae and unholy texts were written down on strips of cloth worn always around his navel. Before leaving Bali the man had sworn that these clothes, or strips of potent cloth, were dead—that he'd given it all up. Now it was clear he had lied. The cloth was still potent.

I said to the Anak Agung, "But you're not afraid of this *leyak*?"

"No!" he scoffed. "He has indeed studied long, but he is a very stupid creature. He could never make a *dangerous* demon."

When an official came down from the embassy to see the group off, we went to the income tax authorities and obtained the necessary clearances and sailing permits. And at last I knew financially where we were. After having paid about 20 per cent of our profits back to the Indonesian Government, the rest I divided quickly among the forty-four of us; but since the group was being ordered to leave at the very stage when our share of the profits were due to roll in—and before we had had a chance to make a film—the Government, in effect, was throwing the benefits of our contract away.

Then came a telegram from Belgium. It was said to give the "protocol" instructions concerning the correct official order in which the members of the group were to descend from the plane on arriving at the Brussels airport. . . .

As soon as this money was in their hands, they went out shopping for the last time. Luce took the three children to buy rubbers and extra clothes against the snow and cold—already they had bought together boxes of panties marked from Sunday to Saturday, some summer frocks and pale green nylon nightdresses—but the other girls would not waste their money on such utilitarian things. With Sampih and the Anak Agung, Tom and I walked round and round the shopping heart of the town, buying airguns, radios, photographs, a film projector and some more copies of our own Columbia Masterworks record. It was at a Miami Bank that the Anak Agung purchased a cashier's cheque on behalf of his family and dependents in the group, to buy for all of them, with the embassy's help, his darling station-wagon.

Came the last thirty-six hours. Amid the potted ferns of the Hotel Patricia I called together the men of the Pliatan club for the last time.

217

In very quiet voices Luce and I took our leave of them, wishing them good luck and a safe journey home. Afterward we spoke again to our oldest friends—to the Anak Agung, to Sampih, to Madé Lebah and to Gusti Kompiang. They were quite resigned to going back via Brussels, Bonn, Paris and Rome—but, ever practical, they wanted to know what advice we could give them.

We reassured them, confidently. I told them of the full reports which Pesik, in the Consulate General, and I had sent to Europe, in which we had detailed their every requirement—the food, the clothing, the hotel rooms, the warmth, the theatres, the guides to assist them. I told them, too, that the embassies would certainly not work under the financial limitations or the timing restrictions which had so hampered us in America. They would be well looked after and Government money squandered if only to prove my fears groundless. Luce and I were also resigned, I said. My old dream had already achieved a success greater than I had ever dared to hope—by their dancing they had built a bridge from the Orient that stood as a lesson to the West in these modern times. Why, only that morning the papers were carrying the news that the National Arts Foundation had voted the Dancers of Bali one of the four outstanding artistic achievements of 1952. It was a miracle, I suppose, that the Government of a country like Indonesia, only three years independent, should have had the vision to allow our plan through at all.

And lastly to the Anak Agung, whose submissive soul we had known so well in Pliatan, I said, "Agung Adji, you may be called upon to dance to a very different tune in Europe, and it may help you to keep silent about our personal friendship. I just want to tell you in advance that you, Sampih, the three children, Luce and myself, will be of one family always. You are no politician, we know. So dance and play where the piper bids you: we shall understand."

On their last evening in America Freddie Schang gave a party at the Shangri La Chinese Restaurant. The food was excellent, but the party was brought to life by a Schang who made little speeches and gave gold bracelets to Raka and the other children, and a silver cigarette case to Sampih and a silver jug of ample proportions to the Anak Agung. Then Freddie danced. He imitated the movements of the Legong dancers. He leapt to take a photograph of Mrs. Volpe, our Miami manager, with a water-squirting camera, and gave the camera to Sangayu; he ran over to put some spectacles on Oka, who could not focus her eyes or eat from her plate with her spoon when she wore them; he slid rubber snakes over the floor, wooden spiders apppeared on the wall, glass ice floated and wouldn't melt in hot coffee and the restaurant became bedlam.

January 8th was the day of their departure. To make things worse, rain poured down in torrents. The plane was the same that had just brought Mr. Churchill across the Atlantic, and it was several hours late. Thus the agony of our farewell was spread over eight hours of waiting in a grey and gloom-filled vestibule. Not only Luce and I were wretched, but Tom, too, was joking in Indonesian to cheer himself up. To the Anak Agung he said, "Now I shall no longer be able to sing in the Barong chorus each night as the curtain goes up on the finale." And to Raka, trying to smile, he said, "You will see me in Bali in five years time, Raka. I'm coming out to kidnap you in true Balinese style." And then Tom and I went out on to the field in the drenching rain to watch the loading of the plane with Gusti Kompiang. Always we were afraid of damage to the gamelan.

Slowly the group weighed in at the B.O.A.C. counter. Commander Dodds had laughed at me when I had suggested weighing the personal baggage. "Couldn't possibly exceed six and a half tons total weight, old boy—they couldn't carry it." But he was wrong. He hadn't met any Balinese. They entered America weighing 4,200 kilos, but they left weighing 6,700—without the station-wagon and electric generator. Each child had gained three or four kilos, and some of the older girls and men had gained more. So much were they carrying with them, that five hundred gallons of gasoline had to be siphoned out before the plane could take off in safety.

Finally, all was ready. We splashed through murky rain across the asphalt and saw them all seated in their places.

"Best of luck to you, friend Indrosugondho. The Balinese are lucky to have you with them. Happy landings, Suprapto—may your patience as their invaluable 'serf' survive just two months more."

And then down the plane Luce and I walked, shaking each Balinese hand. The three little girls were in tears, and our staunch Sampih was speechless with distress. Luce was weeping unashamed, and I, like a coward, clung to my dark glasses. The politics of this parting I cared not a fig for—but with those little girls and Sampih, and with the Anak Agung and that magnificent, life-giving gamelan, part of our hearts were being torn away from us.

"Come quickly again to Bali," whispered our little three. "But *very* quickly."

And so we were standing under our umbrellas out in the grey rain of parting, soaked, dejected, aching, oblivious. This was the bitter price of our success.

"Good-bye little Raka, Oka, Anom," our hearts said silently, as the plane moved over to the runway. "Good-bye Sampih, best of young brothers. Good-bye old Agung Adji and your, *our* glittering gamelan and its perfect music. Take care of them, oh magical Barong —bring them good weather in Europe. Peace on your going! Peace on your journey home!"

A POSTSCRIPT

PARIS, 16-2-1953.

1.

Safe News.

The letter of Jonh and Luse the three of us received with ten fingers spread wide open and with a happy heart, because we had heard news from Jonh and Luse and know how they are now. I feel very unhappy because we have not met for a very long time. Although this is so, my heart will always remember Jonh and Luse.

I ask pardon because I did not carry out my promise that I would send one letter every week. That was not because of my laziness, but because Pa' Ambassador in Roma told us children that Jonh and Luse were now in Paris. Because of that I did not send a letter to America.

2. Now, concerning our journey from Roma to Bon it was in safety and not lacking in anything. It was very lucky that Luse invited the three of us to buy those thick shoes because in Bon there was much snow. I say thank you very much to Jonh and Luse because they brought me up like a child of their own.

On leaving Bon we went straight to Paris. There also we children are well, none of us are sick. Let us hope that Jonh and Luse will come back to Bali as quickly as possible.

Oka,

Thus it is.
Anom,

Raka.

Information

ON THE LANGUAGE, PRONUNCIATION AND CURRENCY, IN BALI AND INDONESIA

Language and Pronunciation

The *lingua franca* of all territories comprising the Republic of Indonesia is INDONESIAN, which is a dialect of Malay, influenced by Javanese and Dutch, and which is still in the beginning of its evolution into a modern, unifying tongue.

In Bali, apart from Indonesia, Balinese is spoken, which is not only a language apart, but consists of a *high* and a *low* language. *High* caste men talking to their "inferiors" use the *low* language; *low* caste men talking to their "superiors" use the *high* language.

PRONUNCIATION:

TJ in Bali is pronounced like CH in Charles in English, but it contains a stronger, deeper dental tone that is more accurately represented by TJ.

DJ in Bali is pronounced like J in James in English, but again has a deeper dental tone that would more accurately be written DJ.

A is generally pronounced short, like U in HUT in English.

E is generally pronounced very short unless accented.

J is generally pronounced Y.

TITLES, ETC.

Pedanda,	Brahmana High Priest.
Ida Bagus,	Brahmana man's title.
Tjokorda,	Ksatriya caste title.
Anak Agung,	Ksatriya caste title.
Dewa,	Ksatriya caste title.

Gusti,	Wesya caste title.
Gusti Biang,	Mother Gusti.
Adji,	Father, Ksatriya or Wesya.
Pemangku,	Non-Brahmana priest.
Tuan,	Mr., Sir.
Nyonya,	Mrs., Madam.
Tribangsa,	Aristocracy composed of Brahmana, Ksatriya and Wesya.
Wayan,	Name prefix of first and fifth-born person of lower caste.
Madé,	Name prefix of second and sixth-born person of lower caste.
Nyoman,	Name prefix of third and seventh-born person of lower caste.
Ketut,	Name prefix of fourth and eighth-born person of lower caste.
Suddhra,	The Lower Caste.
Bli,	Elder Brother.
M'bok,	Elder Sister.
Wo,	Uncle.
Dadong,	Grandmother.
Raja,	One of Bali's eight hereditary rulers.
Punggawa,	Headman of District.
Perbekel,	Head of Village.

ORDINARY SPEECH:

Adoh!	Exclamation of surprise or distress.
Apa kabar?	What news? ("How are you?").
Arak	Strong spirit distilled from the sugar palm.
Balé,	Open-air building, or hall.
Balean,	Balinese herb doctor, magician.
Beh!	Exclamation of surprise, *very* common.
Biasa,	Normal, usual.
Brum,	Sweet pink or white rice-wine.
Bebek tutu,	Smoked duck.
Betel,	Nut of areca palm, pink inside, chewed with leaf of sireh vine, damar gum and lime paste.

Djegeg,	Pretty.
Djegegeg,	Not pretty (slang).
Guru,	Teacher.
Inggeh!	Yes, in language addressed to superior.
Kain,	Batik cloth from Java, normal garment worn by men and women from waist downwards.
Kulkul,	Village drum to summon villagers together.
Lalang,	Tall fibrous grass used for thatch.
Lawar,	Balinese dish of grated, spiced raw meats.
Leyak,	Witch, or spirit, most generally a blood-sucking, flame-dripping female monster.
Masa!	Exclamation, like "Good heavens!"
Melali,	To go out on a pleasure jaunt.
Metjaru,	Religious cleansing ceremony, generally some sort of driving out of devils.
Nyak!	Want, desire.
Oleh-oleh,	Small gift, particularly gifts brought home after a trip abroad or away.
Padi,	Rice growing in field.
Paras,	Sandstone, sold in slabs, used in building temples, also for carving temple figures.
Pemuda,	Literally "young man." Nowadays means young Nationalist.
Penyor,	New Year bamboo-pole, highly decorated.
Puri,	House of man of Ksatriya caste.
Salak,	Astringent fruit with lizard-like skin.
Sarong,	Non-batik cloth for same purposes as kain, but the ends are sewn, and wearer "steps into" it.
Sawah,	Rice-field.
Sebel,	Unclean, ritually.
Sing!	No, in low caste language.
Sundat,	Bitterly aromatic cream-coloured flower.
Tiang, or Titiang,	Yes, in high caste language.
Tjampak,	Polynesian *Champaka* flower.
Tjoba!	Just imagine!
Tjotjok,	Fit well together.
Tuak,	Smoky palm-toddy.

Angklung,   Ancient bamboo percussion instrument, used in orchestra, having only four tones.

Antjur,   Fish-glue paste, for mixing with gold paint, imported from China.

Atal,   Yellow clay, imported also from China, used for dancers' "foundation" make-up.

Djegogan,   Deepest-voiced, five-keyed metallophone.

Gamelan,   Indonesian generic term for orchestra.

Gangsa,   Metallophone—i.e. metal keys strung in xylophone-like manner over framed bamboo resonators.

Gending pokok,   The leading melody.

Gong,   Generally means orchestra; i.e. the Gong Pliatan means the orchestra of Pliatan; but also means a gong in our normal sense.

Gong Gdé,   Full Kebiar orchestra, like our symphony orchestra.

Gupakan,   Gupak is to drum, gupakan is that which is drummed, i.e. a drum.

G'ying,   Leading metallophone, like our violin of an orchestra leader.

Kendang,   Indonesian generic word for drum.

Kantilan,   Smallest metallophone, which plays the fast "flower-parts".

Ontjer,   Part of dancer's costume, a streamer, or piece of cloth which *flows* from hips or body.

Pengisap,   The echo principle governing each pair of instruments in a Gong.

Pengumbangan,   The interlocking principle which governs each pair of instruments in a Gong.

Perada,   Gold paint, liquid or leaf.

Polos,   The "simple" counterpoint pattern in a Gong.

Rebab,   Two-stringed fiddle.

Reyong,   Battery of about twelve gongs of descending size on long low stand; played by four men.

Sangsi,	The "complicated" counterpoint pattern in a Gong.
Sekehe,	(Pronounced: sĕkér.) Music or Dance club.
Semar Pegulingan,	Orchestra of the God of Love, properly used for Legong and Barong performances.
Suling,	Bamboo flute.
Tabuh,	Style of playing, or arrangement of music.
Tandak,	Narrator, who sings from the orchestra the story-accompaniment to a dance.
Tjalung,	Tall, five-keyed metallophone, equivalent of cello.
Tjeng-Tjeng,	(Onomatopaeic.) The cymbals.

CURRENCY:

The currency in use all over Indonesia is the *rupiah*, which is subdivided into one hundred *sen*—(cents.)

One Pound Sterling is worth 32.00 Indonesian *rupiahs*.

One U.S. dollar is worth 11.40 Indonesian *rupiahs*.

One Singapore dollar is worth 3.00 Indonesian *rupiahs*.

In Bali the people love to use the old silver money, *klinting*, which used to be worth from two to three times the value of the new paper money—and still is in their eyes.

Index

*

227